It's **All** a Matter of Perspective!

Our Miraculous Origins

Michael J. Bozoukoff, M.S.

TRILOGY
A WHOLLY OWNED SUBSIDIARY OF TBN
PROFESSIONAL PUBLISHING MEETS POWERFUL PROMOTION

It's All a Matter of Perspective: Our Miraculous Origins

Trilogy Christian Publishers
A Wholly Owned Subsidiary of Trinity Broadcasting Network
2442 Michelle Drive, Tustin, CA 92780

10 9 8 7 6 5 4 3 2 1
Library of Congress Cataloging-in-Publication Data is available.

ISBN 979-8-89041-687-2
ISBN 979-8-89041-688-9 (ebook)

DEDICATION

I have been twice incredibly blessed by God with two exceptional women. This book is dedicated to my late wife, Donna, and current wife, Laurel. They have provided me with inspiration and encouragement to "tackle" this difficult and complex topic. In doing so, I am ever confident in the biblical God as our Creator and Sustainer. I give Him all the praise and glory! He constantly gives me hope for the present and future, regardless of what is happening in the world today.

TABLE OF CONTENTS

FOREWORD

When we think of our miraculous origins, we usually think of ourselves and our position in the universe and, especially, here on Earth. We ask questions and seek some kind of answers to "make sense of it all." Three main initial interrogatory questions are usually asked: Where did we come from, who did it, and how did it happen? God says in Genesis 2:7 and Job 34:14–15 that He made us from the elements of the earth and blew His Spirit into us. In support of this unabashed declaration, scientists have determined that we are made up of twenty Earth elements. If God combined these earthly elements and used His Spirit to "knit" (Psalm 139:13) us together and "awaken" us into life, is it even possible to explain this wonderful and mysterious process yet other miracles? Explaining this phenomenon has been going on since recorded time by historical philosophers, religious theologians, scientists, and all of us at one time or another. As a result, a couple of diverse perspectives or conclusions ultimately emerge — is there a God or no God? However, if God had a "hand" in creating us out of these earthly elements and with His Spirit, how did He combine them to form us into His image as recorded in Genesis 2:5 and Isaiah 49:16 and 64:8?

In attempting to answer this question, one must go back to the very beginning of time as we believe it to be (and not eternal or infinite time before the onset of our cosmic universe) from a biblical and scientific perspective and then move forward to establish how He divinely created everything to ultimately support and establish our human creation. Of all the various monotheistic religions, the Bible openly and clearly declares God as the Creator. This explanation is covered in the book of Genesis (and the Qur'an) and other supporting biblical passages. These scriptural passages provide us with a concise and general account of who and how God "did it" and is the focus in this book. In that regard, the Bible was carefully crafted through God's inspiration to many different authors to be relevant to these ancient Hebrews as well as us today. These scriptures provide us with the logically correct sequence of events that can be verified and validated by most ongoing and vetted scientific discoveries. Yet, this act of creation by God is truly miraculous and yet mysterious by human understanding. Therefore, this belief requires faith in a supernatural occurrence or divine intervention by God to understand it fully. Specifically, the *biblical perspective* gives us the most believable, complete, inclusive, and promising explanation for our beginning as I will elaborate.

In particular, my book takes us back in time and moves forward to see how life was formed from nonlife. It is highly unlikely (think virtually impossible) that life happened naturally or was generated spontaneously or changed gradually even over vast amounts of time as evolutionists believe. Concluding God had us in His "mind" when He created us is more believable (Jeremiah 1:5 and Ephesians 1:4). God's command to create the universe and everything in it (out of nothing) is exemplified by what we see or observe in His creation and is revealed in His Scriptures. His design and integration of all these seemingly unrelated elements and processes have made us who we are! Combining them naturally by chance is highly unlikely. God tells us in Scriptures that He made or engineered us in His image (Genesis 1:26–27).

The Bible reveals that God was and is the Creator of everything. After creating everything else, God created us on the sixth day of creation (Genesis 1:27). We were and are His most marvelous, unique, and special creation! The Bible assures us that He works in our lives (John 14:12 and Ephesians 2:1). He desires a relationship with us (John 3:16 and Revelation 3:20). There are many implications of His offer to us. Following Jesus and His words are what Christians are supposed to do. In doing so, He promises to give us meaning and purpose in our lives (Psalm 57:2–3, 138:8, and Philippians 2:13). This belief must be accomplished through faith in God and exemplified and evidenced by all His miracles for the beginning of creation that continues today in us.

Scientific discoveries alone can never provide meaning or purpose in our lives. At best, these discoveries can provide satisfaction in understanding some of the intricacies of how it was done (such as studying DNA), reinforce, and strengthen our belief in God as the Creator. However, scientific discoveries of understanding the universe outside and inside our bodies provide us only with a "glimpse" of how He brought everything together to form us. I believe this inconceivable and imponderable situation is so that we can adore and appreciate His awe-inspiring creation, give Him the credit, obey and follow His Commandments, shape or influence our daily lives for His glory, and be with Him ultimately and eternally in heaven. The biblical perspective of our creation is truly the "greatest story ever told!"

INTRODUCTION

Background

My trademarked™ phrase "It's ALL a Matter of Perspective"™ can be applied to anything, anyone, or any way. In this case, we consider how it applies to our origins' initiation, formation, and development over time. This book explores and offers five perspectives for a better understanding of our origins. Each view considers the mythological, religious, theological, philosophical, and scientific aspects and ramifications. Invariably, these aspects drive us to the concepts of creation and evolution. In addition, by exploring these concepts, they invariably lead us to higher philosophical and theological concepts, such as the belief in the law of nature or naturalism alone or some divine involvement with a supernatural being, commonly called "God," to provide for our existence.

> NOTE: A single or monotheistic God is originally believed by "Western" (e.g., originated in the Mediterranean region) religions, whereas multiple or polytheistic gods are believed by many "Eastern" (e.g., originated in the Asian, Sub-Asian, Pacific Island, or Oceanic regions) religions.

Ultimately, the question of "God" or gods as the Creator(s) must be addressed by everyone who seeks the truth about our origins. In answering this question, our philosophical worldviews (or what we believe in) and subsequent conduct or behavior in our daily lives need to be considered from various perspectives.

Five Perspectives Explaining Our Origins

In attempting to understand our origins, different views are considered and evaluated. Each of the following perspectives is explored in detail to "make sense of our world":

- Identification of five scientific "cause-and-effect" questions logically leads to various creation and evolution explanations and resulting worldviews.
- Review and hierarchy of the most often debated creation and evolution concepts and interpretations concerning our origins.
- Consolidation of religious/theological, philosophical, and scientific concepts into physical and spiritual pathways leads to individual worldviews about one's belief in "God" or gods as the Creator(s).
- Relevant scientific discoveries folded into each "creation day," as primarily recounted from the biblical book of Genesis chapter 1.
- Origins' historical and philosophical perspectives integrated into a "big" picture summary.

Figure 1 illustrates five perspectives for *"making sense of our world."*

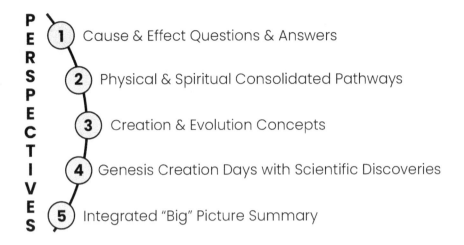

Figure 1: Five Perspectives for "Making Sense of Our World"

Approach

In "*making sense of our world*," the following areas are discussed:

Five origin questions and possible answers are logically addressed. Approaching this complicated area from this perspective provides for our consideration of a wide set of possibilities. Ignoring other perspectives besides the Christian perspective provides an incomplete picture of our religious, theological, philosophical, and scientific landscapes. All these perspectives must be included in any conversation that we might have with others regarding our origins.

The biblical creation story from Genesis chapter 1 and other passages from the Old and New Testaments of the Bible are identified. Addressing some of the significant objections from skeptics, doubters, and critics is crucial to providing legitimacy of the Bible and especially the creation story. Christian responses address these objections.

The creation path is believed by a minority of historical scientists: These scientists employ the concept of supernaturalism or divine intervention, which leads to different creation interpretations. (However, some of these scientists recognize a limited role of evolution, which is directed and controlled by a monotheistic "God.") The Christian religion and its associated theology proclaim "God" as the cause for our existence. This belief is based upon faith and divine revelations from biblical scriptures and God's creation — nature. These scriptures primarily identify "who" did it and "why" He did it! Also, they provide a "high-level" general description of the Genesis six days of creation for those ancient Hebrew believers. In addition, He provides us with the capability to know "how" He "engineered" each of those days in a logical or sequential pattern, which makes sense for scientists and nonscientists to seriously consider. The Genesis account of creation is just as relevant today as it was back then! Believing in this account forms the foundation or basis for believing in everything else contained in the Bible!

The evolution path is believed by most historical scientists: These scientists strictly employ the concept of naturalism, which leads to evolutionary interpretations. Rules and practices of science do not permit the involvement of a supernatural being (e.g., "God") as the cause for our existence. "God" or divine intervention does not enter the scientific process or method of reasoning. Science primarily attempts to answer the questions: "What" happened and "how" did it happen?

Stellar evolution is represented by the "big bang theory," chemical evolution is demonstrated by the "origins of life theory" and experiments, and biological evolution is described by the "common descent theory." They are evaluated for their validity. Chemical and biological evolution theories are the most controversial, especially in evolution versus creation debates as observed in the readings from literature, polls, and the media.

Two pathways are discussed. They include the physical or material realm of reality and the spiritual realm of reality. Each path is associated with concepts that support these realities. In addition, these pathways lead to various individual and collective philosophical and theological worldviews. These worldviews have the potential to influence our daily lives.

Analyses of the evolutionary pathway to humanity and the transition of anatomically modern humans from chimpanzees (i.e., chimps) and hominids (such as Neanderthals) are evaluated from a biological perspective. This subject is arguably the most controversial and "hotly" debated area, especially in the "West."

The dialog method emphasizes the compatibility of the domains of science (based upon empirical data or evidence) and religion (based upon faith, revelation, miracles, and the identification of "God" as the Creator) with regards to the study of our origins and examine: Where did we come from? The intersection of the Genesis six creation days and the validated scientific discoveries provides the possibility for a productive and informative dialog or conversation between all of us in various forums.

A wrap-up includes a "big" picture summary, which provides an integrated origins perspective. Chapter summaries and final thoughts or observations provide a unified conclusion: *the biblical account is the most complete, comprehensive, believable, and inclusive perspective for the understanding of our origins.*

> NOTE: Based upon my research and background as a systems engineer and analyst, the illustrations contained in this book graphically depict, summarize, and integrate these complex concepts and beliefs.

PART 1:

"Direction Determines Destination"

CHAPTER 1:

Our Miraculous Origins — Why Does Understanding It Matter?

Introduction

Who hasn't looked up into a night's starry sky and contemplated the awesome wonder of it all...the mind-boggling possibilities of how it all started, how we came to be, and the mere significance of our existence?

Perhaps Socrates gave one of the most quoted reasons for us to pursue this level of inquiry when he succinctly said, "The unexamined life is not worth living."

From time to time, some of us ponder certain types of "big" philosophical questions about the purpose for our lives. Answering them in a particular way provides some personal meaning to us. However,

most people are usually too busy to go in for that sort of thinking called "philosophical." Their rationale is because they have to spend their time struggling for existence or because they rather enjoy living lives of undisturbed routine. But on rare occasions, a few awkward and irritating individuals with time on their hands ask deceptively simple questions which never seem to have simple answers. [1]

And when we diligently seek answers to these general questions, other more specific questions arise regarding the understanding of our origins that require reasonable explanations, such as:

- Was there a single beginning, multiple beginnings, or no beginning?
- Who or what was involved in creating the universe, our earth, and life?
- What process (or method) has led us to ultimately human life?
- How old are the universe, earth, and various forms of life?
- What is the purpose or meaning for our existence here on earth?

A *biblical perspective* provides the most complete, reasonable, comprehensive, and inclusive explanation when examining these questions and associated answers. Various biblical passages offer critical insight into these difficult, complex, and often controversial areas. Unfortunately, interpretations of these passages can create separations or divisions, especially within the "Western" (Mediterranean-originated) religious communities of faith as well as in the scientific communities at large.

To better understand this divide, we will conduct a brief study of mythologies, religions (and their associated theologies), philosophies, and scientific disciplines, which help us to make better sense of our world. However, when "all is said and done," the bottom line always comes down to whether we believe in "God" as the Creator or not! This dilemma often leads us down two distinct origin paths.

First, there is a scientific approach that is purely physical, materialistic, or naturalistic in substance. This path does not involve a supernatural being or "God" and usually implies evolutionary theories or explanations for our origins, which most scientists believe today. The second path is a spiritual one. This path contains a religious or supernaturalistic belief and primarily involves faith in "God" (or many gods) as the Creator(s). Additionally, it implies various creation accounts, such as those passages provided in biblical scriptures. These scriptures, which describe our origins, are contained in the Old and New Testaments (or covenants) and are believed by most Christians to be the inspired and living "Word of God" as revealed to us for a general understanding of where we "stand" in relation to "God." Specifically, we are told to "be in the world, but not of the world." This is a phrase that is heard a lot in Christian subculture. It refers to what Jesus said as recorded by John, one of His close friends, in John 15:19 and John 17:14–16. This concept is also talked about later in the New Testament by the famous convert Paul (Romans 12:2, Ephesians 4:22–24, and 1 Thessalonians 4:1). These scriptural passages refer to how we should "think" about creation and our relationship with the Creator "God."

My research shows that it is "easier" to believe in a supreme biblical God as the Creator of everything rather than just relying on purely naturalistic (scientific) or evolutionary explanations and concepts. Specifically, the sheer number (e.g., mathematical improbability or odds) of scientific physical events that need to take place in just the correct chronological order at the right time to ultimately form human life is staggering to the imagination! In addition, the majority-approved scientific model of our universe, Earth, and life is constantly changing as new discoveries are found and interpreted by these historical scientists. This "moving target" of scientific evidence often poses serious questions as to the accuracy and reliability of their scientific model. Their model is often changed to fit the scientific facts, which are based upon validated empirical data that is corroborated by different independent and reliable sources.

On another note, public schools find it difficult or challenging "to keep up" with these new scientific discoveries. Often, most science textbooks and curricula do not include the latest scientific findings. In addition, science teachers are not allowed to teach religious creation accounts as an alternative explanation because of various court rulings. In particular, the US Supreme Court has ruled the teaching creation accounts in public schools violates the US Constitution's First Amendment. The "Separation of Church and State" writings of Thomas Jefferson in an 1802 letter to a group of men affiliated with the Danbury Baptists Association of Connecticut provided the basis for their decision. However,

> the U.S. Constitution does not state in so many words
> that there is a separation of church and state. The first
> part of the First Amendment to the Constitution states:
> "Congress shall make no law respecting an establish-
> ment of religion, or prohibiting the free exercise thereof."
> Therefore, it is more accurate to say that the Constitution
> promotes freedom of religion and prohibits the federal
> government from inhibiting its citizens' abilities to
> worship as they wish.[2]

Many constitutional scholars believe the intent of Congress in writing this amendment was for our government not to impose a particular religion on its citizens like the one found in England (e.g., Church of England) or in Connecticut (e.g., Congregationalists) during these earlier times. Because of this decision, this situation has presented a significant challenge for the Bible-believing Judeo-Christian community to teach creation as an alternative to evolution in public schools. (NOTE: The study of comparative religions and their beliefs, such as creation, is rarely taught in public schools, even if this course was offered.) Various organizations refute a purely naturalistic (scientific) evolutionary explanation for our origins. Most of these groups are Judeo-Christian organizations and are very active today in the "West." However, many of their teachings interpret biblical scriptural passages differently. These variations of their interpretations are evident in many articles, books, seminars, media, and conferences that challenge the purely naturalistic (scientific) and evolutionary explanations for our origins.

In addition, these organizations (mainly Christian) believe at some point in our lives that we need to trust and have faith or confidence in the whole "Word of God" that teaches God as the sole Creator of the universe. "God" used a divine command (called "fiat lux" in Latin) to speak or command everything into existence out of nothing (called "creation ex nihilo" in Latin). It is also possible He used selected naturalistic or some "limited" evolutionary means to take place under His authority, direction, and control. Biblical scriptures do not tell us His exact ways of *how* He created everything. So, by rational faith, we have a more than reasonable justification to believe in God's incredible miracle of creation. The (NIV) book of Isaiah 55:9 says:

> *"As the heavens are higher than the earth, so are my ways higher than your ways and my thoughts than your thoughts."*

As much as we try to explain our origins through philosophical and scientific means, we eventually "fall back" on the mystery of how God did it! The miracle of creation and other blessings from God give us a sense of wonderment and gratefulness. Many of us turn to science to provide these answers, while others believe by faith alone. Consequently, in formulating our origins perspective, our lives are often impacted as we attempt to decide to deal with this critical area.

Through solidifying a biblical theological belief or view of creation, we can begin to understand how our actions can impact or influence our behavior, habits, daily conduct in our lives, purpose, and the fulfillment of our needs. Science cannot address this area! Consequently, our attitudes and behavioral activities are often seen or observed through our worldview or philosophy of life.

> "When philosophy gets applied to the stark realities
> and issues of everyday life, it becomes your worldview.
> A worldview is the conceptual framework by which you
> consciously or unconsciously interpret the world around
> you according to your philosophical beliefs."[3]

Additionally,

> we actually have no choice of whether to have a philos-
> ophy or not, of whether to be philosophers or not. We
> inevitably operate out of some philosophical worldview,
> however well informed or incomplete it might be. Our
> choice is between bad philosophy unreflectively absorbed
> from the culture around us and the prejudices of our
> time, or good philosophy built on critical questioning and
> sustained thought… We can be poor thinkers or good
> philosophers.[4]

Our beliefs often result in frustration (inner turmoil) or satisfaction (inner peace). Man's way is through his intellect and five senses. God's way is revealed in the Bible and sometimes contradicts man's reasoning. Man's confused beliefs put him at odds with God. Man attempts to control people and circumstances to win for himself the significance and relationships he craves. God's way promises to give him what he longs for: a sense of purpose and meaningful relationships. Man's misguided efforts are never fully satisfying. Man's (men and women) way binds us to have a marginally satisfying life at best and an utterly unsatisfying one at worst. God's way promises that if we live for Him, He will satisfy us with the fruit of the spirit: love, joy, and peace (Galatians 5:22–23).

Furthermore, the 1646 CE (i.e., Common Era), the Westminster Confession of the Reformed Faith (and later endorsed by the Presbyterian Church) states:

> "Man was created to know God. God created man and to enjoy Him forever. God created man with deep longingly for meaning and love and then planned to meet those longings, fully and eternally, in Himself."[5]

Understanding our origins from a *biblical perspective* is paramount for each of us to pursue and be worthy of consideration by all "thinking" and "seeking" individuals. By objectively examining the various theories, accounts, and concepts about our origins, we must ultimately ask, "What impact has it had on our current cultural worldviews and society in general?" "What have we become in our life's journey?"

However, there are many factors that have influenced this journey. Sociologists, philosophers, and religious leaders have identified many changes that have occurred in our society or culture. Many of them believe:

> "We, as part of 'Western' civilization, are living in a period (*arguably*) called as a 'Post-Modern' and 'Post-Christian' period in which skepticism is promoted or found as the major worldview characteristic."[6]

In addition, many sociologists attribute this situation to secular humanism. Secular humanism rejects religious dogma, a conviction that principles, ideologies, and traditions, whether religious, political, or social, must be weighed and tested by each individual and not simply accepted by faith. Secular humanists do not take the supernatural view of reality. They believe human reasoning is the basis for morality and decision-making.

Secular humanism is a nonreligious worldview rooted in science, philosophical naturalism, and humanist ethics. Instead of relying on faith, doctrine, or mysticism, secular humanists use compassion, critical thinking, and human experience to find solutions to human problems. Secular humanists promote values including integrity, benevolence, fairness, and responsibility and believe that with reason, goodwill, the free exchange of ideas, and tolerance, we can build a better world for ourselves and future generations. Secular humanism calls upon humans to develop within the universe values of their own. Further, secular humanism maintains that, through a process of value inquiry informed by scientific and reflective thought, men and women can reach a rough agreement concerning values, crafting ethical systems that deliver optimal results for human beings in a broad spectrum of circumstances.[7]

The *Humanist Manifesto* of 1933, 1980, and 2003 publications incorporated these articles. It embraced human reason, ethics, social justice, fulfillment, growth, and creativity and continually adapted via a search for objective truth, primarily through philosophy and science, which embodies the concepts of philosophical naturalism and methodological naturalism of science. Philosophical naturalism (e.g., only observable reality exists) is a concern for this life (*as opposed to an afterlife*) and a commitment to making it meaningful through a better understanding of ourselves, our history, our intellectual and artistic achievement, and the outlook of those who differ from us. Practical and methodological naturalism of science is a commitment to the use of critical reasoning, factual evidence, and the scientific method (*e.g.,* *empiricism*) of inquiry in seeking solutions to human problems and answers to important human questions.[8]

Also, these sociologists observe the rise in atheism, agnosticism, pluralism, relativism, and doubt within our Western society. Out of these factors, this so-called "postmodernism" has raised a new challenge to atheism, especially among younger people within the "West." Sociologists have said:

> Atheistic writers have been slow to recognize and reluctant to engage. One of the reasons for this is that atheism has been the ideal religion of modernity — the cultural period ushered in by the Enlightenment Period or Age (*e.g., 18th century*). But modernity is being replaced by post-modernity, which rejects precisely those aspects of modernity that made atheism the obvious choice as the preferred modern religion. Post-modernity has thus spawned Post Atheism. Yet, atheism seems to be turning a blind eye to this massive cultural shift and its implication for the future of its faith. This is because post-Modernism is intensely suspicious of worldviews that claim to offer a total view of reality (*such as the Christian claim for the Bible to be accurate and true especially regarding God as the sole Creator of the Universe*) as inadequate and has a genuine interest in recovering a spiritual dimension to life. This new (*surge of*) interest in spirituality has no necessary connection with organized religion of any kind, let alone Christianity.[9]

Sociologists have also said that these factors or attitudes come from religious pluralism, which accepts all beliefs as equally valid and denies any method of judging between them; relativism, which considers truths about reality or ethics to be dependent on the individuals or cultures that endorse them; and skepticism and doubt, which question our ability to know at all.[10]

However, secular humanism, for all its cultural dominance over the past seventy years, "has failed to offer a robust philosophy of meaning and purpose (*especially among the younger generations*). Secular Humanism did not provide any moral framework for how to act within the world besides being a good person because the alternative is undesirable for everyone."[11]

Today's Western culture seems to be concerned and sometimes even consumed with "righting the wrongs" of society, their traditional institutions, and patterns of behavior and lifestyles. Specifically, this "woke" or cultural awakening movement falls under the contemporary and often derogatory term of "wokeism." This movement has gained momentum since the 1990s primarily due to the increased awareness provided by technology and social media coverage of protests and demonstrations (i.e., Women's Day equality celebrations, gender identity/solidarity and pride [LGBTQIA+] marches, and Black Lives Matter or antiwhite racism and anti-police protests, etc.) The goal of "wokeism" and its culture is to encourage active individual and collective participation to "fight" all forms of political, racial, and gender oppression and diversity and to promote social justice, equal rights, and better protection against formerly discriminated groups. The "wokes" are keenly sensitive to both political and social injustices. Early effects of the "woke" culture are observed in public and private institutions recognizing and promoting tolerance in differences between people and inclusivity in the workplace, educational system, and other institutions through inclusive language in terms of racial and gender identity and equality to protect against human rights violations.

On the other hand, many political and religious conservatives describe this twenty-first-century sociopolitical liberal movement or trend as "left wing" and potentially "dangerous." These opponents consider this "woke" movement, framework, or strategy as sometimes impacting traditional Judeo-Christian principles and values upon which our justice or legal, governmental, educational, and other institutional systems are based upon. Furthermore, they believe "wokeism is *incompatible with the biblical worldview* because it has different interpretations (e.g., perspectives) and leaves no room in the conversation for alternative views of addressing those social and political issues within our democratic process."[12]

> They believe these different interpretations can potentially lead to early stages of a "revolution" of many institutions. Many sociologists attribute this shift in making changes to our current system as a result of "post-Modernism," and "post-Christianity." This shift is heavily influenced by political correctness, cancel culture, cultural Marxism, neo-Marxism, social justice, identity politics, and critical (e.g., race) theory.[13]

In particular sociologist Max Funk has described "wokeism" as:

> A new religion moving like a tidal wave across every facet of western culture, shaping and redefining society as it goes. This religion masquerades under the guise of compassion and with the Christian worldview… If left unchecked, this new religion could lead to a complete unravelling of western culture.[14]

Specifically, the two main differences between the biblical moral framework of Christianity and wokeism are:

- First, wokeism attributes intrinsic guilt or innocence to the individual based on their group identity, regardless of individual action. Christianity attributes our actions to the individual who is responsible to God. Sin or righteousness is not inherited based on one's natural identifiers, like race, gender, or descent (as described in Ezekiel 18:1–3 and 2 Corinthians 5:16). We are to evaluate people based on the moral standards of the Scriptures and treat them as equals created by God. This belief is at the core of Western culture, which states that everyone is made in God's image and is intrinsically worthy of respect (as described in Proverbs 17:15 and 2 Corinthians 5:16).[15]

- Second, wokeism presents the redemptive pattern of various groups vying for power with an inherently oppressive system. In this tribalistic vision of the world, the only thing that exists is power, and if only power exists, then power and control are necessary to tear down a corrupt system. Christianity presents the pattern of the individual in relationship with God as the primary mechanism for the redemption of the world. This pattern culminates with Christ as the perfect man and His sacrifice for the sins of the world. Therefore, the ideal Christian behavior is one of mercy, peace, kindness, and forgiveness (as described in Ephesians 4:32, Luke 6:35, and Matthew 5:7).[16]

This divide or separation on how we view and make changes to our society questions whether Americans have truly turned away from religion. Or have they merely found a new faith (e.g., wokeism)? "A 2016 poll by the Public Religion Research Institute (PRRI) found that 25 percent of all Americans described their religion as 'none.' That description was particularly prominent among elite,

urban, affluent, credentialed, professional, and young Americans."[17]
Let us examine more recent poll results.

Specifically, results from a recent Gallup poll identified three major biological views from 1983 to 2019 on the origin of human beings. They are the (1) percentage of humans that evolved with God guiding, (2) percentage that God created humans in the present form as in the biblical Genesis creation story, and (3) percentage of humans that evolved but that God had no part in the process. The most notable finding from this poll is that the percentage of humans that evolved without God (i.e., view 3) has gone up from 9 percent to 22 percent in about fifteen years, while the other two views have slightly declined! (NOTE: 38 percent to 33 percent and 44 percent to 40 percent, respectively, for views 1 and 2.)[18]

In addition, the results from an early Pew Research Center survey said that "68% of respondents believed that humans evolved (given 40% via Charles Darwin's Natural Selection method plus 28% via guidance or allowance by God) and 31% of them believed that humans always existed in present form." The results from a second later Pew survey said that 81 percent of respondents say that humans evolved (given 33 percent via natural selection and 48 percent via guidance/ allowance by God), and now only 18 percent of them say that humans always existed in the present form![19] The difference in these two Pew results is *how* the questions are asked. The first poll used a two-step approach, whereas the second used a single-question approach.

Today, this situation of how we ask these types of questions presents a real dilemma for Christians. Modern scientific evidence has often "trumped" philosophical or logical arguments and religious or faith claims. Many scientists believe physical evidence, supported by independently verified and validated empirical data from many sources, is more factual because it deals with the observed world. Specifically, these scientists see evolution as a "fact" and not just a "theory" because they say the results and conclusions are testable, verifiable, repeatable, and predictable. Also, many of these scientists conclude that this evidence supports evolutionary theories or conclusions. Likewise, they see religious creation accounts as a myth or story that is either not supportable or inappropriate for scientific investigation. On the other hand, creationists (scientists and nonscientists), who may also believe in many of the contributions of science in the understanding of our origins, are committed to believing in a Creator God, especially as revealed through the Western Abrahamic religions of Judaism, Christianity, and Islam. However, they differ in the "role" of God in the creation process.

Therefore, this situation could be visualized as a spectrum of beliefs where creation alone is at one end, evolution at the opposite end, and some mixed "bag" of creation and evolution concepts at different positions between these ends. For example, some strict or very conservative creationists (tied to a particular religious group) believe exclusively in a Creator "God" who creates and controls everything. Other more liberal or progressive creationists (also connected to a specific religious group) believe in some mixed "bag" of creation and evolution concepts with God, the Creator, guiding and controlling everything. Finally, at the other end of the spectrum, evolutionists believe only in natural means of creation without God or His involvement in any way.

As a result, this subject is "hotly" debated among religious leaders, scientists, and the general public. The debate centers on the validity of the concepts contained within the idea of creation and/or evolution. The two sides can be summarized as follows:

> It (creation) is universally considered religious, not scientific, by professional, scientific organizations worldwide. In the scientific community, evolution is accepted as fact, and efforts to sustain the traditional view (*e.g., Creation*) are almost regarded as pseudoscience... While the controversy has a long history, today it has retreated to be

mainly over what constitutes good science education, with the politics of creationism primarily focusing on the teaching of creationism in public education.[20]

In addition, the debate between creationists and evolutionists is often divided, especially in the "West."

Among the majority of Christian countries, the debate is most prominent in the United States, where it is portrayed as a cultural war. Parallel controversies exist in other religious communities, such as the more fundamentalist branches of Judaism and Islam. In Europe and elsewhere, creationism is less widespread (notably, the Catholic Church and Anglican Community both accept evolution), and there is much less pressure to teach it as fact.[21] For example, Pope Francis of the Catholic Church has stated:

> God is not a demiurge (*e.g., a subordinate deity or lower God*) or a magician (*with a magic wand*), but the Creator who brought everything to life…Evolution in nature is not inconsistent with the notion of creation because Evolution requires the creation of beings subject to direct creation by God of the soul (*e.g., defined as "thinking" self, mind, or consciousness*) and not the product of purely material forces that evolve.[22]

In his speech at the Pontifical Academy of Sciences in 2014, "he (*also*) declared that he accepted the Big Bang theory."[23]

Hence, we face a real controversy because there is a broad spectrum of beliefs, both personally or individually and professionally, especially within the Western scientific and religious communities and the general public.

In a Daily Hope message recently given by Pastor Rick Warren, he defines four popular worldviews that can influence a Christian worldview.[24] They are:

- *Materialism:* What matters most is money. Materialists measure their success by wealth.
- *Hedonism:* Whatever feels good is good. For hedonists, pleasure is their "god."
- *Individualism:* What I want comes first. America is built on rugged individualism, and today that has evolved into a culture of narcissism (e.g., pleasure).
- *Politics as religion.* Politics is the region of people who do not know God. There is nothing wrong with politics, but it should not be your savior.

Exploring these popular worldviews can motivate us to think deeper about this subject. This situation is especially evident when viewed from a historical and philosophical perspective. These perspectives lead us to a personal philosophy and are the foundation for our worldview about life and its significance.

> A worldview that includes "God" will (*should*) cause you to recognize significance and accountability in life. A worldview without "God" may leave you without (*lasting*) meaning or purpose (*especially if you do not believe in life after death*). Your worldview is often determined by what you decide about how the world began with: "God" or gods, no "God" or gods (*or I do not know" if there are a* "God" *or gods*).[25]

In summary, we need to "*be ready for an answer*" to defend our rational faith in a biblical God as the Creator, especially when called upon. Therefore, we need to understand the complexities of this controversial subject to substantiate and, if necessary, defend our position while dealing with alternative views from others. Hopefully, my book will provide an *"overview"* of the major concepts that address our origins for your consideration. This insight will give you confidence and trust to know your biblical worldview is true and accurate while being adequately informed of other worldviews. My hope is that understanding the value God places on us will strengthen our philosophical and biblical perspectives. The book of Genesis 1:27 says:

> *"God created man in his image, in the image of God he created him: male and female he created them."*

Also, Psalm 139:14 declares, "I praise you because I am fearfully and wonderfully made; your works are wonderful, I know that full well."

As mentioned earlier, let us begin by examining the possible answers to these five logical questions. These questions lay the foundation for discussing creation, evolution, and other related subjects relative to the understanding of our origins.

CHAPTER 2:

Survey of Five Origin Questions and Possible Explanations

Answering origin questions regarding our beginnings, causes, processes, age, and purpose gives us the first perspective.

Introduction

Understanding our origins involves many different subjects and associated concepts. These areas have led us to various evolution and creation explanations. In addition, these explanations pose philosophical questions of whether there is a God, and if there is a God, what was or is His role in "creating" our universe, Earth, and life itself? In attempting to answer these two questions, one can logically identify other questions. Such as: (1) Was there a single beginning, multiple beginnings, or none? (2) Who or what was involved in creating the universe, our Earth, and life? (3) What was/is the process (method) that has led us to ultimately human life? (4) How old is the universe, Earth, and various life forms? (5) What is the purpose or meaning for our existence here on Earth?

My approach uses the philosophical and scientific reasoning principles that originate from the scientific and philosophical "law of cause and effect." Logic flow diagrams are constructed for each question using this law, and each possibility is explained. For example, having a beginning or start for the universe can lead to various causes; these causes can lead to multiple processes; these processes can lead to various ages. Finally, these different ages can influence our purpose or meaning here on Earth. This chain or sequence of questions and their possibilities can expand our "big" picture perspective or view of the universe, Earth, and life. Philosophers have said:

> Since the Universe exists (e.g., is an effect), it must have a cause. The existence of the universe is the effect of a cause, and therefore, there must be a beginning. Muslim al-Ghazali, who lived from 1058–1111 CE (Common Era), formulates this argument from an Islamic (a.k.a. Kalam) perspective.

This argument has three steps:[26]

- Whatever begins to exist has a cause,
- The universe began to exist,
- Therefore, the universe has a cause.

Given this rather simple but powerful argument for the existence of the universe, every attempt is made to simplify this review process for the following five basic questions. The fourteenth-century philosopher William of Occam is credited with the "keep it simple" problem-solving principle. The principle is called the "Occam's razor" (e.g., the law of economy or law of parsimony principle). His scientific and philosophical rule, using this logic principle, states "that entities should not be multiplied unnecessarily which is interpreted as requiring that the simplest of competing theories be preferred to the more complex or that explanations of unknown phenomena be sought first in terms of known quantities."[27]

Was There a Beginning?

Scientific discoveries have independently determined and deduced (through corroborated and independently verified empirical data or evidence) that there was a *"single beginning"* at a definite point in time for the start of the universe!

However, this belief has not always been the case. Since the ancient Greeks, the assumption has been that the material world is eternal. Christians have denied this view, based on biblical revelation (book of Genesis chapters 1 and 2, in particular), but secular (before the twentieth century) scientists always assumed the universe is eternal.

> Christians just had to say, well, even though the universe appears static, it did have a beginning when God created it. So, the discovery in the twentieth century that the universe is not an unchanging, eternal entity was a complete shock to secular (*and perhaps some religious*) minds. It was utterly unanticipated. There are two pathways towards establishing that the universe started at some point in the past, one is mathematical or philosophical, while the other is scientific.[28]

Nevertheless, recently to advance this idea of an eternal or infinite universe, several "continuous creation or steady-state" models, theories, or scenarios have been proposed by various twentieth-century scientists to *avoid* a single beginning. They argued:

The universe had no beginning but existed in a steady-state condition, with the new matter being formed from that was already there. These scientists (*essentially*) revived the Hindu (*and perhaps Buddhist and New Age beliefs*) doctrine of a universe that oscillates for an infinite time through cycles of birth, death, and rebirth.[29]

As a result of this belief, six major continuous creation theories were proposed but eventually invalidated by most of the scientific community. They were the (a) steady-state model developed by Sir Fred Hoyle in 1948,[30] (b) oscillating model developed by Carl Sagan in the 1960s,[31] (c) cyclic scenario (vice a model — a permutation of the oscillating model) briefly considered by Albert Einstein in 1930 and then later by other scientists such as Paul Steinhardt and Neil Turok,[32] (d) chaotic inflation theory developed by Andrei Linde in 1983,[33] (e) multi-universe theory developed by Edward Tryon et al. in 1973,[34] and the (f) quantum gravity model developed by Stephan Hawking in 2008.[35]

However, "*no*" indisputable scientific evidence exists to verify these views or theories. These theories attempted to give reasons for a position that there was no beginning to our universe. Today, most of the scientific community "*rejects*" these theories.[36]

Given that the universe is not eternal, two other options are possible. First, the universe is an illusion. This belief claim leads to a view that the universe does not exist (e.g., is an illusion or not real). This option is "*impossible*" by its very definition "since it contains everything that exists, the universe must also exist. If the universe does not exist, then nothing else exists either, and the whole issue does not matter."[37]

Since the universe is not eternal and not an illusion, let us consider the question of a "single" or one beginning of the universe. Scientific discoveries demonstrate a single start. Likewise, the Abrahamic religions of Judaism, Islam, and Christianity agree with this conclusion.

These religious "theists" believe that this occurrence was a supernatural, miraculous event (e.g., caused by God). However, most scientists and most of the scientific community believe it occurred exclusively by natural events. "Their argument for a beginning comes from the 'Big Bang Theory,' which has impressive scientific credentials."[38] Specifically, most scientists and evolutionists believe:

> This (*evolutionary*) theory itself leads us to the conclusion that before inflation of the Universe, which was caused by the "Big Bang," the Universe shrank back to a singularity... the state at which space-time, curvature, along with temperature, density, and pressure becomes infinite... It is the beginning point. The point at which the "Big Bang" occurred... It is the standard paradigm of contemporary cosmology. I would say that its broad framework is very securely established as a scientific fact. Stephen Hawking has said, almost everyone now believes that the Universe, and time itself, had a beginning at the "Big Bang."[39]

A very brief history and description of the "Big Bang" concept states:

> Albert Einstein developed his general theory of relativity in 1915 and started applying it to the Universe as a whole. He was shocked to discover it did not allow for a static Universe. According to his equations, the Universe should either be exploding or imploding. In order to make the Universe static, he had to fudge his equations by putting in a factor that would hold the Universe steady. In the 1920s, the Russian mathematician Alexander Friedman and the Belgium astronomer George Lemaitre were able to develop models based upon Einstein's theory. They (as

well as physicist Richard Tolman in 1922) predicted the Universe was expanding. Of course, this meant that if you went backward in time, the Universe would go back to a single origin before which it did not exist. In 1949, astronomer Fred Hoyle, derisively called this expansion from a single origin of time, the "Big Bang" and the name Stuck! Some of the evidence for the "Big Bang" included Edwin Hubble discovering the light coming to us from distant galaxies appearing to be redder than it should be, and that this universal feature of galaxies in all parts of the sky. He attributed this "red shift" as being due to the galaxies moving away from us… In the 1940s, George Gamow predicted that if the Big Bang really happened, then the background temperature of the Universe should be just a few degrees above absolute zero… In 1965, two scientists accidently discovered the Universe's background radiation (everywhere) at 3.7 degrees above absolute zero… The last piece of evidence for the "Big Bang" is the origin of the light elements. Heavy elements, like carbon and iron are synthesized in the interior stars and then exploded through supernovae into space. But the very light elements, like Deuterium and Helium cannot be synthesized in the interior stars, because you would need an even more powerful source to create them. These elements must have been forged in the furnace of the Big Bang itself at temperatures that were billions of degrees… So predictions about the "Big Bang" have been consistently verified by scientific data.[40]

Specifically, in July 1965, Arno Penzias and Robert Wilson made a discovery that would cement our understanding of how the universe came into being. "Their detection of the Cosmic Microwave Background (CMB), the radiation left over from the birth of the universe, provided the strongest possible evidence that the universe expanded from an initial violent explosion, known as "The Big Bang." Today, the CMB (radiation) is still one of the most important signals that helps us understand the cosmos.[41]

However, suppose the universe is not eternal, not an illusion, and did not have a single beginning. In that case, consider the question of "multiple" beginnings (i.e., many beginnings, destructions, and new beginnings in a cyclical fashion). This view has led to two religious beliefs: First, a cyclical process occurs an infinite number of times and never reaches a final state. This view is primarily an Eastern (e.g., Hindu) religious belief and possibly a "New Age" belief. Or this cyclical process occurs a finite number of times and ends in a final state, often called "Nirvana." This view is also primarily an Eastern (e.g., Buddhist) religious belief and possibly a New Age belief. The New Age view of the world and the universe is monistic and pantheistic, which means that everything that exists is of one essence, and that one essence is God. Everything is a different form of that essence, and the divine force is what holds everything together.[42] Figure 2 provides a logic flow diagram to consider all these possibilities for a finite or infinite beginning.

NOTE: For the following logical flow diagrams, the terms or annotations are Y=Yes; N=No; a white rectangle means a decision needs to be made; a shaded rectangle symbol represents an explanation, concept, theory, or model; and a hexagon symbol means a stop to the logical flow process because it is deemed that there is no other possible way to go in that direction.

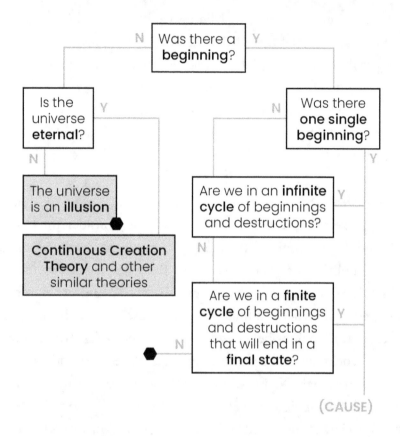

*Figure 2: Logic Flow for Explaining the Beginning(s)
of Our Universe*

Summary of Beginnings

In considering the question of *"Was there a beginning?"* — three choices
are available.

First, the concept of the universe as having an eternal existence
was explained (and *dismissed*) as identified from the six most common
continuous or steady-state theories by various scientists.

Second, the idea of the beginning as an illusion was considered
and *dismissed* since it is not logically possible.

Next, the concept of a single beginning was considered, which
has numerous validated scientific evidences for that possibility.

(Considerable evidence validates this conclusion rather than any other possibilities.) Abrahamic religions support this position and believe God started the beginning.

Finally, if there were multiple beginnings (e.g., birth, death, and rebirth), this view is primarily believed through the Hindu and parts of the Buddhist religions. However, if there were multiple beginnings and then an end or final state (a.k.a. Nirvana), this belief is from the Buddhist religion or philosophy. Lastly, the "New Age" movement can exhibit various ideas of multiple beginnings as well. In any case, these possibilities for at least one beginning can then lead to the question of "*cause*," which is discussed next.

Who or What Is the Cause?

Again, the scientific and philosophical argument of the "law of cause and effect" says:

> Everything in the Universe has a cause... go back further and further in the "chain of causes" you must eventually come to a "First Cause" that got the whole thing going... Without the First "Big" Cause, nothing else would exist... Another way to say it is this: The "First Big Cause" had to be self-existent, or it always had to exist.[43]

In determining "who" or "what" is the first "*cause*" for this (scientifically validated) single beginning, essentially only two possibilities arise — first, an intentional and personal creative act of either a singular (biblical/Qur'an or Western) God or multiple gods (primarily Eastern), which both lead to the worldviews using the theological term theism. This pathway answers the question of "Who?" (NOTE: An unspecified "intelligent designer" is also a possibility and is not necessarily connected with a monotheistic God but could be.) Second, exclusive "blind, random, undirected, mindless, accidental, or by chance" natural forces just happened to start and form the universe. This concept often leads to the worldviews of evolution, evolutionary atheism, and (perhaps?) evolutionary agnosticism (these worldviews will be discussed later). This pathway answers the question of "What?" An example of "what" caused the universe to "spring" into existence suddenly is contained in Bill Bryson's book *A Short History of Nearly Everything*, in which he vaguely speculates on:

> exotic theories about a "false vacuum" or "scalar field" or "vacuum energy" — a sort of "quality or thing" that may have introduced a measure of instability into the nothingness that was and thus sparked the "big bang" through which emerged the entire universe... It seems impossible that you could get something from nothing. But the fact that once there was nothing and now there is a universe is proof that you can. However, where these forces came from is not known by most scientists.[44]

They simply call this evolutionary process of how the universe evolved the "big bang theory" (*and identify the theory* as the "cause").[45] (NOTE: This perspective is prominent among evolutionary scientists today and is detailed later.) On the other hand, the creationists assert that:

> chance (just happened) isn't a choice at all, because it can't cause anything. Only a real force is capable of causation, and chance cannot cause anything because it is not a real force. The philosopher David Hume wrote, "It is universally allowed that nothing exists without a cause of its existence, and that chance, when strictly examined, is a mere negative word and means not any real power, which has anywhere a being in nature."[46]

Figure 3 illustrates the logic flow for explaining these three possibilities for the "causes," which then leads to the question of "method or process."

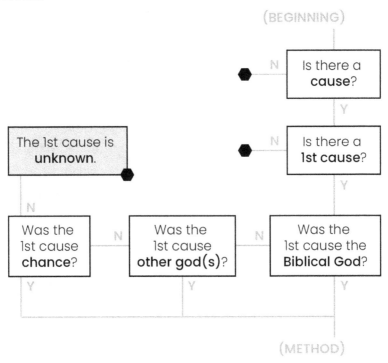

Figure 3: Logic Flow for Explaining the Cause for Creation

Summary of Causes

If the universe is the effect (e.g., composed of matter, energy, space, time, forces, laws, and subsequent entities or structures or living creatures), it must have had a cause for it to have occurred. If the formation of the universe had ultimately the first cause (because there were numerous causes before the first cause — a.k.a. chain of events), then was it the God of the Bible or Qur'an or by other gods, such as the gods of Hinduism, Buddhism, or other Indian or Asian religions? (NOTE: A biblical God as the Creator is the most believable explanation as described in later chapters.) Finally, if the universe just happened to be caused by blind or random forces of nature, then no God or gods would be the cause or even be necessary. There does not seem to be any other choices after these possibilities. Whether the cause was intentional through a God or gods or unintentional through chance, these options lead us to the "process" or method or way that was utilized to form and develop this universe. This question is discussed next.

What Is the Process?

When considering the "process or method" of forming and developing the universe and everything in it, supernatural and natural processes are considered. Various creation accounts explain supernatural processes from different (primarily Western) religions. Most scientific disciplines explain nature through evolutionary theories.

Religion → Creation

The Hebrew biblical Genesis chapters and Muslim Holy Qur'an suras reveal the religious supernatural concept of "fiat lux" or the voice of God commanding everything (time, space, matter, energy, laws, forces, etc.) into existence out of nothing (or creation ex nihilo). This concept is sometimes called the "creation big bang" explanation. NOTE: "The Book of Genesis provides a unified description of creation, the Qur'an does not. Instead, fragmented passages are scattered across many of its 114 chapters ('suras')."[47] A minority of scientists and nearly all religions subscribe to some form or interpretation of creationism.

Science → Evolution

On the other hand, scientific evidence usually interprets their conclusions from a stellar, chemical, and biological evolutionary perspective. Most scientists and the scientific community generally agree with them. In general, the "big bang theory" describes stellar evolution; the "origins of life theory" describes chemical evolution, and the "common descent theory" or "descent with modification" process or pattern describes biological evolution.

In particular, the words "chemical and biological evolution" usually mean the change of nonliving ("organic") chemicals and biomolecules into simpler life forms, more complex life forms, and, finally, into humans. However, the term "evolution" can also apply to nonliving things and different states or events over time, such as those occurring in the universe in general. Almost everything is said to have evolved — the solar system, stars, the universe, social and legal systems, etc. "Everything is said to be a product of Evolution."[48]

Figure 4 illustrates these two paths for explaining the processes involved in determining the origins and development of our universe and Earth. These paths lead to the question of "age."

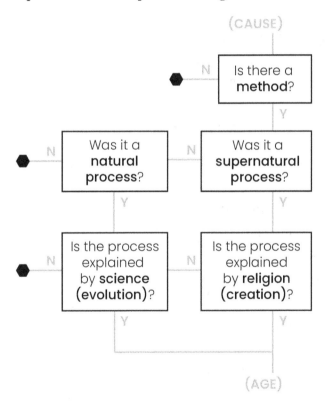

Figure 4: Logic Flow to Explain the Processes Acting on the Universe, Earth, and Life

Summary of Processes

When considering the method or process in which the universe began and was formed, two possibilities exist. They are from a supernatural perspective, which directly leads to various religious creation views (e.g., "creation big bang"), or from a natural perspective (e.g., "big bang theory"). It is also recognized that just because there are religious creation concepts, they can encompass scientific evidence as well and even some limited concepts of evolution, such as microevolution (changes within only the species and possibly the genus level). Evolution is most often associated with biological evolution (and specifically some form of Darwinism such as natural selection), but it is also considered in stellar (e.g., "big bang") and chemical evolution ("origin of life") theories. In either case, both pathways lead to the next question, "Can *age* be determined?"

What Is the Age of the Universe?

In determining the "age" of the universe, the above "continuous creation" explanations, which gave an infinite age, were "*discounted*" and "*rejected*" by most scientists. The "West" has developed different finite age perspectives based on a single beginning. Scientific evidence supports the universe's single beginning. The universe must have occurred or begun at a definite point in time. Two different Christian perspectives or categories have developed in the "West" in the past three centuries to interpret the age of the universe and Earth.

The "Young Earth (Universe) Creationist" or YEC views interpret Genesis 1 age of the Universe and Earth to be between 6,000 and 10,000 years old. Creation Scientists (CS) endorse this literal or conservative view. "It is the most common creationist view brought up by evolutionists as pseudo science."[49]

The "old earth (universe) creationist" or OEC views agree with most of the scientific evidence (if it does not conflict with the Bible). This progressive view supports the age of the universe to be approximately 13.8 billion years old and the age of the earth to be about 4.6 billion years old. This view has two main interpretations:[50] (a) an intelligent designer (ID) scientific view and (b) a progressive (liberal) biblical view with three primary interpretations — gap theory, day-age theory, and the Reasons to Believe (RTB) model.

From an evolutionary perspective (and independently verified and validated by scientific evidence), the universe is at least 13.8 billion years old, but it suggests that it could or should be much older. This long age is needed to support the evolutionist's claim for the gradual transformation of one species into another (e.g., macroevolution) primarily through the processes or mechanisms of natural selection acting on random beneficial or positive mutations of genes (i.e., sections of DNA that "code" for various proteins). From this view, these gene mutations are passed on to their offspring to eventually produce changes from one species into another. The environment in which they live also contributes to these changes. Various Darwinian models support this concept.

Figure 5 illustrates these perspectives on the "age" of the universe, Earth, and life.

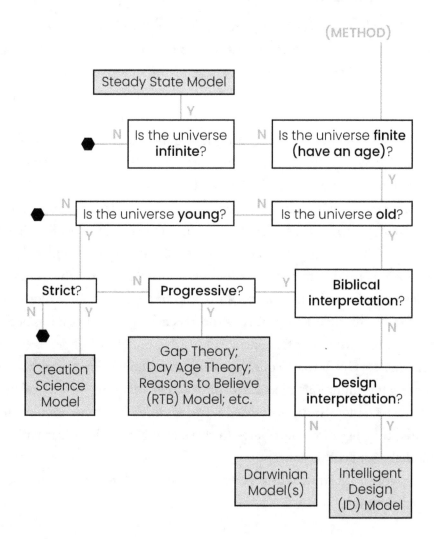

Figure 5: Logic Flow to Explain the Age of the Universe, Earth, and Life

Summary of Ages

The age of the universe and the earth is generally looked at from either an infinite (a.k.a. eternal) or a finite (definite) perspective. The infinite perspective is part of Eastern religions (mainly from some form of Hinduism) and their philosophies but have been recently revived and restructured by leading Western scientists in the past century. One

the creation and evolution concepts or take no position on the subject. (NOTE: These worldviews will be discussed later.)

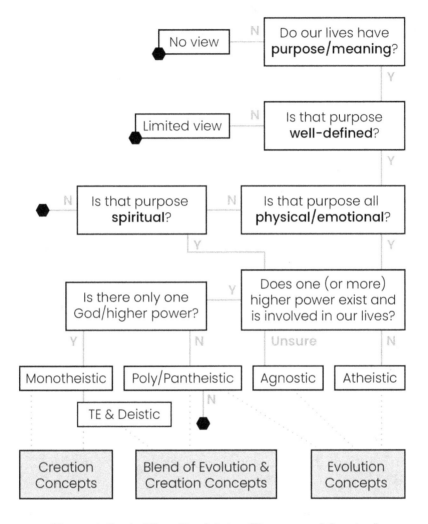

Figure 6: Logic Flow Explaining "Purpose or Meaning" for Our Lives

Summary of Purpose

The question of purpose or meaning in our lives has four options. First, one can simply have no view or perspective on this concept. They may have never really thought about it, even though this is hard to believe but certainly possible in today's secular world. Second, one may have a very limited view. They have tried to avoid or ignore this sensitive and very personal or private topic but have some ideas, usually not organized in any strong belief-claim. Third, some view our purpose here on earth primarily from a physical and emotional perspective. This view often leads to either an atheistic position where God does not exist or is not involved in our lives or is not the creator of the universe. This view is generally explained by evolutionary concepts. Also, if not atheistic, one may take an agnostic position where again evolutionary concepts tend to be accepted over creation concepts. Also, if not atheistic, one may take a theistic position, which basically divides into monotheistic beliefs in a single God or poly or pantheistic positions that believe in satisfying many gods or at least one single or most powerful god out of many. Monotheistic beliefs generally support the creation concept, whereas the theistic evolutionist/deists positions, as a subset of monotheism, tend to support both creation in terms of God initially creating the universe and then allowing the naturalistic evolutionary concepts (which He created) to form everything else. Finally, the poly/pantheists can support both creation and evolution concepts, or sometimes they are not interested in them in terms of practicing their religion and philosophy (e.g., Buddhism).

Table 1 compares and summarizes the explanations for these five origin questions. The following chapters explain these models in more detail.

MODELS	QUESTIONS				
	WHO / WHAT? God or…	HOW MANY? Beginning	WHAT METHOD? Process	HOW OLD? Age	WHY? Purpose
ETERNAL	No God; ultimate reality	None; or multiples	Steady state; oscillating; others	Infinite	Personal

MODELS	QUESTIONS				
	WHO / WHAT? *God or...*	HOW MANY? *Beginning*	WHAT METHOD? *Process*	HOW OLD? *Age*	WHY? *Purpose*
EVOLUTION / DARWIN	No God or gods; just happened	Yes (single)	Natural (random mutation and natural selection)	Billions (agree with scientists, +/- 13.78 BYA or much longer)	Personal; scientific knowledge
CREATION (Young Earth)	Biblical God	Yes (single)	Supernatural flat lux (divine command); Biblical sequence	6,000 to 10,000 YA	Serve God; eternal reward
INTELLIGENT DESIGN (ID)	Intelligent Creator or Designer	Yes (single)	Supernatural designer; scientific design	Billions (agree with scientists, perhaps +/- 13.78 BYA)	Personal; spiritual; scientific
CREATION (RTB / Day-Age)	Biblical God	Yes (single)	Supernatural flat lux (divine command); Biblical sequence	Billions (agree with scientists, +/- 13.78 BYA)	Serve God; eternal reward
CREATION (Gap Theory)	Biblical God	Yes (two: Gen 1:1 & Gen 1:2)	Supernatural flat lux (divine command)	Billions?	Serve God; eternal reward

Table 1: Comparison of Five Origin Questions with Their Models and Theories

CHAPTER 3:

The Biblical Creation Story

Introduction

The book of Genesis is a book of beginnings. Genesis means "the origins, source, creation, or coming into being of something." The Hebrew name for this book is "Bereshit," the first word in the Hebrew text, which translates as "in the beginning" (Genesis 1:1). In discussing our origins, we focus on Genesis chapter 1:1–31, the first description of creation; Genesis chapter 2:1–20, the second description of creation; and Genesis chapter 6:6–8:18, the story of Noah and the flood.

The book of Genesis gives no notice about its author. The early church held to the conviction that Moses, the Hebrew patriarch, wrote the book of Genesis, which was discussed in the Jerusalem *Talmud* and documented by the first-century Jewish historian Josephus.

As a brief overview, when considering our origins from a biblical perspective, we begin with the creation account as described and organized in the book of Genesis, chapter 1, verses 1 to 31. It boldly and clearly proclaims and answers the following key questions:

- Was there a beginning? Yes, one.
- Who was and is the Creator? A monotheistic God, the Creator of heaven and Earth.

- How long did it take? Six days, and God rested on the seventh day.
- What were the events that occurred on each day of creation? *Day 1:* light; *day 2:* sky and waters; *day 3:* land, plants, and trees; *day 4:* stars, planets, moons, etc., appeared; *day 5:* marine and air animals; and *day 6:* land animals and "humans." These days divide into "two sets of threes." In the first group of three days, God organized motionless spaces by separating one from another. In the second group of three days, God formed non-living and living things to fill and rule over those spaces. For example, the sun, moon, and stars occupy and govern the light and darkness; the fish and birds fill and rule the water and air; animals fill the land, and humans rule over all of them.
- Why did God do it? He created men and women in His image to serve, obey, and follow Him. He made us rulers of all the creatures to take care of all His creation. Theologically, as the "Creator of the universe," He is the One who initiated a covenant with His chosen people (e.g., Hebrews). The book of Genesis ties creation with this covenant together in a commanding manner:

The God who initiates covenant is the same God who has created the entire universe. The eternal God and almighty Creator entered covenant with His people (Genesis 1:1; and John 1:1). God's covenant with Abraham is the basic plot of the Scriptures. God's work from that day forward was to accomplish His plan for the worlds' nations through His people Israel, the descendants of Abraham. God's covenant with Abraham (Genesis 12:1–3, 15: 1–2) contains several personal blessings as the father of the faith. But the text's climax is in the words of worldwide import: "And in you, all the families of the earth shall be blessed." The promise is through the person of the Lord Jesus Christ, the Seed of Abraham (Galatians 3:16, 19), through who peoples of all nations and families may enter the joy of knowing the God of Abraham. God's promise is also through the church, in those who believe in Christ.[51]

However, these initial passages do not specify exactly "how" God created everything. Specifically, the Latin concepts of "fiat lux" (i.e., He spoke or commanded everything into existence) and "creation ex nihilo" (i.e., He created something out of nothing) give us some basic understanding of what He did. Nevertheless, this brief description leaves some room for validated scientific conclusions of evidence, especially if they do not violate Scriptures. Interpretations of these scientific conclusions need to support biblical passages. Commentator Gleason L. Archer Jr. says:

> The purpose of Genesis 1 is not to tell how fast God performed His work of creation (though some of His acts, such as the creation of light on the first day, must have been instantaneous). Rather, its true purpose was to reveal that the Lord God who had revealed Himself to the Hebrew race and entered a personal covenant relationship with them was indeed the only true God, the Creator of all things that are.[52]

This chapter lays the foundation for all subsequent events and individuals in the Bible. At least 123 Old Testament and 71 New Testament passages directly refer to His creation. Here are some of the major (summarized) passages that support and amplify the biblical creation accounts. Also, they provide implications regarding our nature and role in this life.[53]

- Genesis 1: The one true God made the universe, the world, and all life.
- Genesis 2: God created humans, marriage, and assigned responsibility.
- Genesis 3–6: Evil entered creation.
- Genesis 6–9: Human creatures became reprobates.
- Genesis 10–11: God dispensed humanity to protect creation.
- Job 9: Creation reveals God's power and design.
- Job 34–41: Creation is complex.
- Psalm 65: God's provision and care for creation are optimal.
- Psalm 104: God gives details of the physical creation chronology.
- Psalm 139: Each human life is a unique design.
- Psalm 147–148: All creation praises God.
- Proverbs 8: Creation is temporal, but God is eternal.
- Ecclesiastes: 1, 3, 8–12: Fixed physical laws govern creation.
- Isaiah 40–51: God gives details of cosmic creation.
- Romans 1–8: God's purpose for creation is redemption.
- First Corinthians 15: Creation and death precede the glory to come.
- Second Corinthians 4: God's light shines through cracked (by sin) "jars of clay."
- Second Peter 3: This creation will end.
- Revelations 20–22: The new creation awaits.

Many biblical scholars believe Genesis 1 is from the perspective or point of view of an observer on the surface of the earth.[54] In addition, these scholars believe that Genesis and the rest of the Bible are God's inspired Word given to men from the "Holy Spirit." Unlike other creation accounts, Genesis records God as the sole or single Creator. By this early and upfront statement in the Bible (and the Qur'an), this monotheistic concept is considered dogma or doctrinal and is based upon matters of faith by the Abrahamic religious beliefs of Judaism, Christianity, and Islam. However, these religions challenge many groups and individuals with different interpretations regarding our understanding of our origins.

Objections and Responses

Skeptics and others believe the creation story, as revealed in Genesis and other supporting biblical passages, is "untrue." They believe the Bible is figurative or metaphorical and symbolic, and, therefore, it should be categorized as a "myth." In addition, they believe the Bible is full of contradictions and errors. The following are some of the major objections with regards to these opponents or skeptics to the biblical creation account:

1. Genesis was copied from earlier ancient writings. Therefore, the Genesis creation account is a myth just like the others.
2. Moses did not write the book of Genesis. It was compiled later by others and is not inspired by God.
3. Genesis chapters 1 and 2 conflict with each other. Which one is true?
4. The "days of creation" cannot each be six literal (twenty-four-hour) days. Scientific evidence and some religious

interpretations say these "days" can be interpreted as more prolonged but finite periods of time.

5. The biblical flood or deluge story was copied from ancient writings. Is the Genesis account not any different?

6. The Genesis creation account does not agree with modern scientific findings. Scientific discoveries are incompatible with Genesis' "six days of creation."

Is the Biblical Creation Story a Myth?

One leading objection to this creation account comes from skeptics, doubters, atheists, agnostics, and others in today's "postmodern and post-Christian" Western culture according to many sociologists. This argument is ultimately based on the historicity and accuracy (or reliability) of the Bible. Many attribute this biblical narrative account to be an adaptation of an ancient written account like the one recorded in the Babylonian creation myth, *Enuma Elish*. They argue that the creation story in Genesis chapter 1 is similar in content to the *Enuma Elish* poem. Is this accusation accurate?

First, skeptics often suggest the Genesis creation narratives were taken (i.e., rather than just influenced) from the *Enuma Elish* creation poem since the original version of the *Enuma Elish* (which was previously taken from the Sumerian Akkadian or *Eridu* Genesis story) was first recorded in the time of Hammurabi the Great, around 1750 BCE (NOTE: BCE means Before Common Era) and may have predated the biblical written version. However, others are not sure which creation version came first. Also, they say that it would be doubtful Moses, who was strictly living and serving a monotheistic God in the

West, would have borrowed the creation story from a polytheistic civilization existing in the East as a source for his story.

The *Enuma Elish* epic poem is summarized below:

> The God, Marduk (or Assur in the later Assyrian versions of the poem) is created to defend the other gods from an attack plotted by the ocean goddess Tiamat. Marduk offers to save the gods if he is appointed as their leader and is allowed to remain so even after the threat passes. The gods agree to Marduk's conditions. Marduk challenges Tiamat to combat and destroys her. He then rips her corpse into two halves with which he fashions the Earth and the skies. Marduk then creates the calendar, organizes the planets and stars, and regulates the moon, sun, and weather. The gods pledge their allegiance to Marduk, and he creates Babylon as the terrestrial counterpart to the realm of the gods. Marduk then destroys Tiamat's husband, Kingu, using his blood to create humankind so that they can do the work of the gods.[55]

If we proceed on the assumption that the Genesis 1 narrative represented a "borrowed" or "embellished" version of the *Enuma Elish*, Table 2 highlights some of these main similar events.

GENESIS 1	ENUMA ELISH
Begins creation story as "in the beginning," darkness proceeds creative acts, and matter exists when creation begins. Shares common ways of thinking.	Begins creation story as "when on high," darkness proceeds creative acts, and matter exists when creation begins. Shares common ways of thinking.

GENESIS 1	ENUMA ELISH
God creates heaven and Earth by dividing waters above and below with a barrier holding back the upper waters (a.k.a. a "firmament").	The god, Marduk, builds the heavens and Earth from the goddess Tiamat's body, once called a body of water.
Light exists before creation of sun, moon, and stars.	Same.
God creates stars and moon to help people decipher days, nights, seasons, etc.	Marduk does the same.
Sequence of creation events: division of waters, dry land, luminaries, and humanity, all followed by rest.	Same.
Assumes darkness and emptiness over the watery chaos (fear of the unknown of the deep).	Implies primeval chaos and unknown monsters in the beginning.
Shows the naming of objects is of importance.	Shows connection between giving names and existence.
Creation is completed on the sixth day and rested on the seventh day.	Creation recorded on seven tablets.
"Man" is created on the sixth day, last, and is special (cosmos is a temple for "man.").	"Man" is created on the sixth tablet, last, and is special.
Hebrew word for sea or "deep" is *tehom*.	Tiamat goddess represents the sea as deep and chaotic.
Earth's existence was from divine intercession by God.	Same, except it was from the actions of Marduk.

Table 2: Relative "Similarities" between Genesis 1 and
Enuma Elish

However, the other perspective explicitly shows significant or "striking" differences between the two! Even though Conrad Hyeres of the Princeton Theological Seminary believes they are both myths, he says:

> Genesis myth polemically addressed earlier Babylonian and other pagan worldviews to repudiate the divinization of nature and the attendant myths of divine origins, divine conflict, and divine ascent, thus rejecting the idea that Genesis borrowed from or appropriated the form of the Enuma Elish. According to this view, the Enuma Elish was comfortable using connections between the divine and inert matter, while the aim of Genesis was supposedly to trumpet the superiority of the Israelite God, Yahweh Elohim (Hebrew generic name for God) over all creation (and subsequent deities).[56]

While it cannot be denied that there are some "relative" similarities between the two creation stories, there are also significant differences between them. Table 3 compares the major differences between Genesis 1 and the *Enuma Elish* creation accounts.

GENESIS 1	ENUMA ELISH
God exists before the beginning of the universe and is separate from His creation. He "stands" over creation and is the Creator of everything.	In the beginning, coeternal gods Apsu (father — seen as freshwater) and Tiamat (mother — seen as salt water) mixed waters to beget gods and their created divine (i.e., not natural) realm.
Creation of natural realm is by the Hebrew or Israelite God, Yahweh.	Creation of natural realm is by the chief or supreme Babylonian god, Marduk.

God is one (monotheistic) with unlimited powers (e.g., all-powerful, etc.). He does not fight over other gods because there are none.	Marduk is one of many (polytheistic gods) with limited powers. He fights with other gods and monsters.
Creation is out of nothing ("ex nihilo") and instantly obeys God's divine "fiat" or command.	Creation of celestial bodies, land, and human bodies by Marduk are made from gods' corpses and blood killed in various battles.
God forms the earth.	Marduk kills Tiamat and splits her body in two, making the sky and the earth.
Creation is in an orderly manner and strict timeline. God sees the events as good and admires His work. He is depicted as a God of peace, quiet, unity, and love.	Creation is out of conflict and chaotic battles. The gods struggle between good and evil, and all creation comes from evil, deceit, and murder.
God forms the heavens and Earth in three days.	Creation of heaven and Earth takes place on the fourth day.
God makes the sun, moon, and stars. He does not regulate them.	Marduk creates the stars and regulates the sun, moon, and weather.
Creation of everything lacks conflict.	Creation is "born" in conflict. Marduk must destroy Tiamat's body to make a new world.
Creation of "man" is created last in God's image and is out of clay or dust. "Man" is the high point of His creation to rule over creation.	Creation of "man" is before animals. Marduk makes "man" out of bodies of Tiamat's followers, and "man" is to be a race of slaves and to give rest to the gods.

Creation events are testable (e.g., scientifically).	Creation events are not testable scientifically.
Creation simply mentions the first humans (Adam and Eve) and the garden of Eden.	Creation unabashedly advances supremacy of Babylon over Mesopotamia.
Genesis 1 clearly depicts a creation epic.	*Enuma Elish* is not primarily a creation story; rather, it is a hymn of praise to Marduk to put him at the head of the pantheon of gods and to exalt the city of Babylon and enhance Hammurabi's power.

Table 3: Major "Differences" Between Genesis 1 and
Enuma Elish

Therefore, considering these significant differences carefully, biblical scholars believe that the Genesis account of creation is "unique" and "distinct" from all other versions of creation, especially the Babylonian *Enuma Elish* poem.

> "The biblical version was not taken from the earlier Babylonian myth."[57]

These findings are significant and often mentioned in evolution versus creation debates as a point of contention. Many skeptics, secularists, and evolutionists postulate that if the biblical creation version is only a myth, how can one believe that anything else in the Bible is true? Therefore, the alternative conclusion implies believing in scientific and philosophical naturalism and evolution alone. So we must give an informed answer to this very critical argument.

Is Moses the Author of Genesis?

The authorship of Genesis and the following four books of the Greek *Pentateuch* (i.e., Exodus, Leviticus, Numbers, and Deuteronomy) has come under severe attack in the past three hundred years by scientific and philosophical skeptics as well as professing Christians and non-Christians. Instead of Moses writing these books, many believe that at least four authors wrote the various portions of these books over many centuries. Then one or more redactors (editors) over many years combined and interwove everything together into its present form. This redactor(s) used the Jahwist (J), Elohist (E), Deuteronomy (D), and Priestly (P) sources, which, in turn, reflect older oral traditions.

> Specifically, various sections of the *Pentateuch* were assigned to multiple authors identified by the letters J, E, D, and P. Hence, it is called the "Documentary Hypothesis" (or the JEDP model). As this hypothesis was developed by several Jewish and theologically liberal Christian scholars in the late seventeenth to the late nineteenth centuries, there were several different proposals of who wrote what and when. But by the end of the nineteenth century, liberal scholars had reached a general agreement. The letters stand for:

> - J documents are the sections, verses, or sometimes parts of verses written by one or more authors who preferred to use the Hebrew name Yahweh (Jehovah) to refer to God. This document dates to about 900–850 BCE.
> - E documents are the texts that use the name Elohim for God. This document dates around 750–700 BCE.

- D stands for Deuteronomy, most of which was written by a different author or group of authors, perhaps around the time of King Josiah's reforms in 621 BCE.
- P stands for Priest and identifies the texts in Leviticus and elsewhere in the Pentateuch that a priest or priests wrote during the exile in Babylon after 586 BCE.

Then around 400 BCE, some redactors (e.g., editors) supposedly combined these four independently written texts to form the Greek *Pentateuch* as it was known in the time of Jesus and modern times.[58]

However, "in spite of the number of modern scholars who reject the Mosaic authorship of Genesis, the traditional view has much to commend it. Both the Old and New Testaments (or covenants) contain frequent testimony to the Mosaic authorship"[59] (Leviticus 1:1–2; Nehemiah 13:1; Matthew 8:4; and Acts 26:22).

Here are some additional reasons why biblical scholars believe that Moses did write the book of Genesis:

It would be difficult to find a person in Israel's life who was better prepared or qualified than Moses to write the history recorded in the Book of Genesis. A man who "was learned in all the wisdom of the Egyptians" (Acts 7:22), Moses was providentially prepared to understand and integrate all the available records, manuscripts, and oral narratives under God's inspiration. Moses may have written the book during the years of the wilderness, wandering to prepare the new generation to enter the land of Canaan. As a prophet who enjoyed the unusual privilege of unhurried hours of communion with God on Mount Sinai, Moses was well equipped with the human race and the nation of Israel. Moses may have finished writing the Book of Genesis not long before his death on Mount Nebo (Deuteronomy 34) before he entered the promised land about 1445–1405 BCE).[60]

As a prophet of God, Moses wrote under divine inspiration (and revelation), guaranteeing his writings with complete accuracy and absolute authority. His writings were endorsed by Jesus and the New Testament apostles, who based their teaching and the truth of the gospel.

In addition, other reasons for rejecting the "documentary hypothesis" (or JEDP model) and accepting the biblical testimony to the Mosaic authorship of the Pentateuch include the erroneous assumptions and reasoning of the liberal scholars and other skeptics such as:[61]

- They assumed their conclusion. They believed the Bible was not a supernatural revelation from God and manipulated the biblical text to arrive at that conclusion. Therefore, they were implicitly Deistic or Atheistic in their thinking.
- They assumed that Israel's religion was simply the invention of man, a product of evolution, as all other religions are. Based on evolutionary ideas, they assumed that "the art of writing" was virtually unknown in Israel before the establishment of the Davidic monarchy; therefore, there could have been no written records going back to the time of Moses. This claim attacks not only the intelligence of the ancient Israelites, but also the Egyptians who trained Moses. Were the Egyptians incapable of teaching Moses how to read and write? Since the documentary hypothesis was first proposed, archaeologists have discovered scores of written records

predating the time of Moses. It is hard to believe that Israel's ancient neighbors knew how to write, but the Jews could not. Liberal Bible scholars allegedly based their theories on biblical text evidence, yet they evaded the biblical evidence that refutes their ideas.

- They used a "pick and choose" approach to studying the Bible, which is hardly honest scholarship in pursuit of truth.
- They arbitrarily assumed that the Hebrew authors differed from all other historical writers. The Hebrews could not use more than one name for God, more than one writing style regardless of the subject matter, or more than one of several possible synonyms for a single idea. Their subjective bias made them illegitimately assume that any biblical statement was unreliable until proven reliable (though they would not do this with any other ancient or modern text). When they found any disagreement between the Bible and ancient pagan literature, the latter was automatically given preference and trusted as a historical witness. The former violates the well-accepted concept known as Aristotle's dictum, which advises that one should give the benefit of the doubt to the document rather than the critic. In other words, the Bible (or any other book) should be considered "innocent until proven guilty" or reliable until its unreliability is compellingly demonstrated.

Although many examples show an ancient Semitic author using repetition and duplication in his narrative technique, skeptical scholars assume that when Hebrew authors did this, it is compelling evidence of multiple authorship of the biblical text. "The skeptics erroneously assumed, without any other ancient Hebrew literature to compare with the biblical text, that they could, with scientific reliability, establish the date of the composition of each book of the Bible."[62]

> No manuscript evidence of the J-document, E-document, P-document, D-document, or any other supposed fragments has been discovered. And no ancient Jewish commentaries mention any of these imaginary documents or their alleged unnamed authors. All the manuscript evidence we have is for the first five books of the Bible, just as we have them today. This evidence is confirmed by the singular Jewish testimony (until the last few centuries) that these books are the writings of Moses.[63]

Do Genesis Chapters 1 and 2 Tell a Different Story of Creation?

Traditionally, conservative biblical scholars attribute the Hebrew creation account to Moses' writings during the Exodus (1446–1406 BCE). Two reports are recorded in Genesis, the first book of the Hebrew Torah or Old Testament. The first version is in Genesis 1, and the second version is in chapter 2. They are different in many respects and are again summarized below.[64]

In Genesis 1:1–2:3, God progressively creates the different features of the world over a series of six days. Creation is by divine command: God says, "Let there be light!" Light is created on the first day. On the second and third days, God separates the waters, sky, and dry land and fills the earth with vegetation. God then (on the fourth day) puts lights in the sky to separate the day from night to mark the seasons. On the fifth day, God creates sea creatures and birds of every kind and commands them to multiply their numbers. On the sixth day, God creates land creatures of every kind. Man and woman are created in the image of God and given dominion and care over all other created things. God rested on the seventh and final day of creation, which He marked as "holy."

In Genesis 2:4–25, the creation of man follows the creation of the heavens and Earth but occurs before the creation of other plants and animals. He is formed from the dust of the ground, and God breathes life into him. God prepares a garden in Eden for man and fills it with trees bearing fruit for him to eat. The man is invited to eat the fruit of any tree but one: the tree of knowledge of good and evil. God commands not to eat of that one tree, "for when you eat of it you will surely die" (Genesis 2:17). Birds and animals are then created as man's companions and helpers, and God presents them to man. The first man (i.e., Adam) gives names to each one but finds none suitable to be his helper, so God puts him to sleep and removes one of his ribs, which he uses to make the first woman (i.e., Eve). For this reason, the text reads, "For this reason a man will leave his father and mother and be united to his wife, and the two will become one flesh" (Ephesians 5:31).

As a result of these two different versions, "higher critics" from the Enlightenment Age (1685–1815 CE), such as the French physician Jean Astruc and the German theologian Johann Eichhorn, have published numerous articles and books undermining the credibility of Genesis. For example, in 1753, Astruc claimed:

> "Genesis contained two contradictory creation narratives, which 'obviously' came from different sources. He asserted that Moses had borrowed and interwoven material from several independent sources."[65]

Later, Eichhorn published the same conclusion (1780) and went on to popularize the notion:

Emerging geological research not only contradicted Genesis chronologies but also the creation date for the heavens and the Earth widely accepted by the church, one proposed by Irish Anglican Bishop James Ussher (e.g., to be 4004 BCE). He and his German colleagues theorized that much of the Old Testament represented a compilation of late, unreliable documents dating from 800–500 BCE. They argued that the Biblical accounts of Creation were edited versions of myths Hebrews borrowed from neighboring cultures.[66]

The impact of these views was very significant. They tended to "cast" doubt in believing in the Bible. Also, they contributed to the "paradigm shift" of many religious leaders, theologians, scientists, and laypeople from a strong belief in creation to one of evolution. Here is a brief description (order) of what and how it changed, especially during the nineteenth century in Europe:[67]

- *Higher criticism:* Bible is unreliable. Belief in God was now subjective, rested on "blind faith," and divorced from reason.
- *Protestant conservative response:* The Bible is God's divinely inspired Word; it cannot be judged as to which parts are genuine or which to ignore. Believing is based solely on the Bible (a.k.a. "Sola Scriptura" or "High View" from the Protestant creed), which is alone accurate and trustworthy, and science is suspect or wrong if it does not agree with the Bible.
- *Protestant liberal/modernist response:* Bible is a significant literary work, "inspired," but not in the strictest sense, and these believers have no respect for history, geography, anthropology, astronomy, or other scientific matters.

- *Higher criticism response:* these Christians would willingly ignore claims of inconsistency and contradiction and hence are naïve, unsophisticated, and intellectually inferior.
- *Scientific reaction:* this resulted in many scientists/others leaving the church and adopting evolution.
- *Peace at any price response:* the Genesis creation accounts should not be "overinterpreted" because they were no more than poetic ballads intended to communicate the beauty and harmony of nature, and they were metaphorical devices to express God's enjoyment of nature and His exhortation to humanity to join Him in appreciating the wonders of the natural realm.

In retrospect, the contemporary astrophysicist and apologist Hugh Ross attempts to shed some additional "light" on why the creation story is repeated and why the second version is so different from the first (e.g., as primarily seen in a different chronological order).

He believes their contents have a different theme and frame of reference. The questions from Genesis 1 focus more on physical creation issues — the what, the where, the how, and the in-what-order of creation. Genesis 1 presents the major physical creation events in a time-ordered sequence but gives just an abridged list of humanity's responsibilities. Genesis 2 zeros in on the why of creation. Genesis 2 lays out humanity's major responsibilities in a step-by-step sequence but provides an abbreviated list of physical creation acts. So, the questions arising from it tend to address theological and philosophical concerns.[68]

Are the "Days of Creation" Six Literal (Twenty-Four-Hour) Days?

Science demonstrates that the creation days are longer than twenty-four hours each day and that some events, as stated in the Bible, are not in the correct order.

This argument raises the question of accuracy and whether these Genesis passages should be interpreted literally or figuratively (e.g., figures of speech or symbolism). In addition, it has to do with the "age" of the universe and Earth and leads to many interpretations of the scientific evidence within and outside the Christian and other communities.

Three significant views seem to emerge from this controversial area:

- First, Genesis 1 presents ordinary twenty-four-hour days (for a total of 144 hours) in the exact sequence of events. This view is taken literally or strictly and is believed by many conservative Christian organizations. The literalist says believe it because that is what is written. They consist of "young earth" (and universe) believers. The creation science (CS) organization mainly supports them. They have developed the concept of the six creation days occurring some 6,000 to 10,000 years ago based on biblical genealogical records of the men (starting with Adam) mentioned in the Scriptures.[69]
- Second, at the other end of the spectrum, the Genesis 1 account of days is symbolic of the length of the days and the sequence of events. Each day is represented by an extended period. Specifically, the word for day or *yom* in Hebrew can be translated as a span or period of more than twenty-four hours for each day. Regarding

the sequence of events, God caused the clearing of the sky on day 4 so that the stars and other objects could be seen rather than making the stars on that day. More progressive Christian organizations believe this view. They consist of "old earth" (and universe) believers. The Reasons to Believe ministry supports the scientific discoveries leading to the universe being approximately 13.8 billion years old and the earth around 4.6 billion years old. The stars and other objects formed after the "creation big bang." They believe Genesis was not designed for scientific accuracy (e.g., sequentially precise). Genesis 1 does not describe how God created. It does not give us the physics of how He separated light and darkness, land and sea; it is not designed to tell whether He created aquatic and land-dwelling insects on the same day. It does not tell us whether the stars existed before day 4 or whether they simply became visible.[70]

- Third, in the middle view, the sequence is correct, but the days are longer than twenty-four hours. Gerald Schroeder, for example, argues that "Genesis presents creation in terms of 'cosmic time,' in which time is relative to the expansion of the universe after the 'Big Bang.'" In this way, he argues that "creation Day one was 24 hours by the cosmic clock, but eight billion years long as we count time today. Day 2 would have been four billion years, and Day three only two billion years. Day 6 would have been only 250 million years long."[71]

Was the Biblical Flood Story Copied from Ancient Writings?

The *Epic of Gilgamesh*, which is described in the epic Mesopotamian/Sumerian poem entitled *"He Who Saw the Deep,"* is taken from the Standard Akkadian version on Tablet 11 — circa thirteenth to tenth century BCE. (NOTE: The Sumerian *Eridu* Genesis, which is from a single clay Sumerian Tablet — ca. eighteenth century BCE — is the earliest known extant flood legend and is like the *Gilgamesh* epic.)

> Gilgamesh (King of Uruk was two-thirds god and one-third man) observes that Utnapishtim (he and his wife are the only humans to have been granted immortality by the gods, and they live on an island) explains that the gods decided to send a great flood. To save Utnapishtim, the God Ea (fountain of wisdom) told him to build a boat. He gave him precise dimensions and sealed it with pitch and bitumen. His entire family went aboard with his artisans and the animals in the field. A violent storm then arose, which caused the terrified gods to retreat to the heavens. Ishtar (goddess) lamented the wholesale destruction of humanity, and the other gods wept beside her. The storm lasted six days and nights, after which all the human beings turned to clay. Utnapishtim cries when he sees the destruction. His boat lodges on a mountain, and he releases a dove, a swallow, and a raven. When the raven fails to return, he opens the ark and frees its inhabitants.[72]

> NOTE: The story of Utnapishtim, the hero of the flood myth, can also be found in the Babylonian *Epic of Atra-hasis.*

By contrast, the Hebrew flood account is found in Genesis chapters 6–9 of the Bible. (The flood story is also contained in two non-canonical Hebrew books, the *Enoch* and *Jubilees*.) (NOTE: The Muslim flood account is found in the Qur'an Genesis suras 11:25–48 and is a similar story to the biblical Genesis account.)

> God selects Noah, a man who found favor in the eyes of the Lord, and commands him to build an ark to save Noah, his family (8 people in all), and the Earth's animals and birds (pairs of each). After Noah built the ark (450 x 75 x 45 feet with three decks), all the fountains of the great deep burst open, and the floodgates of the sky were opened. Rain falls for 40 days, the water rises for 150 days, and all the high mountains are covered. On the 27th of Cheshvan of the year 1657 from Creation, "the earth dried" (Genesis 8:14), completing the 365-day of the Great Flood. The ark rests in the mountains, and the water recedes for 150 days until the waters are gone, and Noah opens the ark. At this point, Noah sends out a raven and then a dove to see if the flood waters have receded. Noah and the animals leave the ark, Noah offers a sacrifice to God, and God places a rainbow in the clouds as a sign that he will never again destroy the Earth by water.[73]

When comparing these two versions of the flood, various themes, plot elements, and characters in the *Epic of Gilgamesh* have "relative" counterparts in the book of Genesis, notably in the stories of the garden of Eden and Noah's flood.

The British professor Andrew R. George

submits that the flood story in Genesis 6–9 matches the *Gilgamesh* flood myth so closely that "few doubt" that it derives from a Mesopotamian account. What is particularly noticeable is how the Genesis flood story follows the *Gilgamesh* flood tale "point by point and in the same order."[74]

In a 2001 Torah commentary released on behalf of the Conservative Movement of Judaism, rabbinic scholar Robert Wexler stated:

> The most likely assumption we can make is that both Genesis and *Gilgamesh* drew their material from a common tradition about the flood in Mesopotamia. These stories then diverged in the retelling.[75]

In conclusion, there are over 600 flood stories in numerous ancient cultures, and scholars widely accept that this is evidence of a significant ancient flood that served as the basis for these stories.[76] If a major flood destroyed a large portion of humanity, it would not be surprising that reports of this massive and destructive flood would be found in many cultures worldwide as humankind dispersed after this disaster. Even though there are major and significant differences in the various flood accounts, the pervasiveness of flood stories in many cultures lends historical credibility to a significant flood.

Besides the pervasiveness of flood stories, their many points of similarity make it likely there is a historical basis behind the stories. For example, both the biblical Genesis flood account and the *Epic of Gilgamesh* agree on these points: a divine judgment came upon humanity; chose a man to build a large boat to survive a flood that brought on the earth; the boat is built to specific dimensions (though not the exact measurements); brought all kinds of animals onto the boat to keep them alive; birds were released to check on whether the water had receded; the ark came to rest on a mountain and then offered sacrifices.

Even though there are many significant differences between the two accounts, many common themes like these appear. Therefore, the flood or deluge stories from the Hebrew Genesis biblical narratives and the Babylonian/Assyrian *Epic of Gilgamesh* poem and the Mesopotamian/Sumerian *Eridu* Genesis tablet "seem to be closely matched and 'few doubt' that the Genesis account is derived from a Mesopotamian account."[77]

The presence of flood stories written down in the Genesis account (and the fact that these stories share some similarities) does not mean the biblical flood account is not historically accurate. The pervasiveness of the flood stories (along with many similar themes) in so many parts of the world (over 600 reports) makes many scholars think that there had to be some major flood in the ancient world (perhaps around 5,000 years ago) to explain this. So this helps us to establish the plausibility of one critical aspect of the biblical flood story: namely, that there was a flood.

Does the Genesis creation account agree with modern scientific findings? The scientific discoveries are incompatible with the Genesis "days of creation."

The Genesis creation accounts were initially written for the ancient Hebrews and were "penned," most likely by Moses, in terms of the words that the Hebrews could understand and follow in their quest to follow God and His commandments to form a covenant between them.

Nevertheless, these biblical creation passages and other related ones in Scripture are probably the most scrutinized words ever written!

Here, a single all-powerful monotheistic God gave Moses these words in general terms to show or demonstrate that He created humans in His image to rule over all creatures, honor Him, and bless them (us) if they obeyed and followed Him.

Taking another perspective, as mentioned before, Genesis is not intended to be a scientific explanation of specifically "*how*" He did it. However, the biblical scriptures are organized logically and agree with the chronological order of events described in the scientific model. Therefore, there seems to be some "room" to explore this relationship without conflicting with a dogma of who and why God did it!

Surprisingly, some Christian interpretations of the ongoing scientific findings or discoveries are consistent with Genesis 1, while others are not. This situation presents a constant "battle or tension" between Christians, non-Christians, and scientists. Unfortunately, this dilemma has divided us, as previously mentioned in the Gallup and Pew polls. Specifically, the polls indicate a downward trend in believing God as the Creator of everything. To counter this "troublesome" trend, I have related the Genesis 1 "days of creation" events to the periods or eras derived from the current scientific discoveries (as discussed in chapter 10).

CHAPTER 4:

Creation Accounts

Supernaturalism

Background

Supernaturalism contains the concept of creation or creationism. Supernaturalism is something above or beyond the idea or notion of naturalism. It is a concept and belief beyond scientific understanding of the laws of nature but includes all aspects of nature. It is usually understood from a religious and theological perspective and involves manifestations or miraculous events considered to be of a supernatural origin. It also implies a divine being(s) that imparts an unlimited amount of power or force that commands or initiates (e.g., creates), controls or intervenes in the formation and development of our universe and everything within it. Theologically, various religions identify this divine source as a single "God" or multiple gods that have distinct characteristics and abilities.

In general, the concept of supernaturalism has a long human history. It probably (arguably) predates the concept of naturalism, which does not involve a God or gods in the formation and development of the universe, Earth, and all forms of life. In terms of creation, these supernaturally provoked, directed, and intended acts are found in the Hebrew book of Genesis accounts (e.g., Genesis chapters 1 and 2), the Sumerian *Eridu* Genesis tablet, the Babylonian *Enuma Elish* creation poem, and the Muslim Qur'an narrative, as previously discussed. Over 200 of these creation stories (some call them "myths") are from nearly every culture that has ever existed on Earth. They include but are not limited to Jewish, Christian, Muslim, Greek, Hindu, Buddhist, Chinese, Korean, Hopi, Maya, Zuni, Cherokee, Iroquois, Germanic, Nordic, African, and other cultures.

> NOTE: Most of these cultures also have a "flood" or deluge story and number in over 600. In particular, the Hebrew Genesis biblical narratives, the Babylonian/Assyrian *Epic of Gilgamesh* poem, and the Mesopotamian/Sumerian *Eridu Genesis* tablet contain these stories. However, as mentioned, the biblical version of the flood story differs significantly from these polytheistic religious stories.

In addition, the theology of supernaturalism relies on the concept of "*theism*," or the study of at least one "God" or divine being (or spirit or force) responsible for creating everything and providing significant meaning to us. This concept generally leads to various forms of creationism. Most creationists believe in some aspect of supernatural theism. Supernaturalism acknowledges that

> theists believe in a supernatural realm of existence. Supernaturalism is a name often given to any belief that there is more to reality than what is found in physical nature. Atheists believe there is nothing above, behind, or undergirding physical nature. Naturalism is thus another name for the (evolutionary) atheistic view that nature is all there is.[78]

In addition, Christian creationists believe

> the main form of philosophically developed theism believed in and by most religious people in the modern

world involves a "God" who not only created the physical reality, but who also acts in the world miraculously...an activist "Creator" who cares for "His" creatures...viewed as the ultimate governor of our universe and is thought of as being responsible for a moral order, as well as the physical structures, we see around the world...we are created by "God," and we all exist under the watchful intent of our "Maker"...who provides for us in this life and also provides a life to come...human persons embody the image of "God"...personhood is more similar to divinity than any form of physicality is... personhood thus resonates with the deepest nature of reality...persons can and will be given an eternal existence alongside "God," whatever may happen to the physical universe in which we have come to be.[79]

Specifically, the concept of a single and sole God involves a divine being who is believed to be separate from (e.g., "transcends" or "eternally exists" outside) His created universe (or world) and all living creatures. Belief in God and His miraculous process of creation is believed primarily by faith. This kind of faith involves a complete trust or confidence in a God who is beyond the natural realm. Believing this concept is primarily based on the doctrines of a particular "holy" and "authoritative" religious source, such as the Bible or Qur'an. Verified and validated evidence to support this belief claim can strengthen one's personal faith in a Creator God. In particular, the Bible provides us with well over 163 miracles[80] performed (eighty-three from the Old Testament and eighty-plus from the New Testament) and 2000 prophesies[81] that were historically fulfilled. Historically, ancient societies did not tolerate anyone who did not believe in their God or gods as the creator or creators (e.g., false prophets promoting other gods or prophets out for personal gain of selfish motive) were killed (Deuteronomy 13:1–5).[82]

Also, during this time of the Old Testament, history shows a departure from this divine concept starting with the Greeks, who began to "think" about other ways (perhaps more logically and scientifically?) of explaining our creation of everything, ultimately including humans. The Greek (e.g., before 300–200 BCE) and then Roman (before 300 CE) philosophers began questioning creation explanations, primarily through the worldview of "essentialism" or the topical thinking described by Plato and Pythagoras by 375 BCE. Essentialism taught that

> all seemingly variable phenomena of nature consist of classes only; each class is characterized by its definition (or its essence); and this essence is constant (e.g., invariable) and sharply demarcated against all other essences. Essentialism was compatible with most agnostic philosophers and with Christians during these periods. It was entirely consistent with the Christian concept of the unique and separated divine creation of "kinds" and that all species members are believed to be descendants of the first pair created by God.[83]

Additionally, Aristotle, an atheist who lived from 384–322 BCE, thought that individual species (which he defined as a breeding group) were fixed or always existed eternally and therefore rejected both evolutionary ideas as well as any creation accounts.[84]

Later, natural philosophers, who were predominately Christians during the later Roman world (300–700 CE) and the Middle Ages (700–1700 CE), tried to integrate the Genesis account of creation with the authoritarian and much-respected view of Aristotle. They typically viewed each species as created by God in the beginning, not just eternal, as Aristotle had said; after that to say that these species remained fixed for all time in a perfect, albeit fallen, creation.[85]

Within the Enlightenment Period (roughly 1700 to 1800 CE), new evolutionary theories began to re-emerge, ultimately leading to "Darwinism." The reaction to this movement of evolution was back to creationism, not creationism necessarily from the Bible but creationism based upon scientific evidence. Specifically, by the 1800s, early morphological (e.g., structural) research on how species were designed and laid out internally was conducted on fossil remains. Georges Cuvier (French Christian naturalist and founder of modern biology) concluded:[86]

> there are only a few basic patterns of animal representation; the various species we see are simply variations of these basic design types (i.e., vertebrates, mollusks, articulates, and radiates).

Species tend to breed true types, with only superficial varieties, because if there was a major change, the individual could not survive; therefore, the origin of new species through evolution was impossible.

Fossils seemed unchanged in the fossil record or recorded history (e.g., no significant change in living organisms over time).

There are sharp breaks in the fossil record, corresponding to epochs in geological history; with each gap or period in the fossil record, he found that each contained a distinct array of fossil types — species that are now in the fossils.

Cuvier broke these epochs into periods from oldest to youngest: Paleozoic, mainly marine invertebrates (perhaps some plants); Mesozoic, giant reptiles with subgroups; and Cenozoic, birds and mammals. He explained these periods by his "theory of catastrophism" such that after each massive catastrophe (perhaps caused by massive floods or ice age), God or some vital force would recreate different forms (i.e., kinds) of life. (NOTE: These periods are still used today.)

This explanation allowed Christians to try to reconcile the newly emerging scientific fossil record with the Genesis account of creation, even though he posited epochs or long periods of geological time. However, to counter this interpretation of long periods of creation time, Bishop Ussher calculated the beginning of creation at 4004 BCE, which was based upon counting past patriarchal generations from the Bible starting with Adam, the first "modern human" mentioned (Genesis 2–7). This explanation has led to different creation interpretations, which are covered later in this chapter. It also has led to "hotly" debated conversations and controversial legal court rulings, especially in America.

Given the relationship between creation and religion, let us examine these areas more closely. In particular, the term creation can have several meanings. First, humans can "create" things, such as readily observed by making, building, constructing, combining, or integrating objects, tools, or things, composing music scores, and generating art forms, producing technologically advanced computer-aided computer and artificial intelligence (i.e., AI) systems or products, etc. However, these items are always created out of something physical or material. Humans use their inherent mental and physical capabilities to "make" or "create" these items. Therefore, our form of creation completely differs from someone or something creating or initiating our universe and everything in it out of nothing! Here, the questions become: "Who or what" did it? "How" and "why" did it occur? Religion and creation primarily answer the "who" and "why" questions by conceiving a supernatural being, such as a single God or multiple gods, to provide this answer. (NOTE: By contrast, science and evolution attempt to answer only the "how" and "what" questions, as discussed in the next chapter.)

These questions are answered by various religions where they identify their God or gods, mainly through oral and written sources, such as their "holy" and "authoritative" scriptures or doctrines. In most cases, these creation stories begin as myths, which tend to lead to religious doctrines and "man-made" or "intuitionally organized" religions. Various religions and their doctrines are the second widely established way to provide a "big" picture perspective of our origins. Religion resembles mythology in that most religions contain stories that may sound and look like mythological stories at first glance. However, religious (e.g., creation) stories, unlike mythologies, include a reason "why" we should believe that they are true: divine revelation can take very different forms.[87]

> Historically, in order to provide an additional support to these accepted and long-standing traditional mythological beliefs, a claim that one of our ancestors, which was very close to the gods (or God) and that they revealed the "truth" of these stories to him. So, when mythological stories are combined with divine revelations, mythology tends to turn into religion.[88]

> NOTE: Philosophers never appeal to divine revelation or tradition in order to show that their theories are true; instead, they appeal to the power of reason. In a broad sense, philosophy can be understood as the attempt to develop a "big" picture view of the universe with the help of reason.[89]

In the most general sense, the French sociologist Emile Durkheim defined different religions as

> an organized collection of beliefs, cultural systems, and worldviews that relate humanity to an order of existence. Many religions have narratives, symbols, and sacred histories that are intended to explain the meaning of life of the universe. From their beliefs about the cosmos and human

nature, people derive morality, ethics, religious laws, or a preferred lifestyle. According to some estimates, there are roughly 4,200 (organized) religions in the world.[90]

Briefly, in his seminal book *The Elementary Forms of the Religious Life*, he defined religion as a "unified system of beliefs and practices relative to sacred things."

Religions and their associated theological beliefs on creation are not only manifested in organized religions but also embraced by individuals not part of any organized religion. For example, atheists and agnostics have their own beliefs on creation. In addition, secular humanism and now wokeism, as mentioned in the introductory chapter, play an ever-increasing and dominant role in many current worldview perspectives about our origins. Secular humanism is compatible with atheism and agnosticism. (NOTE: However, being an atheist or agnostic does not make one a humanist by itself.) Secular humanism rejects religious dogma. It is a conviction that principles, ideologies, and traditions, whether religious, political, or social, must be weighed and tested by each individual and not simply by faith. In 2002, the International Humanist and Ethical Union (IHEU) stated that humanism is not theistic and does not accept supernatural views of reality and religious beliefs as pseudoscience and superstition as the basis for morality and decision making. And lastly, the New Age movement, a broad category, refers to those who think that God is a spiritual, personal guide, or a God that defies specific description or its universal energy.[91]

Specifically, individual theological worldview perspectives of creation are often grouped and described by the main concepts of the various "Western" (e.g., originated from the Mediterranean area) and "Eastern" (e.g., originated from the Asian, Sub-Asian, and Pacific Islands or Oceanic areas) forms of theism, deism as part of monotheism, polytheism, pantheism, agnosticism, and atheism. Here are some of the essential distinctions among these beliefs.

Religious (and Other) Creation Beliefs and Positions on the Existence and Role of God

Theism acknowledges and worships the existence of one or more divinities or deities as the creator or creators that interact with the universe and yet transcends (e.g., is above and separate) his, her, or their creation "works." Some types of theism that can identify with religions of the world include:[92]

Monotheism is the belief in the existence of one God as the sole Creator of all. This belief is seen and practiced primarily in the Abrahamic (from the patriarch Abraham) "Western" religions of Judaism (i.e., Orthodox, Conservative, and Reform), Christianity (i.e., Roman Catholic, Protestant, and Eastern Orthodoxy), and Islam (i.e., Sunni, Shia, and Sufism). In general, God is an eternally existent being that exists apart from space and time, who is the Creator of the universe, and characteristically is omnipotent (all-powerful), omniscient (all-knowing), omnibenevolent (all-good or all-loving), and arguably, omnipresent (all-present everywhere).

Trinitarian monotheism is the belief that there is exactly one (a.k.a. Triune) God who exists in three persons in one Godhead (a.k.a. the mystery of the Trinity — Father, Son, and Holy Spirit as declared in the New Testament). This concept involves a Christian belief in the Triune God, who was and is actively involved in His creations.

Deism is a form of monotheism that believes that one God created the universe, but this God does not intervene in the world or interfere in the world with human life and the laws of nature. A deist believes this one God is like a "watchmaker" or "clockmaker" who created and then wound up the universe and now does not intervene in the universe at all (hence the "watchmaker or clockmaker principle"). Deistic viewpoints emerged during the scientific revolution of the seventeenth century when Europe came to exert a powerful influence during the eighteenth-century Enlightenment Period. For deists, human beings can know God only via reason and the observation of nature, not by revelation (as written in Genesis' account of creation, for example) or by supernatural manifestations (such as in miracles). Deism is related to naturalism because it credits the formation of life and the universe to a higher power, using only natural processes. During the eighteenth century, it paved the way for the understanding of new geologic and fossil discoveries occurring only through biological processes. These discoveries were made by naturalists who became known as scientists.

Henotheism is the belief that multiple deities may or may not exist, though there is a single supreme deity. Henotheism believes that numerous avatars of a deity exist, representing unique aspects of the ultimate creator. Examples are the Greco-Roman religions (Zeus and Jupiter respectively at the head of a pantheon of gods), early and medieval Vedic Hinduism (Indra and then Vishnu and Shiva respectively as supreme gods), and many of the Iron Age religions found in ancient Israel such as the Moabites worshipping the god Chemosh and the Edomites, Qaus, both of whom were part of the greater Canaanite pantheon headed by the chief gods El and Asherah.[93]

Polytheism is the belief in multiple gods and goddesses (some may be half or part-human) involved in the creation and is usually worshiped in temples. Gods are like humans (anthropomorphic) in their personality traits but with additional powers, abilities, knowledge, or perceptions. This belief is seen and practiced in most forms of Hinduism (i.e., Vaishnavism, Shaivism, and Shaktism), Mahayana Buddhism, and Chinese cultural or traditional religions (Confucianism, Taoism, and Shintoism). In the past, various pagan cultures, such as ancient Sumerians, Babylonians, Assyrians, Egyptians, Greeks, and Romans, embraced polytheism.

Pantheism is the belief that God and the universe are the same and there is no division or separation between the two. In other words,

God is equal to nature, the physical universe, or everything is of an all-encompassing, immanent abstract God. It posits a non-interventionist creator who permits the universe to run itself according to natural laws and derives the existence and nature of God from reason and personal experience rather than relying on revelation in sacred scriptures or the testimony of others. For example, God did not make the earth but is the earth and everything else in the universe. Many traditional and folk religions, including African traditional religions, Shintoism (the traditional religion of Japan), forms of Hinduism and Buddhism, and Native American religions, can be seen as pantheistic or a mixture of pantheism and other doctrines such as polytheism animism (i.e., worshiping animals, plants, and inanimate objects that possess a spiritual essence).

> NOTE: In Hinduism and other Asian and Indian religions, polytheism, pantheism, and monotheism can exist together, or they can consist in some combination of them. Also, most of these religions have a dominant philosophical component to their religious belief system.

Other (Irreligious, Nonreligious, and Ambivalent or Mixed Feelings)

Agnosticism believes that the nature and existence of God or gods are unknown and cannot ever be known. This "irreligious" belief contributes to a strong position. A weak agnostic position has no position, pro or con, on the existence of God or gods and has not yet been able to decide or suspends judgment due to lack of evidence. This belief is observed in Buddhism, where there is a lack of carrying or knowing who the Creator is. (NOTE: Agnosticism is not a religion, nor is it associated with any religious group. It is a position on the existence of God.)

Atheism is the belief that God or gods do not exist (strong position), or there is an absence of belief that any deities exist (weak position). This "nonreligious" belief involves some forms of Buddhism, Confucianism, Taoism, and Jainism. In Confucianism, God is not a core concern, and whether God exists (or not) does not affect the Confucian theory. In Taoism, even though they venerate gods, they do not have a God as the Abrahamic religionists do. No omnipotent being exists beyond the cosmos who created and controlled the universe. In Jainism, the universe and its constituents (soul, matter, space, time, and principles of motion) have always existed. Therefore, they reject the idea of a creator deity responsible for the manifestation, creation, or maintenance of the universe. (NOTE: Atheism is not a religion. Atheists do not associate with any religious group. They have their own communities and organizations that foster their beliefs.)

Apatheism is the lack of caring or attitude about whether any supreme being exists or lack thereof. This attitude could apply to members of any religion or belief system.[94]

> NOTE: It is important to see that some of these positions are not mutually exclusive. For example, agnostic theists choose to believe God exists while asserting that knowledge of God's existence is inherently unknowable. Similarly, agnostic atheists reject a belief in the existence of all deities while asserting that whether any such exists or not is inherently unknowable.[95]

Figure 7 illustrates the three basic traditional theistic conceptions or beliefs about "God" as identified by their associated religions and/or philosophies. They are:

Classical "Western" theism focuses on the three main Abrahamic monotheistic beliefs of Judaism, Christianity, and Islam.

Classical "Eastern" Poly/Pantheism focuses on the two Dharmic (Vedic) religious/philosophical beliefs of Hinduism, Buddhism, and other Asian religious/philosophical beliefs such as Confucianism, Jainism, Shintoism, and Taoism.

In addition, New Age beliefs (e.g., spirituality) are now part of the "Western" culture predominately practiced as a philosophy. (Although some individuals may see it as a form of a religious belief system, such as African and Native American cultural tribes.)

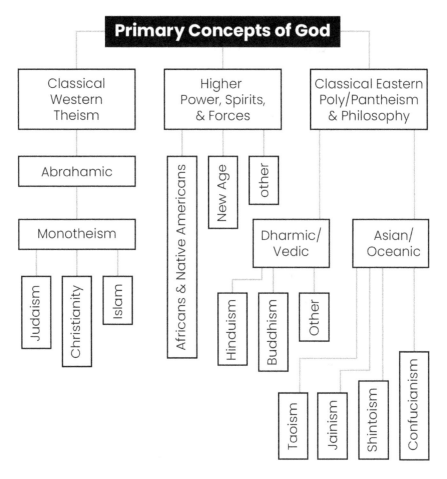

Figure 7: Different Concepts of God Based on Their Religions or Philosophies

Theological Creation Perspectives

Background

These religious creation beliefs are viewed by understanding the divine theological perspectives of general revelation and special revelation, first elucidated in-depth by the Catholic systematic theologian Thomas Aquinas.

> General (or Natural) Revelation is observed in God's creative works of nature. God uses the world (nature) to disclose facts about Himself. Special Revelation is based on authoritative sources, such as the Bible, that reveal the identification and description of the characteristics of a supernatural or divine being, such as God, who created or made the natural world as we know it to be. These concepts can be associated with Creation and evolution interpretations and the theistic, deistic, agnostic, and atheistic worldviews of God.[96]

These divine revelation perspectives, like mythological stories, contain a reason "why" we should believe they are accurate and "why" religious or spiritual experiences are authentic. They take different forms, such as from the prophets or patriarchs (i.e., Moses, Abraham, Mohammed, Jesus Christ, Joseph Smith, etc.) having dreams or directly hearing from "God" or His "angels" to prophesize and perform miracles, believing in the God's "inspired" holy texts and authenticity of holy artifacts (i.e., Bible, Qur'an, LDS, or Mormon Golden Tablets, temples, Qumran scrolls, etc.), or achieving enlightenment through religious experiences (e.g., Siddhartha Gautama or Buddha, the founder of Buddhism), and experiencing a personal relationship with God.

NOTE: Reformed Christian theologians of the sixteenth century, as part of Article 2 of the Belgic Confession, further developed these general and special revelation perspectives and are assumed in this book to apply to these religious areas, but especially to Christianity.[97]

Theology

The study of theology is usually associated with a particular religion, but this is not always the case.

Theology, on the other hand, is the systematic study of the existence and nature of the divine (*i.e.*, *God or gods*) and its relationship to and influence upon other beings. It is a specific branch, undertaken by a specific group which could be non-religious (e.g., feminist theology) or religious (i.e., Christian, Jewish, Muslim theologies).[98]

Religious theology usually has at least three basic tasks:[99]

- First, interpreting the significance of objects, events, and experiences from the perspective of faith. Theology develops the totality of religious teachings (e.g., dogmatics or the doctrine of faith).
- Second, connecting the thinking about faith with everything else in life, such as science, culture, and arts. Theology interprets humanity's existence in the world and determines the norms (ethics derived from faith) for action in the world (e.g., for one's disposition toward fellow humans, societal, political structures, and other institutions).

- Third, assessing what is accurate, intelligible, appropriate, or morally sound concerning these matters. Theology represents its claim to truth (e.g., doctrines of creation or revelation) and then confronts other claims to truth (for instance — relativism or evolution) with other criteria of verification (for instance — apologetics or scientific facts).

Considering these theological implications, we examine the differences between general and special (to include direct) revelations.

General Revelation

In general (or natural) revelation, God communicates His existence, will, power, and glory to us through nature. General revelation "displays" nature's physical phenomena and associated processes of the universe, Earth, life, and ultimately human life (e.g., His creative "works") that are plainly available to all mankind. God reveals Himself by directly implanting knowledge about Himself in all humans. "A working definition would be the revelation of God to all people, at all times, and in all places that proves that God exists and that He is intelligent, powerful, and transcendent."[100] Christian theologians cite biblical references to support general revelation, such as Romans 1:20 and Psalm 19:1–4, respectively.

> For since the creation of the world God's invisible qualities — his eternal power and divine nature — have been clearly seen, being understood from what has been made, so that men are without excuse.
>
> The heavens declare the glory of God; the skies proclaim the work of His hands. Day after day they pour forth speech; night after night they display knowledge. There is no speech or

language where their voice is not heard. Their voice goes out
into all the earth, the words to the ends of the world.

However, one can also view our world from a secular and/or scientific perspective. It is not limited to the beliefs of the Reformed Christian theologians or those practicing other religions. Nature is continually observed or seen by all of us but primarily measured and tested/validated by modern scientists using the scientific method. This method sounds straightforward enough; however, in practice, there is a difference of opinion or interpretation in what the results and conclusions are and what they mean, depending upon one's perspective or bias on their (*providing*) belief concepts of evolution and creation. It has been said that "religion exists to tell us why or what it means, and science exists to tell us how the universe works."[101]

Therefore, besides what the Bible tells us about God as the source for all creation, general revelation can be explained scientifically from two completely different perspectives or opposite ends of the spectrum of beliefs. Understanding nature (via verifiable or valid/testable experiments, reasons, or explanations for repeatable occurrences) can potentially give one a rational basis to:

- First, reinforce, influence, or maximize one's faith in the belief claim for a Creator of the universe, Earth, and life itself (e.g., via a Creator called "God" of the Bible).
- Second, minimize or reject one's faith in the belief claim in a creator of the universe, Earth, and life itself (e.g., no "God" or gods were involved or existed in the creation process).

This breakout "roughly" translates into the concepts or positions of creation and evolution, respectively.

NOTE: However, there are not only degrees of creation and evolution positions, but there are intermediate positions between them, such as in the theistic evolutionary view, which is a selected combination of the two concepts, where supernaturalism dominates in all cases.

These categories complicate our understanding of our origins and are often confusing, especially to the general public, who may have little knowledge of these distinctions. It is also a reason why we have such diverse views and why we may have many misunderstandings.

Special Revelation

Special revelation has been helpful in complementing general revelation to those who have a particular faith or belief system in someone beyond the natural world. Special revelation refers to the more specific truths that can be known about God through the supernatural. Biblically, God is initially identified as the Creator starting in Genesis chapter 1. However, general revelation does not explicitly identify or reveal Jesus Christ or His work of redemption for sinners (e.g., His atonement) as the Creator of the world. Special and direct revelation does. Hebrews 1:1–2 says:

> *In the past God spoke to our forefathers through the prophets at many times and in various ways, but in these last days he has spoken to us by his Son, whom he appointed heir of all things, and through whom he made the universe.*

Special revelation contrasts with general revelation. General revelation refers to the knowledge of God and spiritual matters which can be discovered through natural means, such as observation of nature through science, philosophy, reasoning, conscious, or providence (e.g., the sustaining power of God). Special revelation provides for the belief in God's intervention to make God's will and knowledge available that would not otherwise be available through general revelation. Christian theologians believe disclosure of this "special revelation" is at specific times and to specific persons. This disclosure is generally given through scriptures, miracles, prophecies, dreams, visions, personal experiences, and through the person and earthly life and ministry of Jesus Christ (Genesis 3:8, 18:1; Exodus 3:1–4, 34:5–7; Genesis 38:12, 37:5; 1 Kings 3:5, Genesis 15:1; Ezekiel 8:3–4: Daniel 7; 2 Corinthians 12:1–7; 2 Timothy 3:16–17; and Hebrews 4:12).[102] Theological or spiritual perspectives define special revelation. Here is an example used by evangelical scientists and Christian theologians (e.g., from Article 2 of the Belgic Confession):

> "Making Himself more clearly and fully known to us by
> His holy and divine Word as far as it is necessary for us to
> know this life, to 'His' glory and our salvation."[103]

So, when scientific explanations seem insufficient to explain some observations of the "mysteries" of nature, or we need a "bigger" picture of reality, a theological answer is often (but not always) provided to complete one's understanding of our origins. This is where special revelation often comes into the picture. However, special revelation cannot be explained scientifically. It must be understood and believed through one's faith and subsequent personal or practical religious experiences. This type of faith gives one a rational basis to reinforce, influence, or maximize one's faith in a belief claim for the existence of "God" as the "Creator and Designer" of our universe and everything within it. This belief "roughly" translates only to the concepts of creation and is where the power of philosophy and the concepts of religious faith beliefs, desires, actions, and knowledge come into play.

Philosophical Arguments

Several philosophical (e.g., logical) arguments for the existence of God are associated with the "*case for creation.*" They include:[104]

- *Pascal's Wager* (a self-interest perspective) *argument* (by Blaise Pascal in the seventeenth century): it argued for a belief in God based not on an appeal to evidence that God exists, but rather it is in our best interests to believe in God and is therefore rational for us to do so.
- *Ontological* (a metaphysical perspective) *argument* (by St. Anselm — eleventh century): it argues that part of what we mean when we speak of "God" as a "perfect being," or one of whom nothing greater can be conceived, and therefore that is essentially or inherently what the word "God" means.
- *Cosmological* (a cause and effect perspective) *argument* (from Aristotle to Islamic theologians of ninth to twelfth centuries to its reintroduction by Thomas Aquinas in the thirteenth century): it argues that the existence of the world or universe implies the existence of a being that brought it into existence (and keeps it in existence), that everything that moves is moved by something else, and therefore an infinite regression (that is, going back through a chain of movers forever) is impossible and at some point it stops with the ultimate or final cause or "God."
- *Teleological* (a design perspective) *argument* (from Socrates to Islamic theologians to Thomas Aquinas in the thirteenth century): it argues the appearance of design is far more plausible and far more probable that the universe is the way it is because it was created by God with life in mind rather than ordered by chance.

- *Moral argument*: It argues from the existence or nature of morality to the existence of God. Morality implies that it has a divine origin and consists of an ultimately authoritative set of commands that come from God, who has ultimate authority.
- *Religious experience*: It argues that personal religious experiences can prove God's existence to those who have them. One can only perceive that which exists, and so God must exist because there are those who have experienced Him.
- *Miracles argument:* It argues that the occurrence of miracles demonstrates both the existence of God and the truth of Christianity. If the Bible is to be believed, then Jesus' ministry was accompanied by frequent miraculous signs and His claims and teachings were endorsed by God the Father.

NOTE: There are counterarguments to these philosophical arguments (such as the incompatibility of God and evil and the moral justification for allowing evil). Theologians attempt to answer the challenge of evil by outlining a set of considerations that would show that there can indeed exist a God who is just in allowing the evil that we find in our world. This subject is known as theodicy.[105]

Religious Faith

Religious faith can be tied to the concept of special revelation. Also, understanding religious faith is essential because it is a subset of every belief claim and is, therefore, part of or integral to every religious or philosophical worldview.

Religious faith involves a stance towards some claim that is not, at least, presently demonstrable by reason. It is a kind of an attitude of trust or assent and is ordinarily understood to involve an act of will or a commitment and some kind of implicit or explicit reference to a transcendent source on the part of a believer. The basis for a person's faith usually is understood to come from the authority of revelation either directly through some kind of direct infusion, or indirectly usually from the testimony of another.[106]

Biblically, the most common definition of faith is found in Hebrews 11:1. It says, "Now faith is being sure of what we hope for and certain of what we do not see." The Greek word used most often in the New Testament for faith is *pistis*. It indicates a belief or conviction with the complementary idea of trust. Faith is not a mere intellectual stance but a belief that leads to action. James 2:26 says, "As the body without the spirit is dead, so faith without deeds is dead." Apostle James talks about demonstrating his faith through his works. We often say more about what we believe than what we say.

In other words, from this perspective, faith is essentially equal to a belief claim about someone or something (i.e., "faith = belief claim"). Two concepts rely on religious faith: special revelation holds that faith is exclusively based upon inspiration, revelation, or authority. Fideism states that faith alone is necessary; beliefs may be held without evidence or reason or even in conflict with evidence and reason.

> NOTE: By this definition, religious faith is also called "evidence-insensitive" by philosophers because it relies on faith alone, where faith always "trumps" reason or evidence in interpreting scientific evidence if in conflict.[107]

So, when appealing to the power of reason, reason may be philosophically defined by the following:

> Principles for a methodological inquiry, whether intellectual, moral, aesthetic, or religious; involves some algorithmic "demonstrability" that is ordinarily presupposed and once demonstrated, a proposition or claim is ordinarily understood to be justified as "true" or authoritative.[108]

> [However, the primary] impetus for the problem [or interaction] of faith and reason comes from the fact that the revelation or set of revelations on which most religions are based is usually described and interpreted in sacred pronouncements, either in an oral tradition or canonical writings, backed by some kind of divine authority. These writings or oral traditions are usually presented in the literary forms of narrative, parable, or discourse. As such, they are [somewhat] immune from rational critique and evaluation. [Even attempting] to verify religious beliefs rationally [may be] a categorical mistake. Yet most religious traditions allow and even encourage some... rational examination of their belief.[109]

To deal with these "apparent" unrelated terms, Anglican priest and physician John Polkinghorne et al. have studied the relationship between religion and science, which incorporate the principles of faith and reason, respectively. (Chapter 10 addresses this area in detail.)

However, "the key philosophical issue (or challenge) regarding the problem of faith and reason is to work out how the authority of faith and the authority of reason interrelate in the process by which a religious (*or a scientific*) belief is justified or established as true."[110]

In addition, when looking at these concepts, faith can be related to the evidence. Therefore, the philosophical nature of evidence needs to be further examined in relation to all belief claims.

Evidence

Evidence, broadly construed, is anything presented in support of an assertion (*e.g., proposition*). This support may be strong or weak. The strongest type of evidence is that which provides direct proof of the truth of an assertion. At the other extreme is evidence that is merely consistent with an assertion, but does not rule out other, contradictory assertions, as in circumstantial evidence. In other words, an assertion comes first, and evidence is something that supports an assertion, and evidence is strong, and some evidence is weak.[111]

Evidence can be seen from many perspectives, such as from science, religion, and philosophy. Science relies heavily on empirical evidence, while religion has traditionally leaned on eyewitness testimonials, narratives, symbols, and personal, experiential evidence. Philosophers have pointed out that there are hidden faiths in scientific knowledge; the empiricist creed that all knowledge is derived from sense experience is itself a dogma. The relationship between religion and science is the subject of continued debate in philosophy and theology.[112]

Evidence is usually thought of as coming from the physical or material discoveries of items (*i.e., the DNA structure, fossil record, artifacts, etc.*) through various scientific disciplines primarily using the scientific method or process. In addition, many of these scientific discoveries (*i.e., the age of the universe, black holes, laws of nature, etc.*)

are derived from the massive collection of data from technologically sophisticated devices, such as electron microscopes, land and space telescopes, particle colliders, etc. These findings can be factual or predictable, especially where different but similar and related experiments or discoveries can justify/validate the hypotheses, form theories, and provide conclusions. These conclusions, by scientists, can be interpreted to support the concepts of evolution, creation, or some combination of the two. Specifically, from a secular point of view, most scientists and most of the scientific community see or interpret the universe's origins and its development through natural means only. From a religious point of view, these findings are interpreted by other scientists to see "God" through His creative supernatural work — the universe or cosmos He created.

Personal religious experiences are believed to be "wired in" to us such that morality (sense of "right and wrong") is implanted in each of us. Thinking about "God" (e.g., a spiritual awareness — the "God" idea — has been there since the beginning of time across all cultures) is based on religious inner and/or outer experiences, such as divine revelations (i.e., dreams, direct contact, enlightenment, etc., as previously mentioned). The secular view of personal experiences is not concerned with "God" and His interacting or communicating with us since either He does not exist or is not involved in the creative process. Since personal experiences are not testable or repeatable, their validity or factual nature may be limited from a scientific perspective.

The Stanford Encyclopedia of Philosophy surveys some of the theoretical roles that the concept of evidence has been asked to play and explores some of the relations among them, such as (a) evidence as that which justifies belief, (b) rational thinker's respect for evidence, (c) evidence as a guide to the truth, (d) evidence as a sign, symptom, or mark, and (e) evidence as a neutral arbiter of objectivity, publicity, and intersubjectivity.

Therefore, when combining faith and evidence, a simple yet powerful equation or formula can be written, used, or even modified to establish or correct a belief claim for God through the reasoning process. It can be notionally written as:[113]

Faith + Evidence = Belief (Claim)

If the evidence is strong enough (i.e., well established by personal/religious experiences and/or proven through tested and predicted scientific results), then one's faith is not blind and becomes a rational faith and a reason to believe or accept one's concept or idea. On the other hand, if all or some of the evidence is weak (e.g., opposite of strong), then one's belief claim may also be weak or not as well supported or believed. The "power" of this equation or formula is notionally illustrated in figure 8. It depicts the "leap of faith" concept and can be applied when deciding one's personal views of our origins, specifically in the concepts of creation or evolution regarding our origins. The phrase a "leap of faith" comes from the Latin words *"saltus fidei."* This phrase was created by Søren Kierkegaard, who was a Danish philosopher.

Should I Jump?
— or —
What Should I Believe?

Figure 8: Leap of Faith

As more evidence is accumulated, one can (hopefully) imagine or envision the "gap" getting smaller and smaller so that one can be more confident with a well-supported and reasoned belief claim. In chapter 10, scientific evidence is presented in much more detail, especially in Genesis 1, the six "days of creation." Evidence is usually thought of as coming from purely the discoveries of various scientific disciplines, as it relates to our origins, creation, and evolution concepts. However, scientific results and conclusions can be interpreted to either "add" to the support or "subtract" to the lack of support of religious faith or belief claims (such as "God" as the Creator of the universe). The question (then) will be: Does belief in either the concept of evolution or creation or some combination of the two require a small step of faith or a gigantic "leap of faith"? In other words, is the preponderance of the evidence sufficient, reasonable, or rational to warrant or believe in one position or another or some combination of the two and in "what" way?

The Importance of Belief

Our beliefs are important for many reasons. Wars are fought over beliefs. Deals are made or broken because of beliefs. People gather over beliefs they have in common. They also separate because of divergent beliefs. We chart out our lives in every way in accordance with our beliefs. Many philosophers have analyzed human action as a natural consequence of our beliefs interacting with our desires and have come up with another formula:

Beliefs + Desires = Actions

"What we do in this world is a result of what we believe
and what we want…Having the 'right' beliefs are not just
a matter of intellectual importance, but it is of the utmost
practical importance."[114]

The Idea of Knowledge

We want our beliefs to be true, to connect to reality, to clue us in on what is really happening in the world and in our lives. This is where knowledge relates to beliefs. Knowledge is an attainment concept. Believing is, in a sense, the activity, and knowing is the intended attainment. Philosophers have a traditional analysis of knowledge that says:

Knowledge = Properly Justified True Belief

You cannot know something unless you believe it. Specifically, you cannot know there is a God unless you believe God exists. Belief is necessary for knowledge. But belief alone is not sufficient for knowledge. You can believe something that is false, and you can think you know it. This is where truth comes into play.[115]

The Truth about Truth

The philosophy of relativism claims that all so-called truth is relative, that there is no absolute truth, and different things may be true for me and true for you. This is sometimes also known as "perspectivism." Perspectives differ, this viewpoint alleges, and one is as good as another. Many philosophers insist that, for a state of belief to qualify as knowledge, there must be a link, a connection, a tie between the mental state of affirmation and the state of reality that makes the affirmation true. Furthermore, this link must be of the right sort to properly justify having that belief. This is where reason can connect to truth. We value rationality as a reliable and justified road to truth and, thus, knowledge.[116] In relation to God and His creation, "all [biblical] scripture is God-breathed and is useful for teaching, rebuking, correcting and training in righteousness, so that the man of God may be thoroughly equipped for every good work" (2 Timothy 3:16–17). Christians believe that the biblical account of creation is accurate and true (Jerimiah 30:1–2, 2 John 17:17…). However, there are several interpretations of creation.

> NOTE: This statement is congruent with the main theme of this book, "*It's ALL a Matter of Perspective!*[TM]"

Modern Creation Interpretations

From a creationist perspective, essentially, there are three main interpretation categories. They are the "old earth (universe) creationism or OEC," the "young earth (universe) creationism or YEC," and the "theistic evolution creationism or TEC" perspectives or views. The question of the "age" and "role" of God in and outside of our universe and especially in the earth are the main distinctions between these groups. These distinctions or conclusions lead to other differences or interpretations. Nevertheless, there are also areas of agreement between evangelical OEC and YEC proponents, such as (a) direct supernatural creation (a.k.a. *de nova* or brand-new) of all forms or kinds of life, especially humans. Random mutations and natural selection cannot adequately account for the complexity of life. (b) Opposition to naturalism is seen as a philosophical presupposition of evolution and a belief in a supernatural Creator is called God. (c) Opposition to macroevolution or common ancestry (e.g., no Darwinian "tree of life"). It is more like a "forest of different trees." Microevolution is generally accepted, but macroevolution is not, and (d) The historicity and literal truth of the Genesis origins account is accurate, but there are interpretations of the scriptural passages. Creation of the universe, out of nothing, occurred a finite time ago and included Adam and Eve, from which all of us came.[117]

Old Earth (Universe) Creationism (OEC) Perspective

Old earth creationists usually agree with the mainstream scientific estimates of the age of the universe, humanity, and Earth itself (*as determined by cosmology, geology, biology, and other "historical" sciences*) while at the same time rejecting most of the claims of modern evolutionary theorists with respect to biological evolution, such as macroevolution. This umbrella view is accepted by several Christians.[118] In the past, the old earth creation belief was strong among the nineteenth creationists, although this view dates from at least the fourth century (dating back to philosopher and bishop St. Augustine of Hippo). Today, the prominent contemporary defenders include astrophysicist and apologist Hugh Ross and his "Reasons to Believe" organization, astrophysicist and professor Robert Newman at Biblical Seminary in Hatfield,

Pennsylvania, and physicist and biblical scholar Gerald Schroeder. Most old earth creationists hold that the biblical flood (Genesis 6–8) was a local or regional flood (e.g., not global, covering the whole earth). Four main OEC interpretations or "schools of thought" include day-age creationism, intelligent design (neo)creationism, progressive creationism, and gap creationism.

Day-age creationists believe that the days of Genesis are not twenty-four-hour days and can be read more accurately as years (thousands, millions, or billions of years). (NOTE: Many OEC scholars classify this view as part of progressive creationism.) This theory is considered a more liberal interpretation of Genesis because of the change in the length of the days of creation. However, "Day-Age Creationists are not necessarily any more receptive to Evolution"[119] and is described as:

> A belief that the "days" spoken in the first chapter of Genesis are sequential periods and not literal, 24-hour days. Each day represents a much more extended, albeit undefined period, such as a million or more years. This is rooted to harmonize our understanding of the Bible with what appears to be overwhelming scientific evidence of an "old" Earth. The claim, then, is that the "days" of Genesis 1 are long periods corresponding to the significant periods of evolutionary history. Adherents often point out that the word "day" in Hebrew, "*yom*" sometimes refers to a period longer than a literal 24-hours day. In fact, this happens in the Creation account itself, in Genesis 2:4. There, the entire explanation is described as the "account of the heavens and earth when they were created, in the day that the Lord God made earth and heaven." This is also seen in God's warning in Genesis 2:17, where He warns that man will die "in the day" he eats from the tree. This view tends to support the Evolutionary Theist's or

Theistic Evolutionary and the Progressive Creationist positions.[120]

In Gerald L. Schroeder's updated book *The Science of God*, he argues that Genesis presents creation in terms of "cosmic time," in which time is relative to the expansion of the universe after the "big bang." In this way,

> he argues that "Creation Day," from a biblical perspective, looking forward from the beginning, was 24 hours in length. However, from Earth's perspective, the start of each day in years before the present time was: *Day One* — seven billion years long as we count time today; *Day Two* would have been 3.5 billion years; *Day Three* — 1.8 billion years; *Day Four* — 0.9 billion years; *Day Five* — 0.45 billion years, and *Day Six* would have been only 180 million years long.[121]

In support of this view, the Genesis International Research Association advocates for day-age creationism.

The intelligent design (neo)creationist's position supports or focuses on a scientific design interpretation, which implies the earth, life, and humanity owe their existence to a purposeful intelligent designer. Intelligent design (ID) is a modern adaptation of William Paley's *Argument from Design* (a.k.a. a teleological argument that was previously mentioned) and is a slight variant of progressive creationism. ID presupposes that some biological systems are so complex and/or unlikely that the randomness of evolution cannot explain their existence or function. To solve this problem, ID offers up an unknown intelligent designer. Most scientists argue that ID offers no "undisputed" related scientific research or experimentation to help define this designer or how he/she/it acts on the natural world.

The ID concept stresses the scientific concept of "common design" over "common ancestry or descent" as theorized by evolutionists. They claim that certain features of the universe, Earth, and living things are best explained by an intelligent cause, not an undirected process such as natural selection, as proposed by Charles Darwin. The intelligent design movement (IDM) and organization emerged in the late 1970s and early 1980s by a group of scientists (i.e., Charles Thaxton, Walter Bradley, Roger Olson, and Dean Kenyon) who tried to account for an enduring mystery of modern biology. Specifically, the origin of the digital information encoded along the spine of the DNA (i.e., *deoxyribonucleic acid*) bio or organic molecule.[122]

> These individuals were strongly influenced by several distinguished scientists, philosophers, and design theorists during the 1960s and the early 1970s which began to reconsider the "design hypothesis" and that the laws and constants of physics are improbably "fine-tuned" to make life possible. As British astrophysicist Fred Hoyle put it, the fine tuning on numerous physical parameters suggested that a "super intellect had monkeyed with physics for our benefit."[123]

The intelligent design organization (movement) primarily stresses the concepts of design inference, irreducible complexity, and fine-tuning. Intelligent design proponents believe that these concepts are "scientific" in nature and assert that life could only be created by an intelligent source, agent, or designer beyond us. No specific supernatural source (such as a biblical God) is promoted or endorsed by them as an organizational position. "They sought to avoid legal prohibitions by leaving the source of creation to an unnamed and undefined intelligent designer, as opposed to (*naming*) God."[124] They do not support a particular religion but have Christians and members of other faiths on their staff as part of the Intelligent Design and Evolution Awareness (IDEA) Center. Some of their principles include:

The concept of "intelligent design inference," as explained in mathematician, philosopher, and theologian William A. Dembski's and professor Sean McDowell's 2008 book *Understanding Intelligent Design*, "must pass the test (a.k.a. Explanatory Filter) of 'Specified Complexity' if an object or event happens naturally (through an undirected process such as Natural Selection acting on random variations) or (*supernaturally*) intelligently designed."[125] The ID proponents use information theory to suggest that messages transmitted by DNA in the cell show "specified complexity" — specified by intelligence and that must have originated with an intelligent agent. Therefore, this filter empirically detects the "apparent design" of living organisms, which virtually all biologists acknowledge.[126]

The concept of "irreducible complexity" was first introduced by biochemist Michael Behe in his 1993 book *Pandas and People* and later elaborated in his 1996 book *Darwin's Black Box: The Biological Challenge to Evolution*, in which this notion is a sure sign of design. The "irreducible complexity" concept asserts that all moving and necessary "parts" (cells, tissue, organs, etc.) of a system (like an animal) must be simultaneously in place (e.g., integrated) for it to operate or function properly within a designed body structure or plan. As a much simpler analogy of an irreducibly complex biochemical system, Behe considers the bacterial flagellum.

> The flagellum is an acid-powered rotary motor with a whip-like tail that spins at twenty-thousand revolutions per minute and whose rotating motion enables a bacterium to navigate through its watery environment. Behe shows that the intricate machinery in this molecular motor — including a rotor, a stator, O-rings, bushings, and a drive shaft — requires the coordinated interaction

of approximately forty complex proteins and that the absence of any one of these proteins would result in the complete loss of motor function. Behe argues that the Darwinian mechanism faces grave obstacles in trying to account for such irreducibly complex systems. In *No Free Lunch*, William Dembski shows how Behe's notion of "Irreducible Complexity" constitutes a particular instance of "Specified Complexity."[127]

The concept of "fine-tuning" (a.k.a. the "anthropic principle" for the universe and "Goldilocks principle" for the earth) is described in astronomer Guillermo Gonzales's 2004 book, *Our Privileged Planet*. He points out there are conditions of the universe that need to be precisely set for the emergence and sustenance (e.g., sustainment) of life on Earth.

These conditions include: a "just right" spiral Milky Way Galaxy, a galactic habitable zone for our Solar System, a star (Sun) size and luminosity, planets close to our Sun, surrounding planets for protection of the Earth, especially Jupiter which protects against asteroids and comets and Mars against asteroids, the Earth's moon which stabilizes the Earth's tilt and prevents extreme temperatures, and our planet Earth's size, orbit, core, etc.[128]

ID concludes that mathematically or statistically, these and other key parameters or requirements for life, and especially human life, are essentially "*impossible*" without the consideration of an intelligent designer that exists beyond the natural world.

In 2013, philosopher of science Stephen C. Meyer's book *Darwin's Doubt: The Explosive Origin of Animal Life and the Case for Intelligent Design* tells the story of the mystery surrounding the explosion of animal life (a.k.a. the "Cambrian explosion" or the "biological big bang explosion") some 530 million years ago — a mystery that has intensified, not only because the expected ancestors of these animals have not been found but also because scientists have learned more about what it takes to construct an animal. Expanding on the compelling case he presented in his book *Signature in the Cell* (and later in 2013, *Darwin's Doubt*), Meyer argues that the "theory of intelligent design" — which holds that certain features of the universe and of living things are best explained by an intelligent cause, not an undirected process such as natural selection — is ultimately the best explanation of the origins of the Cambrian animals.[129]

Lastly, in 2005 the US Federal District Court decided in Kitzmiller v. Dover Area School District ruled that ID was a form of creationism (arguably now called neo-creationism) and that it violated the Establishment Clause of the First Amendment to the US Constitution (e.g., "separation of church and state" interpretation).[130] Nevertheless, the ID organization is very active today. Their headquarters is at the Discovery Institute in Seattle, Washington, and has numerous religious followers, many of whom are Christians.

Progressive creationists believe God created new forms of life gradually over hundreds of millions of years. It accepts mainstream geological and cosmological estimates for the age of the Earth and some tenets of biology such as microevolution and archeology to make its case. In this view, creation occurred in rapid bursts in which all "kinds" of plants and animals appear in stages lasting millions of years. The bursts are followed by periods of stasis or equilibrium to accommodate new arrivals. These bursts represent God creating new types of organisms by divine intervention. As viewed from the archeological record, it holds that species do not gradually appear by the steady transformation of their ancestors but appear all at once and "fully" formed.[131] The view rejects macroevolution because they believe it to be biologically untenable and not supported by the fossil record,[132] and they reject the concept of universal descent from a last universal common ancestor.[133] "Thus, they attack the evidence for macroevolution, but affirm microevolution as a genetic parameter designed by the Creator into the fabric of genetics to allow for environmental adaptations and survival."[134] This view dates back to the eighteenth-century French anatomist Georges Cuvier, who proposed that there had been a series of successive creations due to catastrophes such as floods and afterward repopulated the regions with new forms. Many other scientists (geologists and paleontologists) had similar ideas in the 1800s, such as Alcide d'Orbigny, William Buckland, Hugh Miller, and Louis Agassiz. A revival of this view became known as "progressive creationism" in the 1930s and then expanded into modern progressive creationism.[135]

The Reasons to Believe (RTB) organization is one of the leading groups that advocate "modern" progressive creationism. (NOTE: Modern progressive creationism includes the latest biological, chemical, and stellar scientific evidence as it relates to creation, and especially the biblical six "days of creation.") A summary of the main progressive creationist beliefs includes:[136]

- The universe is approximately 13/14 billion years old and came into existence via the "creation big bang,"
- The earth is approximately 4.6 billion years old,
- The days of creation were vast ages, undetermined in length (e.g., because scientific estimates seem to change somewhat with new discoveries),
- The seventh day is continuing now,
- Death, disease, and suffering were present before Adam's fall into sin,
- God progressively created brand new species as old ones died out but did not use evolution as the process for doing so,

- Before Adam, there were soulless hominoids on the earth, commonly referred to as "pre-Adamites,"
- The genealogies in the Bible are not tight but contain gaps (e.g., missing generations),
- Noah's flood was not global but local and was restricted to the Mesopotamian region (NOTE: As mentioned, other local floods were documented but not mentioned in the Bible), and
- The Reasons to Believe Christian organization and ministry emerged in the mid-1980s.

In 1986, Hugh Ross (astrophysicist-turned-apologist) became the leading proponent and founder of the modified (e.g., modern) version of Bernard Ramm's concept of progressive creationism as documented in his 1954 paper "The Christian View of Science and Scripture" (a term developed by Russell L. Mixter in the 1930s), which did away with the necessity for a young earth, a global flood, and the recent appearance of humans.[137] The RTB ministry is located in Covina, California, and is currently led by biochemist Fazale Rana. The RTB ministry believes that faith, reason, religion, and science can be compatible with each other under certain conditions. RTB creationists believe that the six "days of creation," as described in the Bible, basically agree with the major scientific creation events in history. Details of the correlation between these six days and the scientific evidence for each day are illustrated in chapter 10. However, Table 4 gives a very brief overview of a creation timeline from an RTB perspective:[138]

APPROXIMATE TIMES FROM CREATION EVENT	EVENT
0	Moment of creation (some kind of singularity)

APPROXIMATE TIMES FROM CREATION EVENT	EVENT
0 to 10^{-43} seconds	Release of space curvature
10^{-43} seconds	Loss of dimensions
10^{-35} seconds	Strong electroweak separates into the strong and electroweak forces
10^{-35} seconds	Photons and leptons appear
10^{-11} seconds	Electroweak force separates into the weak and electromagnetic forces
10^{-10} seconds	Quarks appear
10^{-5} to 10^{-4} seconds	Baryons and antibaryons appear
0.001 seconds	Annihilation of antimatter occurs
3 minutes	Nuclei appear
300,000 years	Atoms appear; light separates from darkness (outer space becomes black)
365 million years	First stars form
500 million years	First galaxies appear
2 billion years	All manner of quasars and galaxies appear
9 billion years	Solar system appears
10 billion years	Life created on Earth

APPROXIMATE TIMES FROM CREATION EVENT	EVENT
13 billion years	Creation of dozens of new phyla (Cambrian explosion)
13.5 billion years	Creation of dinosaurs
13.73 billion years	Creation of man

Table 4: RTB Creation Timeline

Specifically, the RTB proponents see a compatibility between biblical scriptures and scientific discoveries and attempt to integrate faith and science by exercising and validating an RTB model. RTB progressive creationists believe the biblical sequence of creation events aligns with the scientific findings for the sequence of the origins, the formation of the earth, and the beginning of life.[139]

The RTB model is adjusted with new scientifically validated discoveries as long as they do not conflict with biblical scriptures. They use the term "model" to summarize physical (observational) and biblical data relevant to creation into a coherent explanatory framework. Their model (a) collates all that the Bible says about God's creative work, (b) integrates individual accounts into a coherent picture, (c) presents this interpretation in the form of a scientific model that one anticipates or predicts future findings, (d) evaluates its accuracy considering scientific evidence, and (e) reevaluates both biblical and scientific data and adjust the model if appropriate.

The following foundational beliefs help shape how they interpret the data: (a) the Bible (including Genesis 1:1) is the error-free word of God, (b) the creation account of Genesis 1 follows a basic chronology, (c) the record of nature is also a reliable revelation from God, (d) the message of nature will agree with what the Bible says, (e) the Bible contains a selective summary description of God's creation activity (e.g., no mention of dinosaurs, bipedal primates, quantum mechanics, or the presence of other solar system planets), and (f) God gives humans the privilege to fill in the details, carefully, through patient, ongoing exploration, and increased understanding of the natural realm.[140]

The RTB mission is to "demonstrate that sound reason and scientific research — including the latest discoveries — consistently support, rather than erode, confidence in the truth of the Bible and (*that*) faith in a personal, transcendent God revealed in both Scripture and nature."[141]

Their position is one of the leading progressive creation views that are essentially compatible with a version of the "old universe/earth and day-age theories." Their organization accepts the historical accuracy and inerrancy of biblical scriptures, as well as most findings of modern science. This is accomplished by taking the view that the Genesis account is given from the perspective of someone on the surface of the earth. The appearance of light on the first day is taken to be the modification of the atmosphere to allow light to pass through to the earth's surface. The universe, Sun, Earth, Moon, etc., are all believed to have been created in the event of Genesis 1:1. The subsequent descriptions describe the transformation of the earth into an inhabited world. The order of the events in Genesis and its many predictions of future discovery match remarkably well with the geological (*as well as the cosmological*) record. They endorse common design that the biblical God used, fine-tuning of events that made life possible, and some versions of evolution such as microevolution within species and perhaps in Genera (*e.g., next highest classification level*), but not the common descent or the universal common ancestor concept. Their perspective also holds that species do not gradually appear by the steady transformation of their ancestors *but* appear all at once and "fully" formed.[142]

The RTB model or concept builds and validates its model by doing the following:[143]

- Collating all that the Bible says about God's creative work,
- Integrating the individual biblical accounts into a coherent picture,
- Presenting this interpretation in the form of a scientific model, one that anticipates or "predicts," future findings,
- Evaluating its accuracy considering scientific advances, and
- Believing God's two revelations (Scripture and nature) will agree when correctly interpreted.

If there are any apparent contradictions, the data are reexamined, both biblically and scientifically — recognizing that our understanding is incomplete. Sometimes the scientific data seems unclear or awkward fit with the biblical data, but they see such instances as an opportunity to study both of God's revelations more deeply.[144]

Along with the ID organization, the RTB proponents cite the "Cambrian biological explosion" of major newly formed and complete body plans of animals as a major example of this belief.

The basic creation explanations need not be wholly supernatural in that creation in the Bible also includes God working through the regular laws and processes of nature (general providence). All-natural processes and events are assumed to be fully contingent on the free choice of God. This progression of creation is advanced in degrees by God's activity over a long period of time. For example, the biblical six creation days sequence is compatible with scientific findings and conclusions. RTB accepts the scientifically determined age of the universe, Earth, and life but seeks to disprove Darwinian and atheistic evolution.[145] RTB adheres to a liberal or progressive (vice strict) translation of Genesis 1 and 2 and holds to the principle that "Scripture interprets Scripture" to shed light on the context of the creation account in which he describes the Hebrew word *yom* to have multiple translation possibilities, ranging from a "literal twenty-four-hour day" to long periods — ages, epochs that encompass thousands or millions of years each (*which they endorse*) — and contends that at the end of each Genesis "day," except for the seventh "day," the phrase, "And there was evening, and there was morning," is used to put a terminus of each event. The omission of that phrase on the seventh day is in harmony with the literal translation of Hebrews 4 continuing the seventh day.[146]

The gap theory creationists (a.k.a. restitution or ruin — resurrection creationism) interpret millions of years between Genesis 1:1 and the six literal twenty-four-hour creation days as described in Genesis 1:2. Minister C. I. Scofield popularized "gap creationism" and describes:

> The beautiful Universe and Earth God created "in the beginning" somehow became ruined (the most popular interpretation blames Satan and the rebel angels or demons) and was later repaired by God, as described in the six-day account. They believe that the astronomers, geophysicists, paleontologists, and anthropologists are measuring the ancient ruined Creation, whereas the Bible addresses the recent, repaired Creation.[147]

Specifically, gap theory creationism assumes a vast period elapsed between the first two verses of Genesis. Most variations of this theory interpret Genesis 1:1 as the first creation, which included the creation of the heavens, the earth, plants, and animals, and even a race of humans preceding Adam. Perhaps billions of years then elapsed, during which time Satan and his angels fell (*from heaven*) and corrupted the inhabitants of the earth. God then judged and destroyed the earth and all its inhabitants. Thus, the earth became "formless and void" (Genesis 1:2) and remained that way for eons. The second creation, according to the gap theory, began in Genesis 1:3 with the first day of the familiar six days of creation of the (re)creation week.[148]

Because gap theory allows for an almost literal reading of the Bible, it retains the twenty-four-hour "days of creation" and rejects evolution. It is considered one of the more conservative interpretations of Genesis, but it is still rejected by biblical literalists. The gap theory is easily confused with the distinct (*and often criticized*) term "God of the Gaps."[149]

NOTE: "God of the gaps" is a theological perspective in which gaps in scientific knowledge are taken to be evidence or proof of God's existence.[150]

This gap theory was first introduced in 1814 by Scottish theologian Thomas Chalmers to reconcile the six-day biblical creation account with the newly defined geologic ages being set forth by leading geologists of that era. Chalmers attributed the concept to the seventeenth-century Dutch Arminian theologian Simon Episcopies. More contemporary proponents of the gap theory include Bible teacher J. Vernon McGee and Pentecostal televangelists Benny Hinn, Jimmy Swaggert, Oral Roberts, Cyrus I. Scofield, and Chuck Missler.[151]

From an OEC perspective, theistic evolutionism (TE) is the belief in both evolutionism and theism. The TE interpretation is also known as "God-guided evolution."

God acts and creates through [the] laws of nature. It posits that the concept of God is compatible with the findings of modern science, including Evolution. [TE] is not in itself a scientific theory, but includes a range of views about how science relates to religious beliefs and the extent to which God intervenes. It rejects the strict creationist doctrines of Special Creation, but can include beliefs such as Creation of the human soul.[152]

Geneticist Francis Collins describes TE as the position that "evolution is real, but that it was set in motion by God."[153] Modern TE accepts the general scientific consensus of the age of the universe and Earth, the "big bang or cosmological model," the fine-tuning of the universe, evolution, and natural selection, no special supernatural intervention involved once evolution got underway, humans as a result of these evolutionary processes, uniqueness of humanity and concern for moral law (knowledge of right and wrong), continuous search for God among all human cultures that defy evolutionary explanations and point to our spiritual nature, the origin of the solar system, the origin of life, and evolution itself.[154]

Specifically, TE is the belief that God used evolution as His means of producing the various forms of physical life on this planet, including human life. All theistic evolutionists believe that God performed at least one supernatural act — the act of creating the physical universe from nothing. It is held that Genesis is a nonliteral story written simply to teach that man has fallen and not meant to describe the specific circumstances regarding the origins of the universe. Theistic evolutionists fully accept that evolution is the scientific description of "how" organisms change over time and the result of descent with modification. At the same time, the theistic evolutionist is a theist — who believes in a God who is both personal and concerned with His creation. They could thus belong to any of the three monotheistic faiths or to any other theistic faith.[155] However, this may more properly be called "*deistic*" evolution since there are no miracles involved after the first act of creation. TE tends to believe God set the wheels of cosmic and biological creation rolling at the dawn of creation and then stepped back, letting things unfold as they may. This lack of teleology (direction) to theistic evolution is one major reason for its rejection by conservative creationists.[156] Therefore, there are two other types of TE — deistic evolutionism (DE) and evolutionary creationism (EC).[157]

Deistic evolutionists believe God (e.g., not necessarily the biblical "God") started the universe off with a "big bang" and let it run on its own without further interference. This process is also known as the "watchmaker or clockmaker" principle. The outcome of evolution and other processes are not, therefore, deterministic (e.g., they lack teleology). Some deists believe God ceased to exist or otherwise distanced himself from the material world after setting the universe in motion.

Evolutionary creationists are a conservative take on TE. The EC position holds that evolution and creation can *both* be true, with biblical events taking place outside of normal time. Because natural events are held to be fully controlled by God, EC retains theology (direction in evolution) without requiring any evidence within the material world. "From a scientific point of view, EC is hardly distinguishable from TE…the differences lie not in science, but in theology."[158] Most theistic evolutionists hold to at least two acts of creation: (1) the creation of matter out of nothing and (2) the creation of first life. After that, allegedly, every other living thing, including human beings, emerged by natural processes that God had ordained from the beginning. Some theistic evolutionists do insist that God directly created the first soul in the long-evolved primate to make it truly human and in His image.[159]

The theistic evolutionary creationist's position is dominant among creationists today. Along with the Roman Catholic Church, many mainline or liberal (Protestant) denominations advance the perspective of theistic evolution to one degree or another. Besides Roman Catholicism, Eastern Orthodoxy, Anglican Churches, Judaism, and Islam believe in various views of TE. Specifically, Jewish Reform, Conservative, and Modern Orthodox movements have stated that they feel there is not a conflict between evolutionary theory and the teachings of Judaism, while some Haredi rabbis (of the Hasidic ultraconservative community) have remained staunchly opposed to certain teaching in evolutionary theory. In contrast with the literalist interpretations of some Christian creationists, they expressed openness to multiple interpretations of Genesis through Jewish oral tradition and mysticism. They have also expressed an openness to evolutionary theory in biology, except where they perceive that it conflicts with the *Torah's* account of creation.[160]

Islamic views on creation and evolution are diverse, ranging from theistic evolutionism to evolutionary creationism. The mainstream scientific analysis of the origin of the universe is supported by the Qur'an. Many Muslims believe in EC, especially among Sunni and Shia Muslims and the liberal movements within Islam...Muslims accept science as being fully compatible with Islam and readily accept microevolution and the belief in macroevolution, with the only exception being human evolution... Humans are not viewed as part of the evolutionary scheme but rather as being unique and honored creation of Allah. From an Islamic perspective, everything takes place according to Allah's will and permission and as predestined by Him alone.[161]

The Roman Catholic version of TE is that human evolution may have occurred, but God must create the human soul, and the creation story in the book of Genesis should be read metaphorically.[162]

Finally, many mainline/liberal Protestant denominations have long accepted some form of evolution within the notion of creation. EC (essentially the new term for TE) is increasingly known among evangelical Christians, who strive to keep traditional Christian theology intact. According to executive director of the National Center for Science Education E. C. Scott,

> in one form of another, the view of creation taught at most mainline Protestant seminaries is TE or EC, and despite the Catholic Church having no official position, it does support belief in them. In addition, studies show that acceptance of Evolution is lower in the U.S. than

in Europe or Japan: around 34 countries sampled, only Turkey had a lower rate of acceptance than the U.S.[163]

Young Earth (Universe) Creationism (YEC)

Young earth creationists believe God directly created the universe in six literal twenty-four-hour days. They usually place the age of the earth between 6,000 to 10,000 years ago. They believe in a global flood (around 5,000 years ago) during Noah's day, God's creation of the world with an "apparent" old age, and (often) the existence of a single continent before the flood. They view the book of Genesis as a historical record of what happened, not an allegory or metaphor. They interpret the words *day*, *evening*, and *morning* without symbolism, as a plain term meant to be understood literally. They believe that the

> origin of the earth, the universe, and various forms of life, etc., are all instances of special creation. The doctrine of special creation involves direct divine intervention, suspending the laws of nature to achieve a given result. This doctrine contrasts with a view common among theistic evolutionists that God can work through natural laws… YEC writings tend to focus on attempting to explain why much of modern science cannot be correct…A major YEC endeavor is to explain how the 15 million or more species alive today could have evolved from a much smaller number of "kinds" which they believe were created in Genesis. This project is sometimes referred to as "baraminology," named after the Hebrew word *min*, which is traditionally translated as "after its kind," in passages like "And God said, Let the land produce living creatures according to their kinds: livestock, creatures that move along the ground, and wild animals, each

according to its kind" from Genesis 1:24. A central tenet of Young Earth Creationism is that evolution is possible only within these created kinds, a form of evolution they call *microevolution*, while it is not possible between kinds, which they distinguish as *macroevolution*. This is not the way those terms are used by the scientific community.[164]

Young earth creationism keeps the creation of the plants, sun, and animals in the biblical sequence of Genesis 1:1. Young earth creationists believe that when Romans 5:12 says, "Sin entered the world through one man, and death through sin," the Bible is saying that death did not exist prior to Adam. YEC sees no need to be in harmony with uniformitarian models of the earth's beginnings, especially when such models are usually rooted in a naturalistic worldview. Science demands that evidence be examined and verified. YEC does not shy away from geology, astronomy, biology, or any other field of study. "It is the interpretation of the evidence that makes the difference in Creation beliefs, as discussed above. Proofs for Young Earth Creationism are published by organizations such as the Institute for Creation Research (ICR)."[165]

In addition, YEC advocates are Christian fundamentalists (mainly conservative Protestants). They repudiate the evidence for the "common descent" of humans and other animals as demonstrated and believed by modern paleontology, genetics, histology, and cladistics. (NOTE: Cladistics is an alternative approach to biological classification in which organisms are categorized in groups or "clades.")

They assert these disciplines are based upon the conclusions of modern evolutionary biology, geology, cosmology, and other related fields. Instead, they argue for the Abrahamic accounts of creation and, in order to attempt to gain a place alongside evolutionary biology in the science classrooms, have developed a rhetorical framework of creation science.[166]

As biologists grew more and more confident in evolution as the central defining principle of biology,[167] American membership in (mainly Protestant) churches favoring increasingly literal interpretations of Scripture also rose, with the Southern Baptist Convention and Lutheran Church-Missouri Synod outpacing all other denominations.[168]

The creation science (CS) organization is the main proponent of YEC. Creation science was founded by civil engineer Henry M. Morris, who reacted to the exclusive teaching of evolution in public schools during the 1960s. Creation science principles are based upon geologist and Seventh-day Adventist George McCready's 1923 book *The New Geology*, in which new catastrophism is emphasized. Morris's and theologist John C. Whitcomb's 1961 book *The Genesis Flood* and Morris's 1974 book *Scientific Creationism* revived this concept.

The CS concept promotes a literal or strict interpretation of the Bible. In other words, the universe and Earth were created in six twenty-four-hour days approximately 6,000 to 10,000 years ago and are generally based upon the genealogy/chronology of the patriarchs (*starting with Adam*) of the Bible.[169]

NOTE: This date was initially calculated by Anglican bishop James Ussher and then by John Lightfoot in the seventeenth century by counting the generations backward from Jesus to Adam. Ussher calculated October 4, 4004 BCE (and was later corrected by Lightfoot to October 18, 4004 BCE) as the beginning date of creation. The "Young Earth Creationists often believe that the Universe has a similar age to that of the Earth."[170] Creationist cosmologies result from attempts by some creationists to assign the universe an age consistent with the Ussher chronology and other young earth timeframes based on the genealogies.[171]

The CS belief is consistent with believing in a worldwide or universal biblical Genesis flood (as predicted by many cultures). CS argues that the earth "looks" or "appears" much older than it is and can be explained primarily by Noah's global flood, which dramatically changed the geology of the earth.[172] This view is also known as "flood geology." Therefore, they reject the fundamental principles of modern geology (and modern science in general) and especially the concept of uniformitarianism and radiometric dating, which means applying the same physical and geological laws observed on the earth today to interpret the earth's geological history.[173] They reject common descent and the insufficiency of mutations and Darwin's natural selection mechanism in bringing about the development of all living kinds from a single organism.[174] They especially disagree that the "hominid" ancestor's lineage is evidence for the unique or divine origins of modern humans or Homo sapiens *sapiens*.[175] The CS organizations (such as the Institute for Creation Research, Geoscience Research Institute, and the Creation Research Society) are very active today and have many followers.[176]

In summary, CS includes the scientific evidences and related inferences: (a) sudden special creation of the universe, energy, and life from nothing (creation ex nihilo) by God's commands (fiat lux), (b) the insufficiency of mutations and the natural selection mechanism (mainly attributed to Charles Darwin) in bringing about the development of all living kinds from a single organism (no macroevolution or common descent), (c) changes only within fixed limits of originally created kinds (or baramins) of plants and animals (microevolution accepted), (d) separate ancestry for modern humans and apes (no evolutionary missing links), (e) explanations of the earth's geology by catastrophism, including the occurrence of a worldwide flood (a.k.a. flood geology) as observed by the fossils in the geological column (no uniformitarianism or radioisotope fossil dating methods), and (f) a relatively recent inception of the universe, Earth, and all forms of living kinds within the last 6,000 to 10,000 years ago according to the book of Genesis, which is accurate and inerrant.[177]

> NOTE: Most evolutionists today refer to CS as "the" only interpretation of creationism while ignoring other creation interpretations, as discussed above.

Consequently, the CS proponents wanted public schools to teach their creationist concepts as an "alternative" to the theory of evolution. Based on the 1981 Arkansas Act 590 and the 1982 Louisiana Balance Treatment Act, CS could be taught alongside the teachings of evolution in public science classrooms. However, a 1982 McLean v. Arkansas decision ruled that CS was "simply not science and failed to meet the essential characteristics of science." Nevertheless, the teaching in public schools of CS continued until 1987.[178] In 1987, the

> U.S. Supreme Court's decision in Edwards v. Aguillard affirmed earlier rulings (McLean v. Arkansas and 1968's Epperson v. Arkansas) that 'forced' teaching CS in public science classrooms was unconstitutional because its sole purpose was to advance a particular religious belief. [179]

These teachings were considered religious in nature, were not science as defined by the scientific community, and therefore violated the First Amendment to the United States Consitution.[180] The courts interpreted this Establishment Clause to mean that the government could not establish a particular religion as a state religion and that teaching creation in public school science classrooms violated that clause.[181] In addition, the court concluded that "CS, as defined in the 1981 Arkansas Act 590, is simply not science."[182]

Finally, the overwhelming consensus of the scientific community was that "CS is a religious, not a scientific view, and that it does not qualify as science because it lacks empirical support, provides no tentative hypotheses, and resolves to describe natural history in terms of scientifically untestable supernatural causes."[183]

Creation Summary

The concept of creation contains the idea or reality of a supernatural deity or the belief that caused the universe and everything in it to begin or exist. This belief goes beyond naturalism or the laws of nature and requires a personal faith to believe in the existence of God, and particularly the God of the Bible as the Creator, Designer, and Sustainer. Supernaturalism and various creation concepts are found in all religions worldwide to one degree or another. In particular, the religious creation beliefs in theism have many worldview perspectives — one from the "Western" Abrahamic (biblical) monotheistic God as the sole Creator to the "Eastern" polytheistic/pantheistic gods involved in the process of creation. Other irreligious or nonreligious beliefs, such as atheism, agnosticism, New Age, and secular humanism, were discussed.

Furthermore, these religious creation beliefs can be viewed by understanding the divine theological perspectives of general and special revelations. Several philosophical (e.g., logical) arguments for the existence of God were discussed to support these revelations (i.e., Pascal's Wager self-interest perspective, ontological or metaphysical argument, cosmological or cause and effect argument, teleological or design argument, moral argument, religious experience, and the miracles argument). In addition, a notional belief claim formula was proposed, which contains the key elements of faith and evidence.

Faith + Evidence = Belief-Claim

This equation is valuable, powerful, and necessary when discussing various creation and evolution concepts. Even though empirical evidence (e.g., data) is proven by science, conclusions are interpreted by evolutionary theories and creation accounts. Faith is demonstrated in both religious practices and in the scientific inquiry process; faith is inextricably interwoven into both these "seemingly and arguably" separate areas of study.

However, additional formulas are needed for a better understanding of "how" we process these beliefs. First, any action or decision that we take in our lives is based upon not only those beliefs but the desires (or convictions) we must have to achieve those beliefs. Any action requires both our established or recognized beliefs in something or someone and the associated desire or motivation behind that belief.

Beliefs + Desires = Actions

In addition, for us to have knowledge about something or someone, we must have a properly justified or informed belief. This is where we need to always "seek" the truth in what we believe.

Knowledge = Properly Justified True Beliefs

Finally, most Christian theologians today emphasize three major creation views: They include the old earth (universe) creationism (OEC), theistic evolutionism (TE), and young earth (universe) creationism (YEC) interpretations or perspectives of creation. The OEC perspectives include day-age, intelligent design (ID), gap, and reasons to believe (RTB) interpretations of creation. The TE perspectives include a range of beliefs as well. Besides forms of TE, deistic evolutionism (DE) and evolutionary creationism (EC) are included as a subset of TE. Lastly, the YEC perspective includes the modern creation science (CS) interpretation of creation.

Conclusions

The doctrine of creation is a cornerstone of the Christian faith. The essentials of this teaching have "universal consent" among orthodox theologians. They include the following:

1. There is a monotheistic God.
2. Creation of the universe was *ex nihilo* (out of nothing) by His divine command (*fiat lux*).
3. Every living thing was created by God.
4. Adam and Eve were a direct and special creation of God.
5. The Genesis account of creation is historical, not mythological.

While there is lively debate about the *time* or *age* of creation, all evangelicals agree on the *fact* of creation. There is also agreement as to the source of creation (a monotheistic biblical God) and His purpose of creation (to glorify and obey Him). The exact scientific method of creation is still being discovered; however, "increasingly, the scientific evidence supports a supernatural creation of the universe, the direct creation of first life, and the special creation of every basic life form. Hence, macroevolution, whether theistic or naturalistic, is unfounded both biblically and scientifically."[184]

Let us turn to the other end of the spectrum, which discusses scientific naturalism and the evolutionary path that most scientists believe today.

CHAPTER 5:

Science and the Evolutionary Path

Introduction

Scientific Naturalism Often Leads to Evolutionary Interpretations

Most historical and evolutionary scientists have numerous objections to any creation account, especially from the biblical Genesis "creation" perspective. These scientists study worldly phenomena or events and their effects related to our existence. Their studies are based upon principles of scientific naturalism (vice religious supernaturalism). Scientific naturalism is powerful because of its empirical ruthlessness. Naturalism sees the world as a self-contained system of matter and energy that operates by unbroken natural law...it is assumed that everything in the world happens by chance and necessity with no reference to God. Further, under the concept of naturalism, our world does not need God for the formation and development of our origins. This perspective supports the concepts and relationship of two major forms of naturalism: methodological naturalism and philosophical naturalism.[185]

Methodological naturalism is a systematic and self-correcting process that seeks to produce logical, accurate, reliable, and well-tested conclusions (or scientific knowledge) through repeated experimentations, observations, and (often) measurements of natural phenomena. The practice of science is evidence-based. Science demands solid discoveries that must be verifiable, measurable, and valid. This approach or process is also called the "scientific method" that was first promoted by scientist Francis Bacon. The scientific method progresses from a hypothesis to a theory using testable scientific laws. The concept of testability of the empirical world of natural phenomena is critical in understanding how hypotheses become accepted as theories and scientific knowledge. Only a rational argument combined with evidence can finally justify as a scientific theory. Numerous independent observations and measurements repeat well-confirmed scientific explanations. Repeating or confirming the evidence over time leads to conclusions that are predictable. They serve the scientific community as a reliable theory until new evidence is discovered, which may confirm the current understanding or revise or replace the answers. The answers or explanations must be able to be best falsified and, therefore, could be revised or replaced given new inputs according to philosopher of science Karl Popper. The falsification principle is a way of demarcating science from non-science.[186] A theory in science is the highest form of scientific explanation, not just a "mere" opinion.[187]

In addition, science investigates the occurrence of natural phenomena through various "hard" and "soft" disciplines.

> "Hard" sciences, such as physics, astronomy, and chemistry, are characteristically "simple" in nature because the observations or occurrences can be predicted mathematically (i.e., equations or formulas). "Soft" sciences, such as basic biology and paleontology, are generally more "complex" because there are too many variables to be quantified into equations (in many cases) and are usually less predictable. However, both types of sciences are needed to explain our Origins. They contribute to

the overall understanding of the complex subject of our Origins.[188]

NOTE: Today, many "soft" sciences are becoming "hard," such as genetics, which employs "molecular clock" age methods, and paleoanthropology, which employs radio-metric isotope fossil and artifact dating methods.

As an overall objective, the field of science attempts to obtain (and often does obtain) a broad consensus of agreement from the scientific community in regards to the most likely (best) interpretation of the individual lab/field findings or discoveries subject to numerous peer reviews and criticisms. Science uses "ruthless" independent verification and validation testing methods. Science seeks a "consilience of inductions" (e.g., inductions from different areas of science explained by the same principles or laws)[189] and "converging lines of evidence" (e.g., investigations in various areas of science that dovetail to produce mutually reinforcing explanations).[190]

Based upon these scientific principles, which support methodological naturalism, the concept of philosophical naturalism is often "factored" in, especially by various scientists and philosophers. Philosophical naturalism relies on the belief that no ultimate or supreme being (e.g., God) is responsible for the creation of the universe. However, when combining methodological naturalism with philosophical naturalism in the pursuit of scientific knowledge, scientists and philosophers are more likely to form conclusions that support the theory of evolution rather than creation accounts (e.g., Genesis) for our origins. Philosopher of Science professor Barbara Forrest contends:

Naturalism (vice supernaturalism) is the most rational view of the world, both methodologically (i.e., science is most fruitful when it assumes that all events have potentially discoverable natural causes) and philosophically (i.e., this is an accurate view of reality; there is no supernatural)...Naturalism is committed to a methodological principle within the context of scientific inquiry; i.e., all hypotheses and events are to be explained and tested by reference to natural causes and events. To introduce a supernatural or transcendental cause within science is to depart from naturalistic explanations. On this ground, to invoke an intelligent designer or creator is inadmissible.[191]

However, Thomas A. Gibson, senior editor of *The Stream*, has evaluated Forrest's position in his article "Barbara Forrest and Naturalism" and argues that both science and religion are necessary for gaining knowledge and ultimately discovering truth. Gibson says:

Dr. Forrest, in trying to make a case for philosophical naturalism, makes a big deal of what she sees as science muscling religion out of any claim on truth. Her argument in "*Methodological Naturalism and Philosophical Naturalism*" replays familiar "God-of-the-Gaps" themes, portrays science and religion in a zero-sum game where any advance in science forces religion to retreat. This zero-sum approach is stated concisely here: Under the theistic model, according to (*geologist*) Arthur Strahler, any recognition of natural causation is logically nullified by the simultaneous assertion of supernatural intervention, either actual or merely possible. It is one or the other, there is no shared territory.[192]

NOTE: This topic of compatibility between science and religion and evolution and creation is explored in chapter 10.

Background for the Theory of Evolution

Understanding how nature begins, works, or changes over time (without an intervening God or multiple gods) has been questioned and discussed for a long time. Answers to this question started well over two thousand years ago, especially in "Western" civilizations, such as with the Greek and Roman natural philosophers. These philosophers began to question whether their polytheistic (multiple) gods had the power to cause, determine, or influence natural events.

Here are some of their earlier "crude" evolutionary theories, which lasted up to the 1700s Enlightenment Period in the "West."

In approximately 546 BCE, Anaximander (a Greek natural philosopher) argued that:[193]

- All living creatures arose from water.
- Men evolved from fish.
- There is a single primal substance and a natural law that exerts itself in the world, maintaining a balance between different elements.

Then about 440 BCE, the atomists (e.g., Democritus et al.) theorized that:[194]

- There must be tiny things that finally cannot be "cut" any further; otherwise, the matter could not exist.
- These "uncuttable" atoms move, collide, form new compounds, and are indivisible.

- These atoms explain the objective qualities of the world, like weight, shape, and size.
- Other attributes, like smell, only come into being when the atoms of an object interact with the atoms of the human nose.

In addition, other atomist philosophers proposed crude theories of evolution based on three fundamental ideas:[195]

- There was a beginning to the universe.
- Life started with some sort of spontaneous generation of life (or life from nonlife).
- Pieces could evolve in some way.

By approximately 375 BCE, Plato and the Pythagoreans founded the worldview of essentialism that was universally held until Darwin's time. Essentialism (a.k.a. topological thinking) taught that:[196]

- All seemingly variable phenomena of nature could be sorted into classes.
- Each class is characterized by its definition (or its essence).
- This essence is constant (or invariable) and sharply demarcated against all other such essences.

But it was not until the 1700s that natural philosophers began searching for a natural mechanism to cause or drive this evolutionary change without the need for divine (e.g., God) creation or intervention. Specifically, the Western world entered what historians call the "Enlightenment Period" (roughly 1700–1800 CE). Biblical creationist views of our origins began to be openly challenged by many naturalists, as well as by materialistic philosophers (a.k.a. German idealists or "higher critics"). "Apparent" discrepancies in the fossil geological records were observed. These findings caused many of these natural philosophers or naturalists, now called "scientists," to take a closer look at the age of the earth and the fossil changes in form and structure over time. As a result, they sought to develop materialistic or physical nature-based models solely based upon evolutionary processes, just as these ancient Greek philosophers had attempted to do.

> Especially (seen) in France and then in other countries
> such as England and Germany, where notions of Evo-
> lution and in particular material explanations for life
> began "creeping" back in; that is, Creation by natural
> law (instead of divine causation by God); the notion of
> Spontaneous Generation (life from non-life) seemed to
> be resurrected again.[197]

However, these were turbulent times in England and other European countries right after the French Revolution (1793), where:

> Post-revolutionary France strongly associated Evolution
> with radical scientific and political views, and they were
> widely considered a threat to the established social and
> political order.[198]

During this Enlightenment Period, several French natural philosophers proposed several "highly speculative" materialistic evolutionary explanations with little or no empirical scientific research or evidence to back up their claims. Three individuals are cited.

First, Comte de Buffon (astronomer and biologist) theorized that a comet hit the solar system, which knocked off a bunch of (proto or early formed) planets; a bunch of "mass" flung out, was caught in a vortex, was swirled around in different layers, coalesced into various planets. The origin of species evolved from a few common ancestral types (perhaps created by God); current varieties came to fit their various environments.[199]

Second, Denis Diderot and Baron d'Holbach (biologists) theorized, "Random chance mutations develop living forms from spontaneously generated organisms."[200]

Third, Pierre La Place (astronomer) proposed

> the cosmic view called the "Nebular Hypothesis," where the Solar System was once one giant rotating gas nebula; as it rotated, centrifugal and centripetal forces would pull in a hard center (which became the Sun); as it pulled in, it left little "blobs" of material that coalesced into the various planets.[201]

During the early to mid-1800s, probably the most well-known evolutionist was English naturalist Charles Darwin. Darwin produced four major works: (1) *On the Origins of Species*, with the first edition published in 1859 and five additional editions or revisions, the last one published in 1872, (2) *The Variations of Animals and Plants under Domestication*, published in 1860, (3) *The Descent of Man and Selections in Relation to Sex*, published in 1871, and (4) *The Expression of Emotions in Animals and Man*, published in 1872.

NOTE: Darwin's theory of evolution is discussed under "Classical Darwinism."

Although Darwin was encouraged by the writings of his grandfather (Erasmus Darwin published a book between 1794–1796 called *Zoonomia or the Laws of Organic Life*) and other colleges (John Henslow, Adam Sedgwick, Robert Grant, Alexander von Humbolt, and Sir John Hershel), his works would probably not have been possible without the major influences of:[202]

- Carl Linnaeus' (1735) classification (a.k.a. taxonomy) system depicting the animal kingdom as a *"tree-like structure"* with species (or) families of equal but differing complexity at the ends of the branches (still used today). His hierarchical structure formed the basis for Darwin's view that all life had descended from a single common ancestor.
- German idealist Immanuel Kant, as an early teacher of the modern theory of descent, as well as seventeenth- and eighteenth-century philosophers, such as Leibniz, Descartes, Herder, Goethe, and Schelling, espoused various ideas on evolution.
- Pierre Louis Maupertuis' (1751) writings on natural modifications occurring during reproduction and accumulating over many generations to produce new species and populations. Darwin considered this idea of evolutionary change of species over time according to natural laws.
- Comte de Buffon's (1778) comparative anatomy study of similar embryonic appendages from different species after birth (for example, the five-digit similar pattern of the *"pentadactyl"* limb as manifested in four modern animals [i.e., bats, porpoises, horses, and humans]).[203] Again, Darwin postulated that these similarities or homologies in different animals were best explained as evolving from a common ancestor.
- James Hutton's (1795) *Theory of Gradualism* theorized that the earth's features changed in a slow, gradual, and continual process. Darwin used his theory to describe

natural selection as occurring in a slow/gradual step-by-step process where changes in an organism's form and function are successfully accumulated and passed on to its offspring over a long period of time.

- Chevalier de Lamarck's (1809) evolutionary theory by *transformation* proposed that the environment affected how organisms used their body parts and that what was used was passed on to offspring, but what was not used would not be passed on (e.g., a giraffe's neck would get longer if it was used, and if it was not used, it would not be passed on). "This was referred to as '*Use and Disuse*' and '*Inheritance of Acquired Characteristics.*' Although this theory was disproved, Darwin did employ variations of Lamarck's theory in his later editions of the *Origins* and in *The Descent of Man and Selection in Relation to Sex.*"

- Charles Lyell's (1800s) findings provided geological evidence that the earth was millions of years old and species had changed over time. Darwin became convinced by Lyell's proof that "*uniformitarianism*" provided the correct understanding of the earth's geological history: Gradual geologic changes suggested that organisms would need to adapt to a changing environment, and "*uniformitarianism*" would give ample time for these changes to accumulate. Eventually, Darwin converted to Lyell's "*uniformitarian*" *(a.k.a. gradualism)* view of geology.

- Thomas Malthus's *Theory of Population* for all living things stated that only the fittest can and should survive. (NOTE: The term "survival of the fittest" was coined later by Herbert Spenser in 1860. Darwin converted to this theory.)

- Auguste Comte's philosophical argument (1840s) "that science can now explain natural phenomena by reference to natural laws or strictly material causes or processes and in this way, science can achieve 'positive' knowledge."[204] Darwin was influenced by his argument.

Introduction to Evolutionary Theories

Based upon individual scientific discoveries, which have gone through the rigorous scientific method, scientific evolutionists explain or interpret scientific evidence from an evolution perspective. Scientific evolutionists divide evolution into three basic categories or theories: stellar, chemical, and biological evolution. In addition, most scientists and the scientific community generally agree with these categories. Many of these scientists attempt to understand the "big" picture solely from a naturalistic or evolutionary perspective. However, there are other scientists who believe in the divine intervention of a Creator God. As mentioned,

the story of Evolution leaves no room for a supernatural Creator. Evolutionary processes are supposed to be purely naturalistic. This means that even the need for a supernatural Creator disappears because it is argued that the natural world can create new and better or more complex creatures by itself. The implication of this is very revealing: Evolution means "no God" and if there is no God, then there are no rules — no commandments, no God-given rules which we must obey. We can therefore live our lives as we please, for according to evolutionary philosophy, there is no God to whom we must give an account.

No wonder "molecules-to-man" Evolution is attractive to many, for it allows them to live as they please. This is called relative morality.[205]

The "big bang theory" describes stellar evolution, the "origins of life theory" describes chemical evolution, and the "common descent theory" describes biological evolution (as further defined by the natural selection, microevolution, and macroevolution principles). More specifically, chemical and biological evolution is accepted to mean the change of nonliving chemicals into simple life forms into more complex life forms and eventually into humans. But the word *evolution* also applies to nonliving things. Almost everything is said to have evolved — the solar system, stars, the universe, social and even legal systems. Everything is said to be a product of evolution. Nevertheless, the most common view of evolution is depicted as a "chimp evolving into modern man!"

Stellar Evolution — the "Big Bang Theory"

The "big bang theory" represents or describes stellar evolution. The "big bang theory" is the most prominent scientific or naturalistic view of the universe's origin that is embraced by most scientists. In particular, scientific evolutionists teach that "in the beginning, nothing became something and exploded. Cosmologist's direct support of this idea is that quantum mechanics predicts that a vacuum can, under certain circumstances, give rise to matter."[206]

The "big bang" process explains the initial point source (from which space, time, energy, matter, and laws appeared) of intense radiation energy (suddenly) cooled as it expanded, giving rise to a variety of fundamental particles that internally coalesced into hydrogen and helium after a sudden inflation had further reduced the temperature of the plasma. These gases formed nebulae (galaxies) under the influence of their mutual attraction and collapsed into stars, where they were transformed by nuclear fusion into carbon, oxygen, and other heavier elements. Stars then evolved differently depending on their mass. Some died when they ran out of nuclear fuel, and others blew up, making still heavier elements in the process and spewing the lot in clouds of dust that would, in turn, fall under the influence of gravity to give birth to interstellar matter and new stars. Our solar system was formed this way. The various atoms of the earth and our bodies were produced by the fusion of hydrogen in the cores of stars that were born, lived, and died billions of years ago (BYA).[207]

Chemical Evolution — the "Origins of Life Theory" (or Prebiotic Evolution)

The "origins of life" theory represents or describes chemical evolution and is defined as the crater-covered surface of the moon, which gives us a clue of how the planets were formed by the agglomeration of colliding interstellar matter orbiting the Sun. The moon lost whatever gasses it might have had because of its small mass. Still, the much more massive Earth retained its atmosphere, which initially contained mostly methane (CH_4), ammonia (NH_3), carbon dioxide (CO_2), and water (H_2O) vapor. When intense meteoric activity subsided about four and a half billion years ago, the water cycle from clouds to the oceans proceeded to obliterate the dramatic traces still seen on the moon. Chemicals leached from the land accumulated in the oceans. We can safely speculate that all the chemical compounds that could exist in a stable state under the prevailing conditions came to be formed with the passage of the next five hundred million years. The natural occurrence of nucleic acids was, therefore, not only probable, but it was inevitable. Nucleic acids naturally join up to form chains or polymers that grow from both ends. Eventually, such chains would grow excessively long and break up in pieces that resume growth by scavenging their environment for the required nucleic acids. In this way, these molecules were reproducing the structure that characterized them. The first (ones) did not occur, but those that replicated more efficiently became more numerous and were more successful in attaching the available nucleic acids than less prolific competing molecules. The replicated copies were not always exact. Less efficient mutations tended to disappear, but those that represented a better adaptation to the surrounding "chemical soup" thrived. Their descendants multiplied to dominate each of their respective environments.[208]

The most famous "origins of life" experiment tested the 1924–1928 Oparin-Haldane hypothesis. That is, Sun's ultraviolet (UV) light would transform the simple gases of CH_4, NH_3, CO_2, and water vapor — H_2O — into more complicated compounds and come together to form the microscopic clumps or "primordial soup" that were the predecessors to the first cells. This experiment was conducted in the 1950s by biochemists Stanley Miller and Harold Urey.

> NOTE: "They designed an apparatus that attempted to duplicate these atmospheric conditions of primitive Earth. The Miller-Urey experiments did not produce cells, but they produced several amino acids that are the building blocks of proteins."[209]

Biological Evolution — "Common Descent Theory" (or Biotic Evolution)

The "common descent theory" represents and describes biological evolution. It is probably the most controversial discussed area of these three categories, especially among Christians. The following represents a current and somewhat detailed explanation for biological evolution.[210]

These reproducing chemical structures grew more and more complex over the next 500 million years. They eventually formed membranes to enclose themselves in a favorable environment by controlling the passage of chemicals across their cell wall. These cellular entities, in which many diverse, complex molecules interact cooperatively, can be called the first living organisms. They acquired considerable autonomy by isolating the cell's internal environment from the outside world. Thus, protected inside the cell, replicating molecules could continue developing complex structures that could not have existed in equilibrium with the external environment. Over the next millions of years, cells mutated and brought about the diversity of life required to occupy all available ecological niches. Replicators produced most copies of their cell-making instructions, which dominated each living organism. These replicators are estimated to be about 3.5 billion years old.

These unicellular organisms were the only life forms for another 1000 million years. During this period, the double helix molecule of deoxyribonucleic acid (DNA) became the inherited structure's prevalent replicator. They gave rise to most of today's bacteria. About 2.5 billion years ago, a branch split off by integrating a symbiotic partner to develop new ways of processing energy. The new type of cells, called eukaryotes (cells containing a nucleus and organelles), contain mitochondria structures (*an organelle inside the cell's membrane but outside its nucleus*) specializing in energy production and conversion. Mitochondria contain their own DNA. Over the next 1.5 billion years, eukaryotes had plenty of time to evolve into an innumerable variety of forms containing two or more sets of inherited structures. In the case of blue-green algae, called a chloroplast (a light-collecting molecule like chlorophyll), it used the Sun's energy to power the cell's processes, including the host's reproduction replicator.

Perhaps as early as one billion years ago, mutations in the genetic instructions carried by DNA led to the production of multicellular entities composed of specialized cells cooperating to ensure the replication of their shared genes. After a long maturation period, this new multicellular life model exploded into an infinite variety of forms about 600 million years ago (a.k.a. the Cambrian biological explosion), occupying every possible ecological niche with a multitude of plants, insects, and animal life.

According to this scenario, the specific forms of life that prevailed in each niche were the most efficient agents for reproducing genes (*genes are strands of DNA that "code" for one of more proteins*) in that niche at that time. Successful genes in each niche or place were those whose replication introduced genetic mutations leading to the natural selection of the most prolific mutants. These genes are transmitted to future generations. These factors' actions over several million generations resulted in new varieties and, eventually, new species. After the appearance of multicellular life, the evolutionary process had another 600 million years to set the stage for the emergence of man's first ancestors.

> The first proto-hominids appeared about 8 million years ago. They walked on all fours for 3 million years before Australopithecus *afarensis*, whose brain occupied about 300 cubic centimeters (cc), started to walk upright about 5 million years ago. Two million more years of gradual Evolution passed before the hominid Australopithecus *africanensis* left fossilized skulls showing an increased brain size of 400 cubic centimeters. Another million years later, Homo *habilis* came on the scene with a larger braincase of 600 to 750 cc. We call him "habilis" because he learned to use primitive tools about two million years ago. He was soon followed by Homo *erectus*, whose big brain size (800 to 900 cc) started to develop frontal lobes around. 1.7 million years ago. Homo *erectus* (or Homo *heidelbergensis*) gradually evolved into Homo *sapiens*, with a large 1200 cc brain size about 400,000 years ago. About 200,000 years ago, the Neanderthal branch of Homo *sapiens* (*Latin for wise man*) started spreading out

of Africa. About 130,000 years ago, he was followed by Homo sapiens *africanus*, our ancestors (*which is disputed today and is thought to now be the Homo heidelbergensis*). Mutations of the brain that brought evolutionary advantages enhancing the survival and reproduction of our distant ancestors increased the size of their brains to more than three times that of other larger primates.[211]

Table 5 provides this scientific/naturalistic timetable using the above approximate dates.[212] (NOTE: Many of these events will be covered in later chapters.)

YEARS AGO	EVENT
13.7 - 13.8 Billion	Big Bang: Origin of the Universe
4.5 Billion	Formation of Earth
4 Billion	1st Replicating Molecules
3.5 Billion	1st Simple Cellular Life
2.5 Billion	1st Eukaryotic Cells
1 Billion	1st Multi-Cellular Life
600 Million	Cambrian Explosion of Life
65 Million	Disappearance of Dinosaurs
8 Million	1st Proto-Hominids
5 Million	Australopithecus *afarensis* (300cc Brain)
3 Million	Australopithecus *africanus* (400cc Brain)
2 Million	Homo *habilis* (600 - 750cc Brain)
1.7 Million	Homo *erectus* (800 - 900cc Brain)
400,000	Homo *sapiens* (1200cc Brain)
200,000	Spread of Homo Neanderthals
130,000	Spread of Homo sapiens-*sapiens*
30,000	Disappearance of Homo Neanderthals
8,000	1st Agriculture and Animal Husbandry
5,000	1st Recorded History

Table 5: Scientific/Naturalistic Timetable of Our Universe

NOTE: Most scientists agree with this timetable, including progressive creationist (PC) scientists such as the Christian Reasons to Believe (RTB) organization. However, PC scientists believe that living organisms were "fully" formed by the biblical God, even though microevolution occurred only at the species and possibly the genera next higher level (especially for vast populations of tiny animals such as ants). Also, they believe that "God" created the "creation big bang" and had "His" hand in the natural evolution of the stars, planets, moon, etc.[213]

In addition, the "common descent theory" uses three main evolutionary concepts: microevolution, macroevolution, and Darwinism.

Microevolution refers to minor variations at or below (e.g., breeds) the species level. For example, studies in the Galapagos Islands by naturalist Charles Darwin found that the finch beak's average size and thickness increased during a five percent drought. The surviving birds had more rigid beaks to crack the few remaining hard seeds. When the rains returned and seeds were again plentiful, beak sizes returned to normal. The fact that organisms vary and adapt to changing environmental conditions is not controversial. Microevolution is well supported by scientific evidence.[214]

Macroevolution refers to major innovations such as new organs (like eyes), structures (like wings), or body plans (complete designs with all systems working together). According to Darwin's biological theory of evolution, small and gradual microevolutionary changes in a species can lead to a new species. However, this theory is questioned by many creationists: "Whether gradual, undirected, micro-evolutionary changes accumulate from bacteria to create birds is highly controversial."[215]

Darwinism (briefly described here and initially coined by English biologist Thomas Henry Huxley) is also known as "neo-Darwinism" or "modern synthesis" today and is the most known biological theory of evolution. Darwinism believes the undirected mechanistic process of natural selection acting on random beneficial mutations accounts for both microevolution and macroevolution. Thus, all diverse and complex living organisms exist. Darwinism's key philosophical component is the assumption that "evolution works without either plan or purpose. The National Association of Biology Teachers Statement of 1996 referred to it as "an unsupervised, impersonal, unpredictable, and natural process."[216]

Evolutionary (Biological) Periods and Their Explanations

Classical Darwinism or CD (~1859–1895)

Classical Darwinism describes Charles Darwin's natural selection as the main mechanism for biological evolution to take place. Natural selection of positive character traits within and between species, given the specific environment and other conditions, is seen as the driving force or tool behind evolution. The changes in these species ultimately lead back to a universal common ancestor (UCA) and are represented as a "tree of life." This process or pattern is known as "common descent" or descent with modification." These ideas were very controversial for his time.

"It has been said that he couldn't help becoming a revolutionary in some ways, despite how strongly he resisted. He was born into it."[217]

The making up of Darwin's mind to develop his major theories by purely (naturalistic) materialistic or physical means implied to many natural philosophers, religious leaders, and theologians that God was not needed for life to advance or progress from its initial state and that God might not even be needed at all for creation and progression of biological organisms. "Darwin was acutely aware of this explosive situation and some of its potential implications. He was aware that his theories would be despised, but that does not mean he was afraid of saying what he believed."[218]

Therefore, Darwin spent a tremendous amount of time and effort carefully developing these concepts over twenty years (starting with his concept of natural selection in 1839). His struggle involved conducting extensive research on plants and animals, incorporating the ideas of many of his past and current contemporaries, and observing biological changes in finches, tortoises, and other animals. His travels included his extensive and now famous five-year voyage on the HMS Beagle ship to South America, the Galapagos Islands from 1831 to 1836, as well as other locations and at later times. Another incentive to publish his findings, which were developed from his private papers between 1837 and 1844 and his 1839 book *The Voyage of the Beagle*, was his receipt of naturalist Alfred Russell Wallace's essay in 1858. Wallace's essay also identified natural selection as the prime mechanism for biological evolution, Darwin's key mechanism! This surprise prompted Darwin to "quickly" publish his first comprehensive book (*On the Origins of Species*) earlier ahead of Wallace in 1859! Nevertheless, Darwin is generally given credit for introducing the concept of natural selection because he was able to formulate or propose and demonstrate biological (organic) evolution's first observable, testable, and predictable mechanism (e.g., natural selection).

Ernst Mayr, a modern contemporary evolutionary biologist, further dissected Darwin's conceptual framework, forming the basis for his evolutionary thinking. He partitioned Darwin's evolutionary paradigm into five theories, which later (and current) authors often refer to in some combination.[219]

- *Evolution as such:* This general theory states that the world is not constant or recently created nor perpetually cycling, but rather is steadily changing and that organisms transform or change over time. Darwin took this concept as a "matter of fact" based on his research and other naturalists' or scientists' observations of the fossil and geological column records.

- *Natural selection:* This theory provides evolution's biological process, mechanism, or driving force. It states that "competition" (i.e., struggle for life or, as Herbert Spenser coined it, the "survival of the fittest") exists within species and determines which species live to have offspring and pass their traits on to those offspring. Spencer introduced this phrase in his 1864 book *Principles of Biology*.[220] It determines how these changes occur within a species of like-organisms that reproduce the same kind of offspring to arrive at the pattern of diversity or variations that we observe in specific environments. For example, in Lamarck's argument, when a giraffe is born with a longer neck than its fellows, it gains an advantage because it can reach more food. The long-neck giraffe is, therefore, stronger, lives longer, and is more likely to have offspring (use and disuse principle). These offspring are born with the same long neck as their parent, though some might have longer necks. The cycle continues.

- *Common descent* (e.g., descent with modification): This theory provides the pattern of evolution. It states that every group of organisms (e.g., at the species level) descended from a common ancestor and that all organisms, including mammals, plants, and microorganisms, ultimately return to a single origin (e.g., a reproducing entity) of life on Earth. This single origin of life pattern leads to a last universal common ancestor (LUCA) or universal common descent of a single-celled organism. It is represented by Darwin's original "tree of life," with branches from a common trunk.

- *Population speciation*: This theory states that change in a species occurs within a population as the balance of hereditary characteristics shifts across that population. In our giraffe example above, some would randomly be born with long necks, and this genetic trait (drift) and gene flow would gradually or slowly spread (or accumulate) throughout the population.

- *Gradualism*: This theory states that evolutionary changes occur through the gradual change of populations and not by the sudden production of new individuals representing a new type of species. Evolution is a slow process where positive or successful reproductive changes occur and accumulate in innumerable small steps over long periods.

Impact of Darwinism

I would be remiss if I did not mention the concept of social Darwinism since this concept has had a tremendous negative impact on all of us. In many circles, Charles Darwin is totally blamed for what has happened in our world since his concepts were first developed. Even though Darwin seemed to support the idea of "survival of the fittest" because he incorporated it into his theories, two other individuals should be mentioned (in particular) who influenced the course of history. In the late 1800s, sociologist Herbert Spenser coined the phrases "survival of the fittest" and "laissez-faire capitalism" or unrestrained capitalism during the Industrial Revolution in which businesses were allowed to operate with little regulation from the government. British scholar Sir

Francis Galton launched a new "science" aimed at improving humans by ridding society of its "undesirables." He called it "eugenics."

> Social Darwinism is a loose set of ideologies that emerged in the late 1800s in which Charles Darwin's theory of evolution by natural selection was used to justify certain political, social, or economic views. Social Darwinists believe in "survival of the fittest" — the idea that certain people become powerful in society because they are innately better. Social Darwinism has been used to justify imperialism, racism, eugenics, and social inequality at various times over the past century and a half (e.g., Nazi Germany).[221]

In addition, Darwin, Spenser, and Galton were not the only ones responsible for this "shift" in cultural philosophy (e.g., out of the science lab and into the culture as philosophy as to how you live). Several other influential thinkers were responsible for this transition, such as Nietzsche, Marx, and Freud. In particular, "many intellectual historians agree that these were the dominate figures of the twentieth century for materialism, and the twentieth century saw us work out all the implications of these basic ideas. They have said that:[222]

- Nietzsche proclaimed the death of God,
- Darwin supplied the murder weapon,
- Marx was the architect of the social consequences, and
- Freud played mind games and told us what to think about ourselves.

Neo-Darwinism or ND (~1895–early 1930s)

Neo-Darwinism followed classical Darwinism. Darwin's theory of evolution was revolutionary. It "rocked" the religious, scientific, and political communities and the general public! The time and circumstances were "ripe" to introduce his theories. It was indeed a "paradigm shift" from previous thinking. It presented a comprehensive approach to how evolution proceeded by the *mechanism* of natural selection (and sexual and artificial selection) and the *process* of evolution, which ultimately led to the theory of common descent or common ancestry of a species. These two seminal concepts have survived (and expounded upon) since that time in history and are observed and used in most scientific literature today to explain observed natural findings, events, and phenomena.

Neo-Darwinism updated classical Darwinism with a heavy dependence on natural selection, which argued that it was perhaps the sole cause of all evolution. Other theories contended with natural selection during this time: (a) Neo-Lamarckian evolution says the inheritance of acquired characteristics is modified through "use and disuse" to account for the speeds and direction of evolutionary development, (b) orthogenesis attributes evolution to internal forces within living things that push them back to develop fixed directions and, (c) theistic evolution sees God as a source and guide of variations along lines that are beneficial to the species. These three theories were revived from earlier times as alternative theories for evolution.

However, the scientific community came together to believe in the sufficiency of natural selection alone. August Weismann's germ plasm theory (in the 1880s) cast severe doubts on these specific alternative theories. Also, during this transitional period (the 1880s to early 1930s), other views were attributed to this period, emphasizing natural selection. These explanations included William Bateson's variation theory (1894–1897), Hugo de Vries' mutation theory (1900–1903), Theodor Boveri's and Walter Sutton's chromosome theory (1902–1903), and

Thomas Hunt Morgan's genetic linkage and crossover theory (1913–1915). Their explanations were primarily based on experiments conducted by Gregor Mendel, an Australian monk, mathematician, and botanist from 1856 to 1865. His breeding experiments in his monastery's garden laid the "groundwork" for the science of genetics. In appreciation of his work, he is considered the "Father of Genetics."

Mendel's hybridization experiments tested the "mix or crossing" of over 28,000 garden "pea plants" (*Pisum sativum*) with selected traits over several generations. From these experiments, he deduced two generalizations that later became known as "Mendel's laws of heredity" or "Mendelian inheritance." He described these laws in a two-part paper, *Experiments on Plant Hybridization*, published in 1866, which said:[223]

> After crossing two pea plants which differed in a single trait in the "P" or parent generation (tall stems vs. short stems, round peas vs. wrinkled peas, or purple flowers vs. white flowers, etc.), Mendel discovered that the next generation, the "F1" (first filial generation), was comprised entirely of individuals exhibiting only one of the traits. However, when this generation was interbred, its offspring, the "F2" (second filial generation), showed a 3:1 ratio — three individuals had the same trait as one parent and one individual had the other parent's trait.[224]

From his experiments, three laws were developed — the law of dominance, the law of segregation, and the law of independent assortment that influenced these "Mendelian" scientists. Here are the major points:[225]

> By crossing (pure) purple with (pure) white pea plants (P generation), Mendel found the offsprings (F1 generation) were purple rather than mixed, indicating one color was

dominant over the other (being recessive). This result became known as the "law of dominance."

Mendel's "law of segregation" states individuals possess two alleles for each trait (or phenotype) and a parent passes only one allele to his/her offspring during reproduction or meiosis. (NOTE: An allele is now considered one of several alternative forms of the same gene occupying a given position on a chromosome.)

Mendel's "law of independent assortment" states the inheritance of one pair of factors (genes) is independent of the inheritance of the other pair. If the two alleles are identical, the individual is called "homozygous" for that trait; if the two alleles are different, the individual is called "heterozygous." Also, Mendel crossbred dihybrids (plants that were heterozygous for the alleles controlling two different traits) and found that traits were inherited independently of each other.

Mendel's findings heavily influenced many of these later European scientists after 1900. During this period, Mendel's laws were rediscovered in 1900 by botanist/geneticist Carl Correns, agronomist Erich von Tschermak, and arguably botanist Hugo de Vries. Many of these scientists' plant and animal lab experiments produced offspring with inherited traits or characteristics that followed Mendel's laws of inheritance! These results were a surprise to some and a validation of Mendel's principles to others. The question now became to what extent natural selection played in the inheritance study using Mendel's laws and how other newly discovered concepts, such as mutations, genes, and chromosomes, fit into the overall picture of evolution. (It is interesting to note that Mendel's experimental results of cultivating and crossing over 5,000 pea plants were largely ignored by scientists, even by Darwin, who was aware of his findings but did not consider them in his writings.) However, these concepts were only "loosely" tied together during this period. In other words, the scientific community had not integrated or synthesized these ideas together yet. "Mendelians" (such as Bateson, de Vries, Morgan, etc.) advocated for an early Mendelian inheritance concept. They supported a form of evolution by large "discontinuous" steps or jumps via mutations to change one species into another. Interestingly, this idea parallels the concept of punctuated evolution ("punk eek") or bursts of evolutionary novelty separated by long periods of stasis. This concept was first proposed by evolutionary biologists Stephen Jay Gould and Niles Eldredge in 1972. Since then, there has been an ongoing debate among evolutionary biologists about how significant "punk eek" could be in the evolution of new species. (Remember that they are not arguing about evolution itself but about the relative speed of evolutionary change.)[226]

However, there were opponents to the "Mendelians," and they were called "Biometricians" (such as biologists Karl Person and Walter Weldon). They stated that empirical evidence indicated variations in small "continuous" jumps rather than large "discontinuous" jumps. They were more faithful to Darwin's original version. The scientific community finally resolved this "rift," and the "eclipse of Darwinism" ended with the rise of the modern synthesis theory and associated explanations.

Modern Synthesis or MS (~1937 to present)

Modern synthesis consolidated the efforts of various evolutionists and confirmed that a new synthesis was being formed. Julian Huxley "fused" together the insights from neo-Darwinism (primarily the natural selection and gradualism concepts) and Mendelism through the theory and practice of the new population genetics field (which was mathematically or statistically driven) and some earlier-developed concepts of modern genetics (genes, chromosomes, and mutations) in 1942.

Here are some leading scientists who contributed significantly to developing this synthesis. For early population studies, biologists R. A. Fisher, Sewall Wright, and J. B. S. Haldane; for later population studies, biologists Theodosius Dobzhansky, Ernst Mayr, and George Simpson with Julian Huxley brought together crucial concepts from these population studies. Then, biologists James Watson and Francis Crick (who explained the structure of the DNA molecule), Peter and Mary Grant, H. B. D. Kettlewell, J. L. Hubby, and Richard Lewontin, whose work is still recognized and accepted today by many scientists as the "correct" and "accurate" understanding of the process of evolution. They believe these areas have been incorporated into each scientific field of study, even though they were not in the original concept of modern synthesis.

The term "modern synthesis" (a.k.a. "neo-Darwinian synthesis") is still used today. However, it has created confusion and disagreement, especially within the scientific community. This situation is because new scientific discoveries, such as embryology (the study of the formation and development of an embryo and fetus), were not well integrated into the early twentieth-century synthesis idea. That had to wait for the development of gene manipulation techniques in the 1970s, the growth in understanding of development at the molecular level, and the creation of the modern evolutionary synthesis's successor, evolutionary developmental biology. As a result, a "new" synthesis was proposed to "correct" this situation.

Extended Evolutionary Synthesis, or EES, was proposed at the 2008 Altenberg Conference. Philosopher and evolutionary biologist Massimo Pigliucci called for reexamining or re-evaluating the MS theory, which is based on discoveries after the early 1950s. He proposed a "postmodern synthesis" or an "extended evolutionary synthesis" to include the new areas of embryology, developmental biology, ecology, and genomics or molecular genetics (such as considering the effects of DNA, RNA, amino acids, and proteins). These areas had been discovered after this initial time in the 1940s and were not incorporated into the original framework of the modern synthesis theory. New concepts began to emerge in the 1980s and 1990s, which focused on patterns of ontogeny (origination and development of an organism) and relatively new "growing" fields of evolutionary developmental biology. To amplify this position, here are six critical differences between MS and EES that resulted from the Altenberg Conference:[227]

- MS supports natural selection as the major cause or mechanism of evolution that promotes the adaptation of organisms in their environment in basically one direction; EES supports reciprocal causation that can go both ways between natural selection and the environment for adaptation of the organism.
- MS endorses the concept of genes as the major factor in inheritance; EES supports a more inclusive theory of inheritance of other concepts in addition to genes (such as noncoding portions of the DNA biomolecule).
- MS supports the randomness (i.e., chance) of genes (caused by mutations on the genes) for variations that can enhance fitness/survival; EES supports a nonrandom variation or developmental bias of the organism's phenotypes (traits) that are well-integrated to accommodate fitness/survival.
- MS supports evolution progressing from small, gradual, and accumulating changes; EES supports variable rates of change, from small steps through even large steps/jumps.
- MS supports a gene-centered perspective of evolution based on the changes in gene frequencies brought about through natural selection, genetic drift, mutation pressure, and gene flow; EES supports an organism-centered perspective, which broadens the scope of MS to include developmental systems to facilitate adaptive variation and to modify selective environments.

- MS supports macroevolutionary patterns through the evolutionary processes of natural selection, genetic drift, mutation pressure, and gene flow; EES supports other evolutionary processes besides MS.

In perspective, some evolutionary biologists support this move as it extends the MS framework, while others see this as an "attack" on the MS theory. They believe these newly discovered concepts and biological subjects are "folded" into MS without the need to create new or perhaps "unproven" ideas that have not been fully "vetted."

However, the proposal to extend MS to EES has not gained much of a foothold in the scientific literature and the scientific community, even though several attempts have been made. For example, evolutionary biologist Eugene Koonin proposed a "postmodern evolutionary synthesis" in 2009. He said that MS had "crumbled, apparently, beyond repair, and a new 21st century synthesis could be glimpsed because three interlocking revolutions had taken place in evolutionary biology: molecular, microbiological, and genomics."[228] In addition, philosophers of biology Philippe Huneman and Denis M. Walsh pointed out in their 2018 book *Challenging the Modern Synthesis Theory* the disciplines of embryological development theory, morphology, and ecology had been omitted, and a continuing desire to replace modern synthesis with one that united "all biological fields of research related to Evolution, adaptation, and diversity in a single theoretical network" was needed.[229]

Summary

When historical and evolutionary scientists explain how natural events, living organisms, and observable phenomena occur over time, they invariably see evolution as the answer or explanation for these changes. They conclude that evolution is not only a theory but a fact and can be divided into the categories of stellar ("big bang theory"), chemical ("origins of life theory"), and biological evolution ("common descent theory"). Correspondingly, these proposed theories provide a timetable for these naturalistic events to occur.

Specifically, "biological evolutionary scientists" primarily use the Darwinian mechanism of natural selection and the process of common descent as their explanation for "coupling" scientific discoveries and theories. They link or connect individual or discrete scientific evidence or findings (i.e., from data collected or fossils and artifacts discovered) into an evolutionary path. Biological evolution is especially controversial in the "West." Here, the "evolution of evolutionary" concepts has evolved from ancient theories to more modern approaches. Historically, these evolutionary concepts are identified by the periods of classical Darwinism, neo-Darwinism, modern synthesis, and then to the proposed (but not accepted) extended evolutionary synthesis perspectives.

These theories and concepts, within these periods, attempt to explain or interpret how living species are assumed to be connected/related and evolved over time. They believe that naturally (randomly) selected beneficial or positive gene (from the DNA biomolecule) mutations occur, given the proper environmental conditions, for a species to survive, reproduce, and even change over time into another species (e.g., macroevolution). Microevolution is usually not challenged by creationists, but macroevolution is. Evolutionists say these changes eventually lead back to a last universal common ancestor (LUCA) or a single organism given enough time.

Given these concepts of creation and evolution for our origins, the next chapter consolidates them into a physical path emphasizing naturalism and two spiritual paths emphasizing supernaturalism.

CHAPTER 6:

Consolidation of Religious, Theological, Philosophical, and Scientific Paths

Introduction

The purpose of this chapter is to consolidate the creation and evolution concepts that were discussed from the last two chapters, understanding these origin concepts are viewed from the "Western" perspectives of supernaturalism and naturalism. These perspectives are broken down into specific interpretations of our origins. However, to gain a "higher" perspective, two paths are provided. The physical and spiritual paths provide insight into "why" and "how" we think about our (e.g., created) world. These paths consolidate religious, theological, philosophical, and scientific concepts. These concepts form our worldview perspectives. These worldviews have the potential to influence and shape our daily lives, beliefs, attitudes, behavior, and conduct of living.

Supernaturalism and Naturalism Categories

The biblical creation accounts and their interpretations of supernaturalism fall into either a young earth (universe) creationism (YEC) or an old earth (universe) creationism (OEC) category.

The YEC category is represented by the creation science (CS) interpretation. The OEC category is mainly represented by the Reasons to Believe (RTB) interpretation; however, the day-age and gap progressive interpretations are also mentioned. Also, under OEC, the (arguably) "neo-creation" concept of intelligent design (ID) represents a scientific design interpretation of creation. However, unlike the biblical explanations for creation, ID does not specify who the "intelligent designer" is beyond our natural realm.

In addition, evolutionary theories are based on the concept of naturalism. These evolutionary theories cover three primary areas (i.e., stellar, chemical, and biological theories). The biological or organic area consists mainly of natural selection and common descent (e.g., macroevolution as known today) principles from Darwinism. These principles can be further broken down into four periods in our history that describe evolution: classical Darwinism (CD), neo-Darwinism (ND), modern synthesis (MS), and the proposed extended evolutionary synthesis (EES).

Lastly, when incorporating evolutionary concepts into creation accounts, especially when discussing life and human origins, additional interpretations arise by various religious and nonreligious organizations. This perspective is represented by various interpretations of theistic evolutionism (TE) including evolutionary creationism (EC) and deism. The TE interpretations are considered under the OEC category but connected to evolutionary principles (see solid and dashed lines).

Figure 9 illustrates this consolidated "Western" understanding of our origins and is considered the "*second*" perspective.

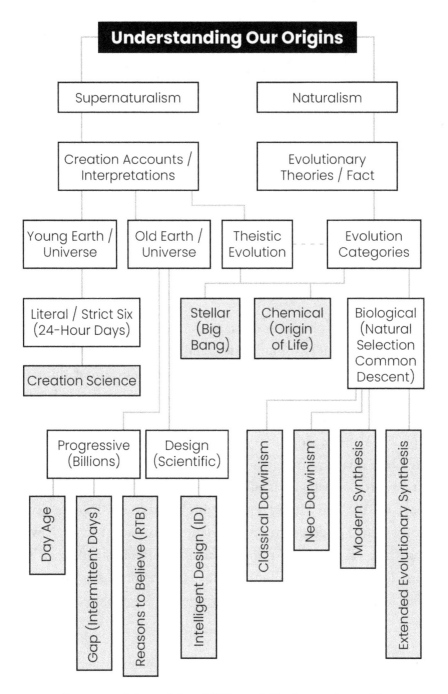

Figure 9: A Consolidated "Western" Understanding of Our Origins

Physical and Spiritual Paths

Introduction

Additionally, to support this consolidation of interpretations under the supernaturalism and naturalism categories, a "*third*" and more detailed perspective is provided. This perspective separates the above concepts of our origins into a physical and two spiritual realms of beliefs.

Believing in a physical realm of existence considers only the "laws of nature" and consists of two forms of naturalism — methodological and philosophical naturalism. Here, empirical evidence is exclusively obtained from the disciplines of science and generally leads to the concept of evolution, which is believed by most scientists today as well as many individuals.

Believing in a spiritual realm takes on a completely different perspective that is related to our understanding of our existence. In the spiritual realm, a spiritual perspective predominates in our thinking. From a Christian perspective, we are spiritual beings that exist in a physical "earth suit," and everything is seen from that perspective (John 17:16–26). More broadly, everything in our universe is related to or created by a divine source, including the "laws of nature." This supernatural source or being(s) is often known as "God" in the "Western" Judeo-Christian and Muslin sense, multiple gods in an "Eastern" sense, or not specified or designated as an intelligent designer sense. Nevertheless, in both realms of thinking about the understanding of our origins, individual philosophical worldviews are formed or influenced by the concepts of creation, evolution, or evolution within creation.

Physical Path

A "purely" or "exclusive" physical or material realm or perspective of reality assumes a lack of involvement of a "God" or a higher power in the study of our origins. This path shows the connections between the philosophical view of reality (e.g., philosophical naturalism); the scientific naturalism approach (e.g., methodological naturalism); the scientific disciplines' interpretations of evidence (via "hard" and "soft" sciences); the acknowledged and generally accepted concept, explanation, and conclusion (e.g., evolution); and the resulting (potential) perspectives that an individual may take or may be inclined to take based upon the linkage between the understanding of these concepts.

This perspective of evolution and its principles that initiate, form, and develop our universe and everything in it tends to lead to or strengthen various philosophical individual worldviews of evolutionary atheism, evolutionary agnosticism, secular humanism, or the possibility of no position taken regarding our origins.

> NOTE: If the sole explanation for our existence is found in scientific theories and their discoveries, this concept is sometimes called "scientism." Scientism addresses nature as the only form of reality for an individual.

Evolutionary atheism or atheistic evolution assumes that life emerged naturally from preexisting, nonliving building blocks exclusively under the influence of natural laws. Also, in EA, there is no God, and the origin of those natural laws is not explained. Furthermore, scientific evidence from "hard" and "soft" scientific disciplines gives a complete and reliable knowledge of reality and is the primary perspective and source of knowledge for evolution.

Evolutionary agnosticism is the position of the "acceptance of biological evolution, combined with the belief that it is not important whether God is, was, or will have been involved."[230]

Secular humanism is a philosophy, belief system, or life stance that embraces human reason, secular ethics, and philosophical naturalism while specifically rejecting religious dogma, supernaturalism, and superstition as the basis of morality and decision making.

Philosophically, secular humanists are naturalists. That is, they believe that nature is all that exists — the material world is all that exists. There is no God, no spiritual dimension, no afterlife. Astronomer Carl Sagan said it best in the introduction to his *Cosmos* series, "The universe is all that is or ever was or ever will be."[231]

Philosopher Roy Wood Sellars concurs. "Humanism is naturalistic," he says, "and rejects the supernaturalistic stance with its postulated Creator-God and cosmic Ruler."[232]

> Secular Humanist beliefs in the area of biology are closely tied to both their atheistic theology and their naturalistic philosophy. If there is no supernatural, then life, including human life, must be the result of a purely natural phenomenon. Hence, secular humanists must believe in Evolution. Julian Huxley, for example, insists that "man … his body, his mind and his soul were not supernaturally created but are all products of Evolution." Sagan, Lamont, Sellars, Kurtz — *all* secular humanists agree on this.[233]

NOTE: Religion and theology are not in this path or perspective because the assumption is that there is no divine involvement and that science always prevails! This path tends to support the "incompatibility" model that separates science from religion.

Figure 10 illustrates the physical path/perspective (without divine involvement) of our origins.

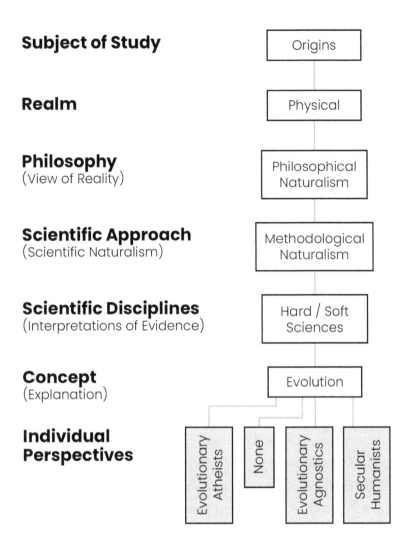

Subject of Study — Origins

Realm — Physical

Philosophy
(View of Reality) — Philosophical Naturalism

Scientific Approach
(Scientific Naturalism) — Methodological Naturalism

Scientific Disciplines
(Interpretations of Evidence) — Hard / Soft Sciences

Concept
(Explanation) — Evolution

Individual Perspectives — Evolutionary Atheists | None | Evolutionary Agnostics | Secular Humanists

Figure 10: Physical Path/Perspective (without Divine Involvement) of Our Origins

Spiritual Paths

Introduction

A spiritual realm or perspective of reality assumes that a higher being(s) above humans (e.g., supernatural in existence and essence) is responsible for creating our universe and everything in it and is involved to various degrees in this process. Therefore, supernaturalism, the philosophical and theological views of reality, considers two distinct paths. Both paths incorporate philosophical, religious, theological, and scientific concepts relating to our origins.

Path A

From a "Western" spiritual realm perspective. This philosophical view of reality encompasses the overall or overarching concept of supernaturalism. The theological supernaturalism concept incorporates a biblical "God" as the "Creator" and is defined by general revelation. General revelation looks at nature's physical phenomena and associated processes of the universe, Earth, life, and ultimately human life. However, one can view it from a religious, secular, and/or scientific (natural) perspective.

In addition, when "God" (e.g., which is generally believed to exist) is not involved, unknown, or defined differently in our understanding of creation, principles of natural revelation (a.k.a. general providence) are considered. Natural revelation observes and evaluates nature's physical phenomena and is explained through the associated "hard and soft" scientific evidence. However, in both cases of revelation, "hard and soft" scientific evidence is interpreted differently. Specifically, in general revelation from a Christian perspective, individuals observe all forms of creation, evolution, or evolution within creation as the "handiwork" of a biblical "God." For natural revelation, evolution alone is believed by others without the involvement or consideration of God.

> It (*e.g., Creator God*) is not limited to the beliefs of the Reformed Christian theologians or those practicing other religions. Nature is continually observed or seen by all of us but primarily measured and tested/validated by modern scientists using the scientific method. This method sounds straightforward enough; however, in

practice, there is a difference of opinion or interpretation in what the results and conclusions are and what they mean, depending upon one's perspective or bias on their (providing) belief concepts of Evolution and creation. It has been said that religion exists to tell us why or what it means, and science exists to tell us how the universe works.[234]

When combining the perspectives of general revelation with natural revelation, the interpretations and conclusions come from examining the "hard and soft" scientific evidence. Differences in the interpretation of the evidence provide three ways to (a) reinforce the concepts of creation and "God" as the Creator, (b) exclude "God" in creation by supporting evolution alone, or (c) include evolution within creation.

Believing in creation alone or with very minimal involvement of evolutionary mechanisms such as microevolution tends to result in individual perspectives contained in the various religious worldviews of theism where religious and theological doctrines always "trump" scientific conclusions (e.g., called "fideism" or faith alone), especially when evolutionary theories conflict with them.

As previously discussed, believing alone in evolution through natural revelation and physical interpretation of the "hard and soft" scientific evidence tends to lead to the individual philosophical worldviews of evolutionary atheism, evolutionary agnosticism, and secular humanism.

When considering the involvement of evolution within creation, through both general and natural revelations and mixed interpretations from "hard and soft" scientific evidence, individual perspectives tend to take on some form of theistic evolutionism (TE). Specifically, within TE, there is a spectrum of beliefs that include evolutionary creationism (EC) and deism.

Figure 11 illustrates this spiritual path that supports both the compatibility models (both integrative and dialog), where principles of evolution are contained within creation, and the "incompatibility" models, where creation and evolution are separate domains between religion and science.

NOTE: The shaded areas represent differences in how they are perceived or interpreted. Should they be allies or adversaries? Here, faith-based religions and philosophers are not mentioned.

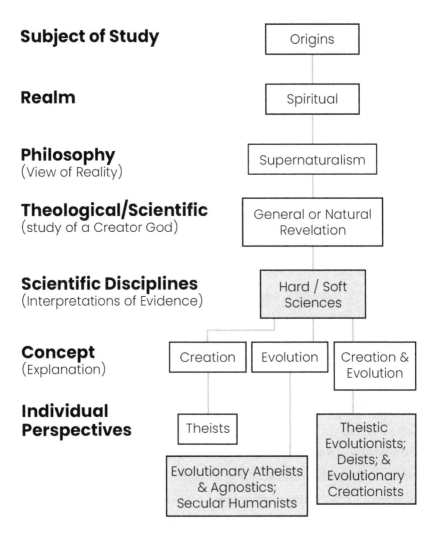

Subject of Study	Origins
Realm	Spiritual
Philosophy (View of Reality)	Supernaturalism
Theological/Scientific (study of a Creator God)	General or Natural Revelation
Scientific Disciplines (Interpretations of Evidence)	Hard / Soft Sciences
Concept (Explanation)	Creation · Evolution · Creation & Evolution
Individual Perspectives	Theists · Evolutionary Atheists & Agnostics; Secular Humanists · Theistic Evolutionists; Deists; & Evolutionary Creationists

Figure 11: Spiritual Path/Perspective of Our Origins (Path A)

Path B

A second spiritual perspective with supernaturalism as the dominant philosophical view of reality is considered. The theological concept is exclusively from general, special, and direct (e.g., directly revealed) revelations from "God." General revelation is described in the previous illustration. However, when it is combined with special revelation and direct revelation, various Western and Eastern religions and their philosophies must be considered to give a "big" picture. As discussed in chapter 4, in special revelation, an authoritative source reveals the identification and description of the character of a supernatural or divine being (e.g., biblical God) who created or made the natural world as we know it to be. In addition, direct revelation, like mythological stories, contains a reason "why" we should believe these "holy" sources (e.g., being or beings) are telling the truth and "why" their religious or spiritual experiences are authentic. They take different religious forms, such as from the prophets or patriarchs (i.e., Moses, Abraham, Mohammed, Jesus Christ, Buddha, etc.) having dreams or directly hearing from "God" or His "angels," discovering holy texts and holy artifacts (i.e., biblical, and Islamic scriptures, LDS or Mormon Golden Tablets, etc.), or achieving enlightenment through religious experiences (e.g., Siddhartha Gautama or Buddha, the founder of Buddhism).

These specific and unique kinds of revelations lead to multiple belief claims and doctrines from various "Western" and "Eastern" religions. They are mainly from the Abrahamic, Dharmic (Indian), Asian (Chinese, Japanese, Korean), and Oceanic religions and their associated theologies and philosophies, as previously discussed in chapter 4. These belief claims are uncontested and deemed to be true, accurate, and absolute and may include strict religious interpretations or a combination of religious and "hard and soft" scientific interpretations to support or enhance their concepts of creation, evolution, or evolution within creation. In some "holy" texts, the "Western" view of creation or evolution is not mentioned and there seems to be no real concern over deciding on the validity or verification of these concepts (such as in Buddhism).

Believing in creation alone or with very minimal involvement with evolution tends to result in individual and collective perspectives and practices contained in the religious worldviews of theism, where religious and theological doctrines always "trump" "hard and soft" scientific conclusions (e.g., "fideism" or faith alone), especially when evolutionary findings conflict with them. This theological view of creation is found in the concept of theism. Theism includes monotheism, polytheism, pantheism, or some combination of them.

In particular, the monotheistic Western religions of Judaism, Christianity, and Islam define a single "God" as the sole creator. In Christianity, many different interpretations were identified, such as the creation science and Reasons to Believe perspectives. In the Eastern religions of polytheism (i.e., forms of Hinduism, Buddhism, Confucianism, Taoism, Shintoism) and pantheism (i.e., African traditional religions, Shintoism, forms of Hinduism and Buddhism, Native American religions), many gods are involved in creation.

Besides a "strict" belief in creation or creationism, some individuals support evolution within creation. These individual and collective interpretations are also contained in the Abrahamic, Dharmic, Asian, and Oceanic religions. Worldview interpretations include forms ranging from theistic evolutionism (TE), evolutionary creationism (EC), and deism, as described above. (NOTE: Deism is a secular understanding of our creation and not a religious view.)

Finally, some Eastern religions (such as Buddhism) have no specific written concept of creation or evolution. These individuals may consider themselves either atheists (i.e., a nonreligious position) or agnostics (i.e., an irreligious position) with respect to their beliefs in the "Western" concepts of creation and/or evolution. In addition, this area might include the "New Age movement" of the 1960s as especially observed in the Western society and culture. This movement is a broad category that refers to those who think that God is a spiritual, personal guide or a God that defies specific description or its universal energy.

This pathway (figure 12) supports the "incompatibility" models of creation and evolution as separate domains of religion and science and the "compatibility" models of evolution within creation as there is some overlap between the religion and science domains.

> NOTE: The "shaded" areas recognize the potential differences between various religious creation belief claims strictly based on faith with minimal or no involvement with science (e.g., "fideism"), evolution belief claims ("none category") strictly based on science, reason, and evidence with no involvement with religion (e.g., "scientism"), or evolution within creation belief claims based on a combination of faith, reason, and evidence.

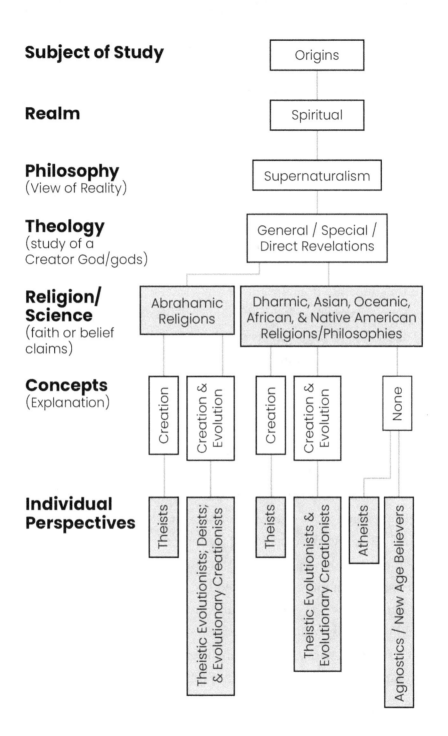

Subject of Study	Origins
Realm	Spiritual
Philosophy (View of Reality)	Supernaturalism
Theology (study of a Creator God/gods)	General / Special / Direct Revelations

Religion/Science (faith or belief claims)

- Abrahamic Religions
- Dharmic, Asian, Oceanic, African, & Native American Religions/Philosophies

Concepts (Explanation)

- Creation
- Creation & Evolution
- Creation
- Creation & Evolution
- None

Individual Perspectives

- Theists
- Theistic Evolutionists; Deists; & Evolutionary Creationists
- Theists
- Theistic Evolutionists & Evolutionary Creationists
- Atheists
- Agnostics / New Age Believers

Figure 12: Spiritual Path/Perspective of Our Origins (Path B)

Summary

In studying our origins, there are essential connections (or intersections) between religion, theology, philosophy, and science. All four disciplines are needed to provide a "big" picture or perspective of our origins. Leaving any of them out does not give us an accurate or realistic view of how to perceive our origins. These perspectives or paths consolidate previously discussed concepts, provide insight into our understanding of our origins, and (hopefully) facilitate dialog and discussions on this important subject. This ultimately leads to the study of the incompatibility and compatibility domains of religion and science. Are they separate domains, or do they intersect in some way? This is the main "struggle" or "tension" between these two subjects regarding any discussion of the concepts of origins in relation to the explanations of creation and evolution.

In addition, these models and pathways can shed "light" on "why" individuals have certain worldviews, which has the potential to influence their personal lifestyles, beliefs, and conduct or behavior.

From a physical realm perspective, if one believes human beings evolved exclusively from evolutionary principles, then their Western worldviews tend to be categorized by some form of evolutionary atheism, evolutionary agnosticism, secular humanism, or no opinion formed regarding the question of our origins.

However, from a spiritual realm perspective, the individual views tend to be much more complicated because there is a specific distinction between just general or natural revelation and general revelation combined with special/direct revelation.

General or natural revelation interprets the evidence from the "hard and soft" scientific disciplines differently. These different interpretations lead to the conclusions of creation alone, evolution alone, or evolution within creation. Their conclusions tend to support the individual philosophical worldviews of theism for creation; evolutionary atheism, evolutionary agnosticism, and secular humanism for evolution; and evolutionary theism, deism, and evolutionary creationism for evolution within creation.

General revelation combined with special and direct revelations interprets the "hard and soft" scientific disciplines primarily from the Abrahamic, Indian, Asian, and Oceanic religions (e.g., including theologies and philosophies) perspectives. They include creation alone or evolution within creation. Creation alone leads to the philosophical worldviews of theism, as discussed (i.e., monotheism, polytheism, and pantheism). Evolution within creation leads to theistic evolution and evolutionary creationism and deism. Also, as a matter of perspective, believers in forms of Buddhism and possibly the "New Age movement" could be considered atheists or agnostics because they do not address or care about the "Western" concept of creation or evolution.

Finally, as stated in Proverbs 23:7 (NKJV), "For as he thinks in his heart, so is he" (or becomes). From a Jewish and Christian perspective, our "hearts" become our reality. In believing in your (metaphysical speaking) heart, you will see the glory of the Lord and not be limited by your own thinking. Possibility thinking (vice positive thinking) determines destination and direction. Philosophical worldviews are shaped by our interpretations of our physical or spiritual paths, which are defined by the concepts of creation and evolution. These six chapters have demonstrated that direction in life determines your destination. They provide a review of the various possibilities in which one can take.

Now, we focus on part two, the biblical path for creation. In the author's opinion, this belief gives the reader the most complete and believable origins explanation for creation. Evolution alone is not the answer. Discounting evolutionary theories and considering the compatibility of science and religion or evolution and creation is further demonstrated to form a "big" picture of our origins.

PART 2:

"The Biblical Path Gives the Most Complete and Believable Origins Explanation"

CHAPTER 7:

Evaluation of the Stellar and Chemical Theories of Evolution

Introduction

The previous chapters provided a general overview or survey of key concepts regarding the study of our origins. Now, we turn to specific areas to justify the belief that "the biblical path gives the most complete and believable explanation" for the understanding of our origins. These areas include the (a) evaluation of the stellar and chemical theories of evolution, (b) evaluation of the biological theory of evolution, (c) discounting the evolutionary pathways of humanity, which includes separating modern humans from chimps and Neanderthals, and (d) showing how the biblical Genesis account can be compatible with most scientific discoveries and their conclusions.

Carefully examining the evidence to assess the validity of connecting scientific discoveries or findings about our origins into an evolutionary path is the goal. Historical researchers in cosmology, astronomy, astrophysics, planetary, chemistry, biology, geology, paleontology, anthropology, archeology, and other related disciplines evaluate the evidence, which is ongoing and subject to change as new scientific discoveries are made.

If the evidence is "strong" enough, then a case for evolution is possible and needs further examination. If the evidence is "weak" or "missing" for the case of evolution, serious consideration of alternative explanations should be considered. In other words, if significant changes from one event, object, or state to another can be explained and verified by natural processes alone, then evolution (in some form) is at least possible or perhaps even likely. Other possibilities, such as divine intervention, must be considered when evidence is minimal, lacking, or problematic. In particular, the biblical explanation for our origins, whether stellar, chemical, or biological, should come under serious consideration.

Stellar Evolution — The "Big Bang Theory"

Initially, the scientific evidence for understanding the initial state and the development (e.g., expansion) of the universe, including the galaxies, stars, planets, moons, and other cosmic objects or images, is measured, mapped, and evaluated by using highly sophisticated ground and space (satellite) computer-controlled telescopes as well as other sophisticated and complex ground instruments or techniques (i.e., such as using particle accelerators/colliders or radiometric isotope dating methods). Data are collected, analyzed, and independently validated by several different "trusted" sources. Consequently, by using the proven scientific method, this information becomes highly accurate within a high degree of probability (e.g., likelihood), but it is always subject to future findings according to the rules of science. Figure 13 is an artist's rendition from NASA of the "big bang." The illustration depicts the beginning and expansion or "unfolding" of the universe from a known and proven beginning point in time and under certain assumed conditions. This view of the universe is from a satellite's perspective and is portrayed as an envelope or section of space.

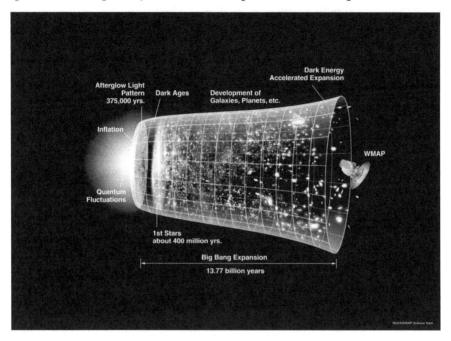

Figure 13: "Big Bang" Formation and Expansion of Our Universe, NASA / WMAP Science Team, WMAP # 060915, https://map.gsfc.nasa.gov/media/060915/index.html

The illustration shows the timeline of the metric expansion of space, where space (including the hypothetical nonobservable portions of the universe) is represented at each time by circular sections. This is one of several diagrams that represent the "evolution" of the universe over 13.7 billion years.

The far left depicts the earliest moment we can now probe, when a period of "inflation" produced a burst of exponential growth in the universe. For the next several billion years, the expansion of the universe gradually slowed down as the matter in the Universe pulled on itself via gravity. More recently, the expansion has begun to speed up again as the repulsive effects of dark energy have come to dominate the expansion of the Universe.[235]

In particular, "The far left depicts the earliest moment…of '[hyper] inflation'[that] produced a burst of exponential growth [*of first stars and then the development of galaxies, planets, etc.*] in the universe." (NOTE: Size depicts the vertical extent of the grid in this graphic.) For the next 7 to 8 billion years, the universe's expansion gradually slowed as matter in the universe pulled on itself via gravity. This period is known as the "matter-dominated era." After that period, the expansion (rate) of the universe began to speed up again as the repulsive effects of dark energy (a mysterious and invisible repulsive energy force thought to be evenly distributed across the universe) came to dominate (*over matter*). This period is known as the "dark-energy-dominated era." During this period, matter density fell below the dark energy density influence, and the expansion of space began to accelerate and is continuing today. The afterglow "light" from radiation, as seen by the Wilkinson Microwave Anisotropy Probe (WMAP) satellite images, was emitted about ~400,000 (perhaps 377,000) years after inflation and has traversed the universe largely unimpeded since then. The conditions of earlier times are imprinted on this light. It also forms a backlight for later developments of the universe. (NOTE: This light or glow phenomenon is known as cosmic microwave background or CMB radiation and was further measured by other satellites via their powerful telescopes. NASA's Cosmic Background Explorer [COBE], European Space Agency's [ESA] Planck, and now the James Webb satellites have independently produced and validated the same data.)

From these events, most scientists deduce that changes from one phenomenon to another are by natural means only. From this perspective, these events are interpreted to "evolve" from previous events that lead back to the very beginning of the "big bang." While scientific discoveries provide validity for many of these individual events, can evolutionary scientists explain how these events are connected to one another? This is where the stellar theory of evolution comes into play.

Evolutionists assume that with the right natural states, mechanisms, and forces, given large amounts of time (millions to billions of years), stellar changes in the naturally occurring events can and will eventually (gradually and sometimes rapidly) occur and form space objects. Galaxies containing stars, planets, asteroids, comets, debris, and other space phenomena (e.g., "black holes") will form and "evolve" (e.g., through a death and birth cycle) over time.

Evaluating Stellar Evolution

In general, astrophysicists and cosmologists propose an initial "big bang" at or very near the beginning of time, where quantum fluctuations of plasma cause fundamental subatomic particles to form and coalesce into simple elements of hydrogen and helium. Under extreme conditions, these gases form primitive (proto) stars and nebulae (e.g., an enormous cloud of dust, gas, and debris occupying the space between early stars and acting as a nursery for new stars under gravitation pull). These early stars, where nuclear fusion takes place in them, form carbon, oxygen, and other heavier elements. Some of these supergiant stars blow up. As a result of these explosions, gravity pulls in these heavier elements to form new stars and galaxies (e.g., like our solar system located within our Milky Way galaxy).

Evaluating the "Big Bang Theory"

First, the initial event of the beginning of the universe is not well understood. In fact, theoretical physicist Paul Sutter has said, "In the beginning there was a question mark. All else followed…The 'Big Bang' is not a theory of creation of the Universe. It is a scientific cosmological model of the history of the Universe, tracing the Evolution of the cosmos to the earliest moments."[236] For these earliest moments after the "big bang," cosmologists and astrophysicists have designed theories to cope with the conditions before the universe was even 10^{-43} seconds old. This period is known as the "plank time" — which is less than a quadrillionth-quadrillionth-trillionths of a second — and is the smallest unit of measurement that physicists use to measure the shortest lengths of time that can exist. Even though these conditions are considered in the quantum gravity era (which is very near the "big bang"), many leading scientists

> honestly admit that no consistent theory of quantum gravity yet exists which theorizes the effects of gravity on the smallest bits or elemental particles of the Universe. Finally, no physical technology, existing or future, advances will permit astronomers to observe phenomena earlier than 10^{-35} of a second… Even the most powerful particle accelerators cannot duplicate the energy densities of these particles.[237]

However, there is substantial evidence for the existence of sub-atomic particles. Discovery of fundamental or elementary particles such as photons, neutrons, quarks, leptons, bosons, and fermions at their expected masses, including the Higgs boson (a wave-like particle), is demonstrated by particle accelerator experiments with well over thirteen independent experimental proofs for Einstein's special and general relativity theories. These elementary particles are directly observed in the Large Hadron Collider (LHC), the world's most powerful particle collider and the largest machine in the world. The LHC was built by the European Organization for Nuclear Research (CERN) between 1998 and 2008. Since then, the LHC has discovered fifty-nine elementary particles called hadrons.[238]

Cosmic hyperinflation, expansion, and subsequent cooling of the universe is an expected outcome from the "symmetry breaking" of the separation of these fundamental four forces (i.e., weak and strong nuclear forces, gravity, and electromagnetism). Inflation would leave an unmistakable signature in measurements of the polarization modes of the CMB radiation. In particular, accurate measurements of the "E-mode" (e.g., a transverse magnetic mode) signals in the CMB maps would reveal this signature called the "spectral index." Sophisticated computer-controlled telescopes from NASA's Wilkinson Microwave Anisotropy Probe (WMAP), Cosmic Background Explorer (COBE), and James Webb satellites, the European Space Agency's Plank satellites, and the South Pole Telescope provided CMB image analyses. These analyses have determined that there is less than one chance in 900,000,000 that the universe did not experience an inflation event very early in its history. The South Pole Telescope team found the average certainty to be 95.93% +/- 0.67. The error estimate, 0.0067, implies that there is less than one chance in 900,000,000 that the universe did not experience an inflation event very early in its history.[239] Also, using these satellites (plus the earlier Keck and Hubble Space Telescopes) to measure the distance and time for CMB radiation or light to travel to Earth, their measurements indicate this event occurred approximately 380,000/400,000 years after the "big bang" or 0.003 percent of the universe's age.[240]

Scientific discoveries of subatomic particles and CMB radiation seem to validate the "big bang" theory. However, several questions remain. First, who or what caused the initial or quantum state for this transformation? Evolutionists simply answer this question as the "big bang." After the initial state, who or what mechanism(s) caused the newly formed matter to ultimately form our inorganic and organic elements and compounds necessary for life?

Given the complexities of the processes to form our elements and organic compounds, it seems *unlikely* that it "just" happened by chance, exclusively through the laws of nature and the direct interaction of the four fundamental forces (i.e., gravity, electromagnetism, weak and strong nuclear energy).

Therefore, it seems likely these natural laws were created by a supernatural being, such as "God," to evolve the universe as described. Also, the possibility of "God" creating the universe via a "creation big bang" where He had His "hand" in providing the right direction and ultimate conditions for life to form on Earth must be seriously considered.

In conclusion, it appears stellar evolution involves natural and supernatural events that are directly initiated and controlled by "God." Metaphorically speaking, we are indeed in the "hands" of God. God "holds, causes, and protects" His universe to stay together for our benefit. He has the whole world in His hands. Luke 1:37 and 18:27 say:

"For no word from God will ever fail."

and

"What is impossible with men is possible with God."

Even though this artist's rendition from NASA is quite spectacular and revealing, it is also extremely hard to fathom how our universe evolved without having some degree of "faith" without God's involvement! This illustrated path or trajectory in time has many implications. For example, did all these events occur randomly and naturally (e.g., through an "unguided" and "mindless" process by random chance), or were they part of a cause-and-effect scenario that could imply some involvement in the naturally occurring "forces" that is initiated, directed, and controlled by a supernatural intelligent maker or designer?

Specifically, many biblical creationists, such as those from the RTB organization (and many CS and ID individuals etc.), see this cause-and-effect scenario or path as a distinct possibility for a divine or supernatural intervention. They attribute these events to a "creation big bang." From a Christian perspective, this supernatural "creation big bang" was and is under the initiation, control, direction, and development of the God of the Bible (e.g., see Genesis 1). Biblically and scientifically speaking, God supernaturally created all initial elements, such as space, matter, energy, time, laws, constants, and all natural processes. Additionally, God ultimately prepared and provided a specific path for life and human life to begin, exist, and flourish. In other words, these events are not from a "big bang" explosion (which implies destruction or chaos) but from an intentional and divinely planned and ordered "cause-and-effect" set of natural and supernatural events that eventually support life on Earth.

Consequently, these creationists observe the universe and Earth as "fine-tuned" to support and sustain life. They believe the occurrence of these successive and numerous events is mathematically impossible to produce life without divine or supernatural intervention. Creationists call these deterministic sequences (e.g., or just right) of events the "universe's anthropic and earth's Goldilocks principles." The anthropic principle is attributed to the theoretical astrophysicist Brandon Carter. In 1973, at a symposium, he reacted to the "Copernican principle," which states that humans do not occupy a privileged place in the universe and that all large regions and times in the universe must be statically identical.

Since then, these principles have been extended by cosmologists John D. Barrow and Frank Tipler to include many cosmological constants and parameters. These philosophical principles argue that even any slight percentage deviation (e.g., any differences in the tolerances) from any one of these universe and Earth event parameters would cause a catastrophic and destructive situation and consequently disrupt the possibility of the existence of life itself as we know it to be today.[241]

Astrophysicist Hugh Ross, in his book *The Creator of the Cosmos*, provides an estimate of the probability for attaining the necessary parameters for life support. According to his calculations, the probability for the occurrence of all 128 parameters is 1×10^{166}, and the maximum possible number of planets in the universe is 1×10^{22}. Thus, less than 1 chance in 10^{144} (or a trillion multiplied by itself twelve times) exists that even one such planet would occur anywhere in the universe.[242] Some of these factors for life to exist on Earth are the right galaxy cluster (location of Milky Way galaxy residing in a loose grouping of galaxies called The Local Group, which is located on the far outer edge of the Virgo supercluster of galaxies), the right galaxy (only 5 percent of the galaxies are spirals with the solar system positioned in just a spiral arm at the right distance from the center of the galaxy and known as a galactic habitable zone), the right star (our middle-age Sun in a sufficiently stable burning phase and at the right distance to Earth), the right planet (water vapor, liquid water, and frozen water are all stable and abundant), right temperature and surface gravity, right rotation period and axis, right planetary companions (such as Jupiter and Saturn protecting us from asteroids and comet debris), the right collider (a right-sized asteroid hitting the earth) and eventually forming the Moon, which eliminated a life-suffocating atmosphere, produced a replacement atmosphere thin enough and of the right chemical composition to permit the passage of light to Earth's surface, boosted the mass and density of Earth high enough to retain (by gravity) a large quantity of water vapor for billions of years, provided the right chemicals and nutrients on Earth, stabilized the tilt of the earth's rotational axis, and many more.[243] The RTB, CS, and ID organizations agree on these and other factors or parameters that make the universe, Earth, and life unique and a special place. The odds are against a set of natural events randomly occurring in the right sequence to ultimately provide for life on Earth. A purely evolutionary pathway has not been established. Our universe, Earth, and life appear to be designed by a Creator God because they were.

Chemical and Prebiotic Evolution — the "Origins of Life" Theories

Eventually, according to chemical and geological evolutionists, the planet Earth (unlike our Moon) retained its atmosphere, which was assumed to initially contain methane (CH_4), ammonia (NH_3), carbon dioxide (CO_2), and water (H_2O) vapor predominately. From these chemicals, a primitive or primordial "soup" formed and survived on Earth under the right (or less hostile) environment. This "soup" contained all the "ingredients" (i.e., elements, compounds, and biomolecules) necessary for life to begin. From the chemical "soup," simple or primitive cells (e.g., protists) formed, survived, grew, and adapted to their specific environments. These very "simple" organisms eventually "morphed" into more complex single-celled organisms. They had limited metabolic or energy functions for survival and reproduction. The most adaptive organisms survived, reproduced, and evolved into different multicellular organisms having complex and advanced body features, plans, or types.

Specifically, chemical changes will evolve spontaneously from inorganic chemicals to initial prebiotic organic (carbon-based) compounds and then into the primitive (first) protocells. These primitive first cells will consist of single-celled organisms (e.g., such as prokaryotes or bacteria having no nucleus for the DNA), which have minimal metabolic functions. These simple cells will evolve into more complex single-celled organisms (e.g., eukaryotes or animal, plant, fungi) having a nucleus for DNA which surrounds many organelles. These advanced and complicated cells will evolve into various multicellular organisms containing multiple and different functions. These very advanced organisms, such as animals and humans, contain complete body plans or types containing tissues, organs, and systems all integrated and simultaneously functioning together. A textbook or technical description of life's natural origins is summarized as follows:

> Under high energy conditions or sources (catalysts such as lightning, ultraviolet radiation, solar and volcanic heat, cosmic rays, and ionizing radiation from radioactive decay), Earth's early reducing atmosphere (gases such as water vapor, ammonia, methane, carbon dioxide, and nitrogen without oxygen present) formed simple and small prebiotic molecules (hydrogen cyanide, formaldehyde, etc.,), which accumulated in Earth's ocean to make up a prebiotic "soup." The prebiotic molecules within this soup reacted under condensation to form more complex biomolecules (such as amino acids, sugars, fatty acids, purines (a unique DNA double ringed structure), and pyrimidines (a unique DNA single-ringed structure). These molecules, in turn, functioned as building blocks for more complex molecules that eventually led to the biomolecules (DNA, RNA, and proteins) found in all cells today. This scenario continues with the eventual production of a self-replicating molecule. The increasing concentration of complex molecules in the probiotic soup supposedly prompted their aggregation into protocells. These entities possessed partial cellular properties and served as a predecessor for the first actual cell. The first cells that emerged as random chemical and physical events caused the self-replicators to transfer self-replicating capability to the protocells. Evolutionary processes (for example, Natural Selection) have transformed the protocells, gradually increasing their capacity to self-replicate and carry

out various metabolic processes. As this occurred, the protocells gained in complexity. Finally, these protocells yielded an organism called the Last Universal Common Ancestor (LUCA). Presumably, the LUCA resembled modern-day prokaryotes (e.g., single-celled organisms that do not contain a nucleus for their DNA and have a lack of other internal cell organelle structures, like bacteria) and archaea bacteria. They evolved to yield life's three major domains: eubacteria (actual bacteria containing a nucleus for DNA and internal organelles), archaea (single-celled organisms superficially resembling bacteria, but biochemically different), and eukaryotes (complex multi-cellular eukaryotic organisms such as plants, animals, and fungi).[244]

Evaluating "Origins-of-Life" Prebiotic Chemical Theories

Scientists and evolutionists have offered several theories and hypotheses to support chemical evolution. They include vitalism theory, reductionism theory, chance hypothesis, and the self-organization or biochemical predestination theory.

Vitalism Theory

Philosophically, for centuries, the "vitalist" and "reductionist" proponents have argued whether a qualitative distinction existed between living and nonliving matter. These "abiogenesis" proponents believed life came from nonlife (a.k.a. "spontaneous generation"). The vitalists maintained living organisms contained some immaterial "vital force or spirit" that distinguishes them qualitatively from nonliving chemicals. For example, the "protoplasmic theory" of the 1860s stated that attributes of living things are derived from a single vital nitrogen-rich substance called protoplasm, which is inside the walls of cells.[245] Later, Thomas Huxley's contribution to this theory elaborated a simple two-step chemical process that forms protoplasm: simple elements such as carbon, hydrogen, nitrogen, and oxygen first react to form common compounds such as water, carbonic acid, and ammonia. He believed these compounds then combined under unspecified conditions to form protoplasm, the chemical essence of life.[246] Then, Ernst Haeckel proposed the existence of ancient creatures that occupied an intermediate position between life and nonlife. He called these predecessors to life "monera" and thought them to be formless lumps of gel capable of reproduction. Shortly after Haeckel advanced this hypothesis, Huxley provided observational support for the idea. He detected gelatinous lumps in ocean-floor mud and interpreted them as monera remains.[247]

Evaluation of the Vitalism Theory

"Origin-of-life" researchers have *never* found this immaterial "vital or spiritual force" that distinguishes life from nonlife and *reject* this theory! Scientists discovered that the cell derives its energy from the mitochondrial organelle located inside the cell wall membrane's cytoplasm (a gel-like substance).

> This chemical energy is from the Adenosine Triphosphate (ATP) compound, which is produced from the Krebs cycle (e.g., a 10-enzyme glycolysis pathway). When ATP is hydrolyzed (with water taking away a phosphate group) and converted to Adenosine Diphosphate (ADP) from this cycle, energy is released. (ATP is composed of three phosphate groups (PO_4), the nucleotide base Adenine, and the 5-ringle Ribose sugar molecule.) ATP provides the energy for the cell's metabolism, waste elimination,

signaling for all communications within and between cells, and other critical functions.[248]

Reductionism Theory

Reductionists held that life represented merely a quantitatively (vice qualitatively) more complex form of chemistry.

> Thus, in their view, living organisms, like complex machines, functioned as the result of processes that could be "reduced" or explained solely by referencing the laws of physics and chemistry. The molecular biological revolution of the 1950s and 1960s seemed to confirm the reductionist perspective. Watson and Crick discovered the DNA (Deoxyribonucleic Acid) structure in 1953. This ("*large*") biomolecule contains the mechanism for storing and transmitting information in the cells, in terms of the ordinary concepts of physics and chemistry or rather simple extensions of them.[249]

Also, Aleksandr Oparin's "evolutionary abiogenesis theory" (1922–1928) stated that an early atmosphere containing ammonia (NH_3), dicarbon (C_2), cyanogen (CN), steam (H_2O), and simple hydrocarbons like methane (CH_4) and methylene (CH_2) would react with the iron carbides arriving at the surface of the earth because of lightning strikes and UV radiation from the Sun. This process would have formed heavy energy-rich hydrocarbons, the first organic molecules. These hydrocarbons would react with ammonia (NH_3) to create various nitrogen compounds such as amino acids, which then would link together to form amino acid chains (a.k.a. polypeptides) and proteins. Then, organic molecules would be transformed into living things. Specifically, primitive structures of fat clusters that encase carbohydrates and proteins (called "coacervates") would form and grow in complexity through natural selection and eventually form into the first living cell.[250]

Evaluation of the Reductionism Theory

The most famous "origin-of-life" experiment tested the 1924–1928 Oparin-Haldane "abiogenesis' hypothesis" (e.g., life from inorganic molecules or chemicals). Sun's ultraviolet light transformed the simple gases of CH_4, NH_3, CO_2, and water vapor — H_2O — into more complicated compounds. They came together to form the microscopic clumps or "primordial soup" that were the predecessors to the first cells. This "spark-discharge" experiment was conducted in 1953 by biochemists Stanley Miller and Harold Urey. "They designed an apparatus that attempted to duplicate these atmospheric conditions of primitive Earth. The Miller-Urey experiments did not produce cells, but they produced only two amino acids (glycine — 1.05% and alanine — 0.75%) that are the building blocks of proteins."[251]

Also, "origin-of-life" researchers cannot identify any location on primordial Earth suitable for producing prebiotic molecules! Those scientists studying the unique and overriding problem of "homochirality" cannot explain how the uniform "handedness" of amino acids, nucleotides, and sugars could emerge in any so-called "prebiotic soup." Data from geological, geochemical, and fossil records all place impossible constraints on naturalistic scenarios. Life arose rapidly and early in Earth's history — as soon as Earth could support it. "Origin-of-life" researchers recognize that life had no more than tens of millions of years to emerge. Life also appeared under amazingly harsh conditions — conditions that would not allow life to survive, let alone originate. Earth's first life was complex chemically, though simple morphologically (in its form). Consistent with this, investigators have discovered that life in its most minimal form requires an astonishing number of proteins that must be spatially and temporally organized within the cell.[252]

Specifically, biochemist A. Polanyi *refutes* the concept of "reductionism." He shows that a communication system within the DNA biomolecule *defies* reduction to physical and chemical laws.[253] This concept is known as the "gene expression system." Further, reductionism does not determine or explain the specific arrangement or sequencing of the DNA molecular bases (i.e., specifically the nucleotide bases of adenine [A] are connected to thymine [T], and cytosine [C] is connected to guanine [G]). In addition, this gene expression system requires freedom from chemical determinism or constraints to effectively "instruct" or "code" for functional proteins into an exact functional configuration. See figure 14 for the double helix configuration of the "large" DNA biomolecule. The DNA biomolecule contains a sugar-phosphate backbone and these four nucleotide bases. (NOTE: The RNA biomolecule contains a single helix configuration sugar-phosphate backbone, but uracil [U] replaces thymine.) These nucleic acids resemble "steps or rungs" on a ladder.

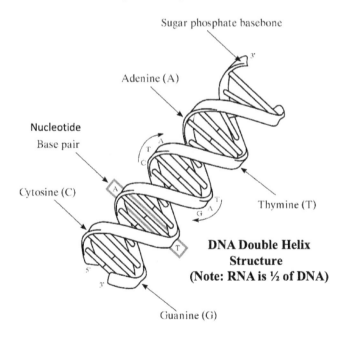

Figure 14: Structure of DNA

NOTE: As a background, Watson and Crick's "sequence hypothesis" suggested these bases functioned like alphabetic letters in an English text or binary digits in software or machine code where their specific order (e.g., instructions) determines the arrangements of amino acids and, in turn, determines protein folding and consequently a functional 3D protein structure.

Philosopher of science Steven C. Meyer realized the significance of this "gene expression system," which Polanyi suggested. Meyer concluded:

> The information in DNA does not reduce to or derive from physical and chemical forces. This realization implied that the information in DNA did not originate from such forces. He also realized that this was highly specified and complex information, which was tightly processed to ensure accuracy of the outcome, and produced functional proteins.[254]

In addition, these (supposedly) proven mechanisms do not answer the "origins-of-life" question. Often, it comes down to the "chicken-and-egg" dilemma. Specifically, and simply put, as an example, the chicken (e.g., DNA) directs the production of eggs (e.g., proteins), but proteins are needed to support DNA. The cell needs proteins to process and express the information in DNA in order to build proteins. But the construction of DNA molecules also requires proteins. Which comes first — DNA or proteins?[255] This dilemma has led scientists to redefine the question of the "origins of life."

Various scientists have attempted to explain the origin of the information processing system that the cell requires to maintain itself.

Meyer detailed four approaches: First, random molecular interactions by chance alone. Second, law-like forces of necessity. Third, a combination of chance and necessity. Fourth, an intelligent designer (ID). Due to the specified complexity and causal adequacy (e.g., power to produce the kind of effect, feature, or event in need of explanation) of making proteins from genes, he cites ID as the "inference to the best explanation" to (solve) the DNA enigma.[256]

Chance Hypothesis

The "chance hypothesis" envisions amino acids or nucleotide bases (i.e., A, T, C, G, and U), phosphates, and sugars "knocking" into each other in an ocean-sized "soup" until the correct arrangements of these building blocks arise by chance somewhere and somehow. Such an environment would have generated many opportunities for assembling functional proteins (via amino acids) and DNA (via genes) molecules. This hypothesis assumes by chance that all these chemicals are available in the right quantities and come together naturally to produce functional or useful proteins.

Specifically, in a hypothetical prebiotic "soup," could information-rich biomolecules (proteins, RNA, DNA, etc.) randomly react with one another to form amino acid chains if heated in condensing agents?

> Some researchers speculate these conditions could have occurred when tidal waters evaporated at the shoreline of volcanic islands, leaving behind prebiotic compounds. Lab simulation experiments designed to mimic these chemical reactions on early Earth show proteins that form by heating amino acid solutions to dryness, have a random amino acid sequence. However, some selective enrichment occurs for a few amino acids.[257]

This observation means that any proteins formed under prebiotic conditions would have consisted of random sequences of amino acids. The production of biologically meaningful proteins, then, becomes a probability problem. Some random proteins produced by prebiotic pathways would have been "junk," while others would have potentially beneficial biological properties. Therefore, the question is: What is the likelihood that the proteins needed to carry out essential life functions could form through the random assembly of amino acids?

NOTE: This probability problem is also known as a "combinatorial problem" by mathematicians. It refers to the number of possible ways that a set of objects can be arranged or combined. Most scientists calculate the probability of a single functional protein of average length by the probability of each of the other necessary proteins arising by chance. The product of these probabilities determines the probability that all the proteins necessary to service a minimally complex cell would come together by chance. Most "origin-of-life" scientists analyze the odds of arranging amino acids into a functional protein.[258]

Evaluation of the Chance Hypothesis

Before addressing these probabilities or odds, the additional problems of homochirality, cell membrane limitations, and carbon-based exclusive life formations are considered.

Homochirality must precede the origins of proteins. In other words, the naturalistic assembly of proteins, DNA, and RNA is prohibited without preexisting reservoirs of exclusively "left-handed" amino acids and exclusively "right-handed" sugars.[259] (NOTE: Imagine a mirror image concept of bringing our hands together, as in the right-handed and left-handed configuration of the generic amino acid example illustrated in figure 15.) Each configuration determines a different function. Amino acids consist of a primary amino group (NH_2), an acidic carboxyl group (COOH), hydrogen (H), and a specific side chain (e.g., R = CH_3 is the amino acid alanine), all attached to the same carbon atom.

HOMOCHIRALITY

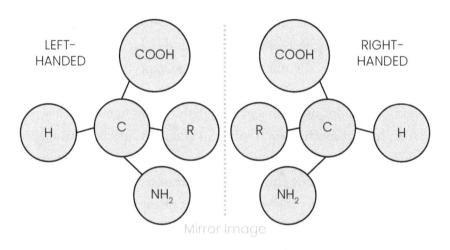

"R" designates a specific amino acid

Figure 15: Amino Acid Homochirality

In nature, every amino acid found in proteins (with one exception — glycine) has a distinct mirror image of itself (a.k.a. homochirality); specifically, there are nineteen left-handed versions, or L-forms, and one right-handed version, or D-form. These mirror-image forms are called "optical isomers." Functional proteins tolerate only left-handed amino acids, yet in abiotic amino acid production in the lab, the right-handed and left-handed isomers are produced with roughly equal frequency. In addition, in nature, only right-handed (or D-chiral) sugars are used in the DNA backbone. This condition presents two questions. First, what served as the original template for biasing the production of one enantiomer (*describes one of the pairs of mirror images of a chiral object*) over the other in the chemically austere and presumably racemic environment of the prebiotic world? And second, how was this bias sustained and propagated to give us the biological world of single chirality that surrounds us?[260] "This homochirality situation presents a real challenge to life occurring naturally without any 'supernatural divine' direction."[261]

All attempts to synthesize amino acids and sugars in laboratory simulation experiments produce racemic end products only.[262] In other words, prebiotic synthesis of amino acids and sugars, whether on Earth or anywhere else in the universe, would be expected to produce only racemic mixtures (e.g., 50 percent right-handed and 50 percent left-handed). Therefore, hope for a natural path toward homochirality must lie in a physical mechanism. Only two (known) means drive racemic mixtures of amino acids and sugars into a homochiral configuration. First is an effect called "chiral magneto anisotropy," which links chirality and magnetism. The second astronomical mechanism uses circularly polarized ultraviolet light emanating from neutron stars and black holes. However, based on particle accelerator experiments and calculations from observations, neither mechanism is strong enough to change or drive the racemic mixtures into the correct configurations for life to be formed.[263] Also, as mentioned, right-handed (homochiral) sugars make up the DNA biomolecule (a six-ring sugar — deoxyribose) and the RNA biomolecule (a five-ring sugar — ribose). This sugar is critical for naturalistic "origin-of-life" scenarios. Scientists have yet to detect any of these respective six-ring and five-ring sugars in the nonbiological world. "The absence of these homochiral sugars is as difficult for the naturalistic research to deal with as is the absence of homochiral amino acids."[264]

In addition, the homochiral molecules of amino acids and sugars are subject to the second law of thermodynamics — the "law of entropy." This law guarantees that time and heat (via UV, X-ray, and gamma-ray radiation) will drive any set of homochiral molecules into a racemic mixture (fifty-fifty) unless some direct repair work occurs, such as that in the molecular machinery inside a living cell.[265]

Also, even under controlled and pristine conditions, scientists, such as chemist Robert Shapiro, have not been able to produce in the lab from "spark-discharge" experiments the nucleotide bases of cytosine (C)[266] and adenine (A)[267] and the high-energy phosphate group (PO_4). These bases are used in the DNA backbone to provide energy and used by the cell to power its operation. He has concluded that their formation on early Earth could not reasonably have occurred because of the harsh conditions on primitive Earth. Studies on possible pre-biotic production of these compounds demonstrate that even though researchers have identified chemical pathways to them, the lack of available starting materials, plus chemical interference by other environmental materials and rapid decomposition, would have precluded formation. In other words, viable chemical routes to these key life molecules have not been found.[268]

Another area presumed by chance is the formation of the first protocells. Here, within the evolutionary framework, the emergence of cell membrane systems is a necessary stage in life's origin and the initial step toward forming the first protocells. The cell membrane's structure and associated functions are incredibly complex. It comprises two lipids (mainly phospholipids) layers and integral and peripheral proteins between/inside the lipid layers. This "well-guarded" cell border keeps harmful materials from entering the cell and sequesters the beneficial compounds inside it. Proteins embedded in the cell's membrane act as border patrol agents, regulating the traffic of materials in and out of the cell — the advances in membrane biophysics challenge natural-process explanations for cell membrane origins. While a wide range of amphiphilic compounds (e.g., "ambivalent" in its likes, such as soaps and detergents) could serve as lipid components for primitive biological membranes to self-assemble into bilayers, this self-assembling process requires just the right conditions (i.e., temperatures and pressures) and the just-right molecular compounds (carbon monoxide and hydrogen). It is unlikely that such conditions would exist or persist for long on early Earth."[269]

Also, life molecules must be carbon-based. Only carbon possesses a sufficiently complex chemical behavior to sustain living systems. Carbon readily assembles into stable molecules comprised of individual and fused rings and linear and branched chains. It forms single, double, and triple bonds. Carbon also strongly bonds with itself and oxygen, nitrogen, sulfur, and hydrogen.[270] Prebiotic lab experiments have demonstrated that certain amino acids based on carbon, such as arginine, lysine, and histidine, have not been produced. Adenine and guanine nucleotide bases require freezing conditions for their synthesis, and cytosine and uracil bases demand boiling temperatures. For all four building blocks to take shape simultaneously, the prebiotic soup must simultaneously freeze and boil.[271] In addition, recent advances now indicate that Earth's earliest atmosphere was *not* reducing but neutral, consisting of nitrogen (N_2), carbon dioxide (CO_2), carbon monoxide (CO), and water vapor (H_2O). This atmosphere could not have sustained the production of prebiotic molecules. Prebiotic molecular synthesis can occur in this type of atmosphere only if high hydrogen (H) gas levels are included. Since molecular hydrogen escapes to outer space because of its low molecular weight, it most likely rapidly escaped early Earth's atmosphere. From this perspective, lab experiments are irrelevant to the origin-of-life question.[272] Another exciting aspect is the presence or absence of oxygen in prebiotic chemical pathways. Physicist Ivan Draganic points out that "between 3 to 4 billion years ago, the intensity of radiation from radioactive decay of uranium, thorium, and potassium-40 must have been much more significant than today. Continuous oxygen production means Earth's kitchen never cooked a prebiotic soup."[273]

Ironically, oxygen's absence would also have turned off prebiotic chemistry due to a lack of an ozone layer, where UV radiation would have broken apart the chemical bonds of prebiotic molecules.[274] Finally, geochemists found that from all carbon-13 to carbon-12 ratio radio-isometric measurements of carbonaceous deposits formed from the remains of once-living organisms — *none* of the deposits formed from prebiotic material. Researchers concluded:

> No known abiotic process can explain the data…With this accumulation of data, the primordial "soup" hypothesis evaporates. In addition, the same findings were made when researchers examined the nitrogen isotope ratios of nitrogen-15 to nitrogen-14. This evaluation confirmed that *no* primordial soup ever existed on (or in) Earth.[275]

So how valid is this hypothesis? Or in other words, what is the probability that the information necessary to build the first living cell would arise by chance alone? Based upon minimal-complexity experiments, some scientists speculate (but have not physically demonstrated) that a simple one-celled organism might survive with as few as 250–400 genes and with around 1200 nucleotide base pairs for each gene. (NOTE: Genes are specific sequences of DNA that "code" for proteins.) These genes would build a sizable preexisting suite of proteins and RNA molecules — polymerases, transfer RNAs (tRNAs), ribosomal RNAs (rRNAs), etc., all that function together in a tightly integrated way. The cell would also have required some semipermeable membrane or a cell wall to protect itself and enable the chemical reactions inside it.[276]

Given these minimal requirements, chemical engineer Douglas Axe calculated the probability of a single functional protein of average length arising by chance alone and the corresponding genetic information appearing by chance. Axe conducted a series of site-directed mutagenesis experiments on a 150 amino-acid protein-folding domain within a B-lactamase enzyme and published the results in the *Journal of Molecular Biology* in 2004... In addition, he calculated the probability that a single protein — any working protein — would have arisen by chance on the early earth as one chance in 10^{74} attempts (e.g., 10^{74} is a one with seventy-four zeros after it). This calculation considers the right sequencing of 150 amino acids that form a chain with each amino acid connected by a peptide bond. (Several chains or polypeptides undergo a four-step folding process to produce a stable and functional 3D protein structure.) Axe concluded that though proteins tolerate a range of possible amino acids at some sites, functional proteins are still extremely rare within the whole set of possible amino-acid sequences. His work confirmed earlier studies that the odds are prohibitively stacked against a random process producing functional proteins.[277]

Also, chemists Charles Thaxton, Walter Bradley, and Roger Olsen have rigorously addressed this problem.[278] They argued that in the absence of any chemical competition with non-amino acids and non-biologically relevant amino acids (which is considered the best-case scenario), the probability of getting the right amino acid in a specific position in a protein molecule is 1.25 percent.[279]

NOTE: There is a 50 percent chance of natural processes randomly selecting a left-handed chiral amino acid (instead of a right-handed chiral one), a 50 percent chance of joining the two amino acids with the appropriate chemical peptide bond, and roughly a 5 percent chance (one in twenty essential amino acids) of selecting the correct amino acid. This gives us a 1.25 percent chance by multiplying each of these percentages (also, the probability of undirected processes assembling a protein a hundred amino acids long becomes roughly one chance in 10^{191}).[280]

In effect, there is *no chance* that even a relatively small protein, which is made up of a specified sequence, could ever form by undirected processes.

Since then, several additional "chance" experiments have been conducted to determine the mathematical probability that new life would appear. Here are just a few more examples.

In the 1990s, Robert Sauer, a molecular biologist,

performed a series of experiments that first attempted to measure the rarity of proteins within amino-acid sequence space…Based on a set of mutagenesis experiments, Sauer and his colleagues estimated the ratio of functional (i.e., favorable or beneficial for survival and reproduction) to non-functional amino-acid sequences (harmful which would lessen, if not destroy, the functional these functional capabilities) at about 1 to 10^{63} (meaning one chance in 63 zeros that it would occur) for a short protein of 92 amino acids in length.[281]

Hubert Hockey, an information theorist,

performed later experiments on the Cytochrome c proteins (*proteins involved in the biochemical pathways that generate energy in cells*) in different species and determined the ratio of functional to non-functional sequences to be about 1 to 10^{90} for amino acid changes of this length (100 amino acids)."[282]

In 2007, Douglas Axe determined the probability of a 150-amino-acid compound assembling in the correct order by random interactions in a prebiotic soup to make a functional protein. He multiplied three independent probabilities by one another: the probability of amino acids forming peptide bonds between other amino acids (1 in 10^{45}), the probability of incorporating only left-handed amino acids (1 in 10^{45}), and the probability of achieving correct amino-acid sequencing to produce stable protein folds (1 in 10^{74}). Multiplying these separate and independent probabilities involves adding their exponents. This calculation gives the odds of 1 in 10^{164} attempts to produce any functional protein from a prebiotic soup.[283] And if it is assumed that a minimally complex cell needs at least 250 proteins of, on average, 150 amino acids and that the probability of producing such protein is 1 in 10^{164} as calculated above, then the likelihood of making all the necessary proteins needed to service a minimally complex cell is 1 in 10^{164} multiplied by itself 250 times, or 1 in $10^{41,000}$.[284] Therefore, the conclusion by Axe is that it is essentially *improbable* that chance alone can produce genes and proteins!

In conclusion, philosopher of science and ID advocate Steven C. Meyers concluded regarding the chance hypothesis:

> Following many leading "Origin-of-Life" researchers,
> I came to the same conclusion about the first life and
> even the first genes and proteins: it is much more likely
> than not that chance alone did not produce these phe-
> nomena. Life, of course, does exist. So do the informa-
> tion-rich biological macromolecules upon which living
> cells depend. But the probability that even one of these
> information-rich molecules arose by change, let alone the
> suite of such molecules necessary to maintain or build a
> minimally complex cell, is so small as to dwarf the prob-
> abilistic resources of the entire Universe. The conditional

probability that just one of these information-rich molecules arose by chance — in effect, the chance that chance is true — is much less than one-half. It is one in a trillion trillion (e.g., 10^{12} x 10^{12} = 10^{24}). Thus, I concluded that it is more reasonable to *reject* the Chance Hypothesis than to accept it.[285]

Biological Predestination or Self-Organization Hypothesis

In response to the "chance hypothesis," evolutionists took another approach to reduce these improbable odds. "Necessity" or "biological predestination or self-organization" would explain the "origins-of-life" mystery. Here, "self-organization" refers to a spontaneous increase in the order of a system due to some natural processes, force, or law — ones that can be described mathematically as laws of nature. This deterministic process could help overcome the otherwise long odds against the "origin of life" occurring by chance alone. These theorists formulated theories that either tried to explain or circumvent the need to explain the "DNA enigma." Aleksandr Oparin's scenario describes how life might have arisen through a series of chemical transformations in which more complex chemical structures occurred from simpler ones. Dean Kenyon's model considers those simple monomers (e.g., amino acids, bases, and sugars) arise from simpler atmospheric gases and energy; polymers (proteins and DNA) arise from monomers; primitive membranes form around their polymers, and primitive metabolism energy inside these polymer membranes interact chemically with one another. Unlike Oparin, who relied on chance variations to achieve some of the chemical transformations, Kenyon relied more exclusively on deterministic chemical reactions based upon different affinities that imposed certain constraints on the sequencing of amino acids, rendering specific sequences more likely than others.[286]

However, Kenyon did not attempt to explain the information in DNA since he favored a protein-first model. Unfortunately, he could not explain the DNA molecule since DNA provides the template of information for building proteins and not the reverse. Information flows (strictly one way) from DNA to proteins. Moreover, there are several good reasons for this asymmetry. Each triplet of DNA bases, such as ATG (and the corresponding RNA "codons" of TAC), specifies exactly one amino acid during the transcription and translation processes. Yet most amino acids correspond to more than one nucleotide triplet of RNA codon. This feature of the genetic code ensures that information can flow without "degeneracy" or low "specificity" in only one direction, from DNA to proteins, and not the reverse. Based on the structure of the DNA molecule, Keyon doubted that DNA possessed any self-organizational properties analogous to those he had identified in amino acids and proteins.[287]

NOTE: DNA splicing and transcription processes occur within a cell's nucleus, where a gene's DNA sequence is copied (transcribed) to make a messenger RNA (e.g., mRNA) molecule. Translation is the process through which information encoded in the mRNA molecule directs the addition of amino acids during protein synthesis. Translation takes place on the ribosome organelles located in the cell's cytoplasm, where mRNA is read and translated into the string of amino acid chains (a.k.a. polypeptides) that make up the synthesized 3D protein using a complicated four-step "folding" process.

Regarding chemical evolution (as the precursor to biological evolution), Christians seem even more skeptical that natural "forces or mechanisms" work alone to produce and sustain life without divine input. Lab experiments validate this conclusion. Specifically, they believe randomly and gradually changing inorganic chemicals into organic (e.g., carbon-based) chemicals and biomolecules into "simple" life to "complex" life and then to "advanced" life (i.e., animals and humans) seem *virtually impossible* without direct divine (e.g., God) intervention.

Summary

Based upon the above studies, many of these scientists have concluded *"it is highly improbable"* for natural processes alone to have (a) initiated, formed, and developed the universe and (b) produced all forms of life on Earth, even in its simplest form (e.g., a single-celled organism that can survive and reproduce). Specifically, it is *"doubtful"* that simple elements and compounds in a presumed primordial "soup" could survive under harsh environmental conditions on Earth. If this "soup" could survive, the "ingredients" inside it would need to keep on colliding until they formed organic (carbon-based) compounds. These compounds would then need (naturally), by chance, necessity, or both, to develop into a very stable but flexible, adaptable, and unique DNA biomolecule. This seems very unlikely since the DNA's double-helix configuration is composed of a durable and stable phosphate plus a right-handed chiral sugar (ribose) backbone and unique chiral nucleotide bases attached to the backbone or spine. DNA serves as a "blueprint" to "code" for the formations of specific functional proteins in only one direction.

"Origins-of-life" lab experiments and mathematical calculations have shown that the evolutionary theory of how the first cell came to exist and survive is "virtually impossible" without divine intervention. Lab experiments show that the vitalist and reductionist interpretations are equally "*flawed*" and unlikely to be possible. Evolutionary hypotheses (chance and biological predestination of self-organizational) were addressed and dismissed as improbable as well. That is, going from early Earth's atmosphere to simple prebiotic molecules to a prebiotic "soup" to prebiotic molecules to biomolecules to protocells to simple cells and to the last universal common ancestor (LUCA) was seen to be highly unlikely (effectively "*zero*") to have occurred. Many biochemists and geochemists agree with this conclusion. They have made several discoveries that show the "shortfalls" of biochemical evolution. They are the uniqueness of amino acids, sugars, and nucleotides with their homochirality restrictions, the most likely early Earth atmosphere that would provide additional limits of available chemicals for life, the harsh environmental conditions eliminating or breaking down certain chemicals for life, the complexity and tightly controlled DNA (gene) to protein synthesis process, and the complexity of the cell membrane to allow only certain chemicals to go in and out of the cell. Besides these scientific findings, calculations show the improbability of all these events happening together from an evolutionary perspective. The results indicate that they could not have occurred without some external input.

The bottom line shows these stellar and biochemical evolutionary mechanisms and processes are highly improbable to occur through natural means alone, even if there are unlimited amounts of time. The evidence for evolution alone is just not there! Evolutionary theories have been partially validated for stellar evolution. However, evolutionary theories have not been validated for chemical evolution. As an alternative, divine intervention from an intelligent designer or biblical Creator God needs to be seriously and objectively considered to initiate and direct these events to occur. Faith and reason play an essential part in coming to this conclusion.

Next, an extensive evaluation of biological evolution is presented. This topic is the most controversial subject regarding our origins. The next three chapters cover the Darwinian concepts of natural selection and common descent.

CHAPTER 8:

Evaluation of the Biological Theory of Evolution

Introduction

Let us move on to biological evolution, where scientific evolutionists say the first cell evolved into multicellular and advanced organisms. What is the likelihood that these changes will evolve on their own?

Specifically, the Darwinian biological mechanism of natural selection, which contributes to the "macroevolution or common descent" of one species changing into another and ultimately to a common ancestor (i.e., last universal common ancestor or LUCA), has come under intense scrutiny. Discoveries from the scientific fields of genetics, molecular biochemical, and biogeological research of fossils that were found in their isolated geological strata have shed additional "light" on the theory of biological evolution. Gene or genomic research casts *doubt* on this evolutionary scenario.

Evolutionists assume, based upon environmental conditions and population size and location, natural selection randomly selects beneficial and survivable mutations within genes to gradually evolve one species into another species. (NOTE: Neutral mutations are also selected and passed on but do not necessarily contribute to any changes, although some scientists today say they do.) Also, evolutionists assume the right kind and number of organic chemicals and biomolecules are available under the right environmental conditions to have natural selection act upon them to evolve one species gradually into another. However, many creationists and some scientists believe the sequence of these natural events to produce life is impossible without divine or "God's" intervention.

> NOTE: As a review from the last chapter, genes are specific sections or sequences of the DNA biomolecule. Each parent contributes their portion of DNA through their forty-six chromosomes (i.e., twenty-two autosomal pairs and two sex pairs — XX for the female and XY for the male). DNA is structured in a double-helix or ladder configuration. Portions of the DNA biomolecule (e.g., genes) are responsible to "code" for the formation of specific proteins. This unique DNA (gene) structure has the inherent replication capability to provide for the instructions to produce thousands of different functioning proteins that our bodies need for existence and survival. Proteins help to repair and build our body's tissues, allow metabolic reactions to take place, coordinate bodily functions, provide our body with a structural framework, maintain proper pH and fluid balance, keep our immune system strong, transport and store nutrients, and can act as an energy source if needed. Through four tightly controlled sets of processes, genes "faithfully" produce these correct functional proteins to a very high degree of accuracy. These unique processes to produce proteins from genes include gene splicing, transcription, translation, and

protein folding into a (*functional*) 3D structure. It is estimated that the human body may contain over two million proteins, coded for by only 20,000 to 25,000 genes.[288]

Since there is reasonable collaborating scientific evidence for some form of stellar evolution to have occurred, the question becomes, "Did the universe occur or evolve naturally alone or supernaturally with divine involvement?" Chapter 7 demonstrated the virtual impossibility of the universe to begin and evolve without "God" initiating, controlling, and guiding certain events or states to eventually form the environment and conditions for modern humans to begin, reproduce, and survive. This was covered under the anthropic and Goldilocks principles of "fine-tuning." Chapter 9 elaborates on our beginnings and evaluates our evolutionary path from a scientific perspective.

In particular, the most debated and sensitive area is whether archaic and modern humans (e.g., Homo sapiens *sapiens* or sometimes just called Homo *sapiens* by historical scientists such as paleoanthropologists) are considered the highest form of "animal" life. Evolutionists believe this perspective to be true and demonstrate this concept through the "missing links" of previous so-called "archaic" hominids or "humans." On the other hand, many creationists believe modern humans are unique or special and made in the image of God by God Himself, "fully" formed!

> So, God created man in his own image; in the image of God, he created them; male and female he created them.
>
> — Genesis 1:27

Also, Christians believe humans have been given or endowed by God with special abilities not found in any other species, such as the ability to "create" things that have led to the development of technologically advanced civilizations and cultures. Evidence supports this conclusion through rigorous scientific genomic, molecular, paleoanthropological, and other studies. These studies reveal humans are unique and special from all other hominid species. Specifically, analysis of fossil remains indicates that many genes are entirely different from other hominids. (NOTE: Modern humans are classified in the hominid genus taxa by these scientists.) Scientific discoveries show this conclusion to be particularly important and relevant, especially with the findings of highly increased and advanced brain function activity and morphological or structural superiority for conducting highly advanced functions in modern humans.

Contributing to these discoveries, biblical theologians and philosopher scholars believe we are "wired" with the ability to seek and know "God" or a "higher being" as part of our consciousness and thinking processes, unlike other species. Additionally, Christians believe God created us to love Him.

The reason that God desires that we know Him is because He wants us to love Him. And you shall "love the Lord your God with all your heart and with all your soul and with all your mind, and with all your strength" (Mark 12:30). This is the first commandment. The more we come to know God, the more we come to know love because God is love.

All traditional Christian creationists believe our purpose in this life is to acknowledge who God is (e.g., the Trinity or triune Godhead composed of the Father, Son, and Holy Spirit) and to love, follow, and obey Him. Our rewards are not just limited to this life but to gain an eternal life with Him in heaven. (Nevertheless, I believe God delights in us when we try to "figure out" some of the scientific details regarding the creation of our origins and then give Him the credit for His miraculous creation!)

Biological Evolution

According to biological evolutionists, organic chemical structures (i.e., nucleic acids, amino acids, etc.) combined and grew to form complex large biomolecules, such as deoxyribonucleic acid (DNA) and ribonucleic acid (RNA), over very long periods (millions or billions of years). These biomolecules eventually form primitive protocells with membranes or walls to enclose themselves. Cell walls protect their cells from harsh environments. Additionally, the walls control and protect the passage of chemicals in and out of these cells. Eventually, different cells multiply within specific environments. They became diverse in function and interact cooperatively to form the first living organisms. These unicellular or single-celled organisms (called prokaryotes because they have no nucleus for the DNA) are the only forms of life where the DNA molecule becomes the inherited structure's prevalent replicator. According to these scientists, this event occurred about 3.5 to 3.8 billion years ago. These simple but chemically complex and very early organisms give rise to most of today's bacteria. From these bacteria, a branch splits off by integrating with a symbiotic partner to develop new energy production methods. These new types of cells are called eukaryotes (because they have a nucleus that contains most of the DNA, a small amount of DNA in the mitochondria organelle, and other organelles [such as ribosomes] that contribute to the functioning of the cell).

According to these scientists, the eukaryotes give rise to blue-green algae called chloroplasts (e.g., a light-collecting molecule like chlorophyll). The chloroplasts use the Sun's energy to power the cells' processes, including the host's reproduction replicator or DNA. Then, mutations in the genetic (DNA) instructions lead to the production of multicellular entities composed of specialized cells cooperating to ensure the replication of their shared genes. After a long maturation period (about 3 billion years), this new multicellular life model explodes into an infinite variety of forms about 600 million years ago (a.k.a. the "Cambrian explosion" or the "biological big bang") and occupies every possible ecological niche of multiple plants, insects, and animal life.

Within this biotic evolutionary scenario, specific forms of life prevail in each niche. Successful genes in each niche are those whose replication introduces genetic mutations leading to the natural selection of the most prolific or beneficial mutants. Then these genes are transmitted to future generations of species. These factors' actions occur over several million generations and result in new varieties and, eventually, new species. After the appearance of multicellular life, the evolutionary process has another (approximately) 592 million years to set the stage for the emergence of man's first ancestors, according to evolutionary scientists.

> NOTE: The first proto-hominids appeared about 8 million years ago. So, within this "human tree of life," here is a brief description of these hominid genera according to evolutionary scientists: After about 3 million years, the hominid Australopithecus *afarensis* group (or genera) started to walk upright about 5 million years ago. Two million more years of gradual evolution passed before the Australopithecus *africanensis* group appeared. Another million years later, the Paranthropus group appeared. Later, the Homo group appeared, including Homo *habilis*, Homo *rudolfensis*, Homo *ergaster*, Homo *erectus*, and distinct species such as the Homo sapiens *idaltu*, Homo sapiens *denisova*, Homo sapiens *neanderthalensis*, and the modern humans or Homo sapiens *sapiens* came on the scene.[289]

Biological evolution is evaluated and is based on scientific discoveries. In addition, as a contrast, creation explanations provide an alternative when evolutionary principles are weak, missing, not observed in nature, or cannot be demonstrated in scientific discoveries and selected experiments.

> NOTE: For convenience and understanding, evolution is defined and represented by the stellar, chemical, and biological theories. However, according to evolutionary scientists, evolution is considered a continuous process where distinct events and objects naturally evolve from one state or condition or event to another without any divine input.

Scientific Evaluation of the "Common Descent" Theory

Evolutionary scientists most often refer to Darwin's "common descent" theory to represent biological or biotic evolution.

Scientific evidence for first life started approximately 3.8 to 3.9 (billion years ago or BYA) is observed through the fossil record and geochemical data recovered from some of the world's oldest rock and sediment strata formations by paleobiologist William Schopf. For example:

Fossilized cyanobacteria, single-celled filament-shaped microorganisms, have been found in the Warrawoona Group strata of Western Australia and were preserved in ~3.465 BYA embedded in cherts (microcrystalline sedimentary rocks). The same strata have also preserved stromatolite mats, an organic accretionary growth structure usually indicating the presence of bacteria, within slightly younger dolostone sediments of ~3.45 BYA.[290] These were single-celled "primitive" or "primordial" prokaryotic organisms. Then, (~3.0/2.5 BYA) eukaryotic organisms such as bacteria, stromatolites, algae, and microfossils appeared and were observed to be morphologically or structurally simple. But, as seen from genetic investigations, they were biochemically complex in terms of precise processes for genes to code for proteins through specifically arranged DNA, RNA, and amino acid biomolecular sequences. Hundreds of different proteins are needed for cells to form and perform metabolic, reproductive, and life-sustainment functions. These functions depend on each type of protein's exact 3D folding structure. In addition, these functions depend upon other structures of the cell (a.k.a. epigenetics), such as the ribosome and other organelles in the cytoplasm of the cell, as well as the importance of the cell's bilayer membrane to establish the boundaries and gate-keeping activities of various nutrients and liquids, moving in and out of the cell.[291]

Numerous fossils and traces of fossils have been discovered, especially during the Cambrian and post-Cambrian periods, by paleontologists and other historical scientists. These findings indicate a significant "jump" in sophistication with a "sudden" and "dramatic" increase in the structure and functionality of numerous organisms. Paleontologist Kevin Peterson "characterized this significant 'pow' as an apparent quantum leap in organismal and ecological complexity."[292] Through radiometric isotope dating methods, scientists have determined that these changes occurred over a relatively brief period of geological time (perhaps less than 5–6 million years in some cases). What is somewhat unexpected for geologists and paleontologists to find is that these changes have occurred after a little less than 3 billion years of "stasis" of relatively no change from single-celled microorganisms![293]

Based upon these scientific findings, new plant and animal multicellular life forms seem to "suddenly" appear on Earth over a relatively short geological time! These life forms or biota are found in the following biological periods in millions of years ago or MYA:

- Ediacaran (~635–543 MYA)
- Cambrian (~543–485 MYA)
- Post-Cambrian (~485 MYA to present)

Description of the Ediacaran Biota

Paleontologists, geologists, and geochronologists refer to this rather sudden appearance of these "enigmatic" (e.g., puzzling, since we do not see most of them today) multicelled organisms found just "before" the Cambrian explosion as Ediacaran. These Ediacaran faunas or biota fossils (from the Ediacaran Hills) are from the Neoproterozoic (geological) era (~635–543 MYA) and were dated by the surrounding sedimentary rocks and zircon crystals using the uranium-to-lead radiometric isotope dating method. These Precambrian fossils contained more than one type of cell and had a significantly increased anatomical structure and functional or physical capabilities. These fossils appear to have been "radiated" from the Avalon (oxygen) explosion around ~575 MYA after the earth had thawed from the Cryogenian period's extensive glaciations in ~582 MYA. Some major examples of them include sponges, Dickinsonia (flat air mattress-like body), trace fossils (remains of animal activity such as tracks, burrows, and fecal pellets), Kimbrella (primitive mollusks), corals, worms, and jellyfish phyla. Many scientists believe these multicellular organisms were the precursor to the Cambrian animals.[294] (NOTE: The Cambrian period was first named by Adam Sedgwick in 1835.)

Description of the Cambrian Biota

In addition, during the Cambrian explosion period, geologists and paleoanthropologists discovered fossils from the Burgess Shale in British Columbia, Canada, the Mao Tianshan Shale near Chengjiang, China, and other regions around the world.[295] This metazoan (e.g., refers to animals with differentiated tissues) fossil specimens were well preserved. During this "explosion" of fauna, representatives of about twenty of the roughly twenty-six total phyla present in the known fossil record made their first appearance on Earth. They were "fully formed" in the Cambrian strata and representatives of other fundamentally different body plans and designs of equal complexity. Here is a brief description of these fossilized metazoan animals that were discovered or appeared during the Cambrian explosion (*approximately 541 to 530 MYA*) phyla:[296]

- Brachiopods are marine invertebrate animals that have hard valves or shells on the upper and lower surfaces.
- Echinoderms are marine invertebrate animals with radial symmetry, such as starfishes, sea cucumbers, sea lilies, sand dollars, sea stars, and sea urchins.
- Annelids are animals such as ragworms, earthworms, and leeches possessing a body cavity, movable bristles, and a body divided into segments by transverse rings.
- Ctenophores are marine invertebrate animals with a gelatinous and translucent body like a modern ciliated comb jelly.
- Hypoliths are extinct animals with small conical shells.
- Chordates are a group composed of all vertebrates, including humans and all mammals, fish, and birds possessing a notochord, a dorsal nerve cord, pharyngeal slits, an endostyle, and a post-anal tail.
- Arthropods are invertebrate animals such as shrimp-like trilobites, insects, lobsters, crabs, spiders, mites, centipedes, and millipedes. They have an exoskeleton, a segmented body, and paired jointed appendages.

NOTE: In 1758, naturalist and botanist Carolus Linnaeus developed a classification or taxonomy system for plants and animals that is still used today by most scientists. His "top-down" classification system of this hierarchy starts with domain, then kingdom, phylum, class, order, family, and finally, to the species level for botanical and zoological organisms. This classification system was based on Aristotle's approach of essentialism. Essentialism was a system declaring that elements of nature or quality, including species, had an ideal and constant essence that did not change. He built his taxonomy on the presence or absence of selected (*fixed or permanent nature of species*) and predetermined characteristics. He was the first to group organisms more or less in parallel rather than along a single, linear scale of progression. He scrapped any concept of the *scala naturae* — Aristotle's organization of hierarchical, linear fashion, from the least perfect atom to the epitome of perfection — man. Linnaeus's animal kingdom (*and phyla*) splayed out into a tree-like structure, with species of families of equal, if differing, complexity at the ends of the branches. He contributed a great deal to the theory of evolution, even though unintentionally.[297]

Description of the Post-Cambrian Periods

The post-Cambrian periods also saw an additional sudden appearance (a.k.a. speciation) of new animal phyla (perhaps nine) observed in the fossil record.[298]

In the "Paleozoic period," which lasted from ~542–252 MYA, there were:

- Jawed and bony fish, arthropods (invertebrate animals with exoskeletons, segmented bodies, and jointed appendages) from the Ordovician-Silurian transition event (~444 MYA),
- Fish species, four-footed animals, and insects from the Lau event (~424 MYA) and the Devonian explosion (~420–359 MYA),
- Amphibians and marine invertebrates from the end of the Devonian explosion and the beginning of the Carboniferous period (~359 MYA), and
- Reptiles, crawling, flying insects, cockroaches, beetles, and true bugs from the rainforest collapse and the Permian era (~305 MYA).

In the "Mesozoic period," which lasted from ~252–66 MYA, there were:

- First birds, mammals, and lizards from the Jurassic period (~201–146 MYA) and
- New groups of birds, mammals, bees, and other pollinating insects, first ants, termites, aphids, grasshoppers, and lizards, including the Tyrannosaurus Rex and other

famous "terrible lizards" (a.k.a. dinosaurs) from the Cretaceous period (~144–66 MYA).

In the "Cenozoic period," which lasted from ~66 to 0 MYA, there were:

- New kinds of advanced birds and mammals during the Paleogene recovery event (~66–23 MYA) and
- First hominid and "human" life forms (starting ~7 to 8 MYA to present).

Evolutionary scientists see these new vertebrate forms as a "parade" of evolutionary progress going from less complex to more advanced and highly complex organisms to modern man. This "parade" perspective is summarized as follows:[299]

- Fish (cartilaginous, bony, lobe-finned — prehistoric sharks) >
- Tetrapods (four-legged skeletal fish out of water possessing fingers, claws, and paws) >
- Amphibians (prehistoric, first to colonize dry land — lay eggs in water; now represented by frogs, toads, and salamanders) >
- Terrestrial reptiles (land lizards — pelycosaurs, archosaurs — prehistoric crocodiles and first dinosaurs, anapsids, prehistoric turtles, and prehistoric snakes) >
- Marine reptiles (fish lizards — ichthyosaurs, long-necked plesiosaurs and pliosaurs, sleek and vicious mosasaurs) >
- Pterosaurs (skin-winged lizards — small to large archosaurs) >

- Birds (dino-birds or prehistoric bird-like dinosaurs — Archaeopteryx and Epidexipteryx) >
- Mesozoic mammals (small, mouse-sized mammal-like reptiles) >
- Cenozoic mammals (prehistoric cats, dogs, mammoths/ elephants, horses, whales, camels, rhinoceroses, hippopotamuses, beavers, wombats, marsupials, etc.) >
- Primates (gibbons, orangutans, gorillas, chimpanzees, bonobos, and "hominids") >
- Humans.

Evaluation of the "Common Descent" Theory

Scientists have endeavored to explain this sudden appearance of new body plans and designs in the "Cambrian explosion" from fossil remains with lab experiments and various theories. However, since most scientists base their explanations on scientific materialism or naturalism alone, they usually take an evolutionary view to understand how this remarkable increase in complexity happened. They have proposed two primary "missing link" theories as the "artifact" and "deep-divergence hypotheses."

Artifact Hypothesis

Many evolutionary biologists and paleontologists believe that some of the Ediacaran biota are "missing links" or "transitional intermediate forms" that gave the sudden rise to the Cambrian biota, starting approximately 542 MYA. They seek to explain the Cambrian explosion as an "artifact" of incomplete sampling of the fossil record and is therefore called by geologist Charles Doolittle Walcott the "artifact hypothesis."[300]

Evaluation of the Artifact Hypothesis

However, with the development of offshore drilling technology in the 1940s, 1950s, and 1960s, geologists evaluated these drill cores and found no Precambrian fossils.[301] Other versions of this hypothesis, which proposed that the rocks had not preserved the fossils or that they may have been too small or too soft, or both to have been preserved, have been *discounted* due to lack of findings of single-celled filament-shaped microorganisms in Precambrian rocks by geologists, paleontologists, and other historical life scientists.[302]

Deep-Divergence Hypothesis

The other primary explanation is known as the "deep-divergence hypothesis," which holds that "a rather 'long fuse' of animal evolution and diversification lasting many millions of years leading up to what 'looks' like an explosion of animal life in the Cambrian. Still, this evolutionary history was hidden from the fossil record."[303] Biologists have attempted to reconstruct the Precambrian-to-Cambrian "tree of life," mapping the course of evolution during a cryptic period before the Cambrian using a method of analysis known as the "molecular clock" studies. These studies assume that the extent to which DNA sequences differ in similar genes in two or more animals reflects the time since those animals began to evolve from a common ancestor.[304] "Their studies concluded that the common ancestor of animal forms lived ~1.2 BYA, implying that the Cambrian animals took some ~700 million years to evolve from the 'deep divergence' point before they first appearing in the fossil record."[305]

Evaluation of the Deep-Divergence Hypothesis

Again, this hypothesis is based upon the absence of Precambrian ancestors due to their soft-bodied forms, rendering their preservation unlikely. Therefore, "many paleontologists and evolutionary biologists now concede that the long-sought-after Pre-Cambrian fossils necessary to document a Darwinian account of the origin of animal life are missing."[306]

Creation Interpretation

Common Design Hypothesis

Other scientists (such as High Ross and Fazale Rana [from the RTB organization]) and philosophers of science, such as Stephen C. Meyer (from the ID organization), explain this sudden increase in complexity through the concept of "Common Design" from a biblical God or intelligent designer (or agent) perspective that intervened in this progression of life (e.g., from single to more advanced multicellular types) by the manipulation of genetic information especially during the Cambrian explosion (~530 to 525 MYA). Meyer believes that new information was manipulated by an "intelligent agent" (such as he recognizes "God" as the agent) to build a new form of life from a simpler preexisting form and is, therefore, *the* cause of this sudden increase in biological complexity in various microorganisms. This new information is found in the unique and tremendous increase in the number of common biomolecular sequences of DNA, RNA, amino acids, genes (portions of the DNA molecule that "code" for proteins), and specific functional proteins (e.g., "unique 3–D folding patterns") to produce all anatomical and functional characteristics of a life-form as well as the information not stored in genes, called "epigenetic information."[307]

Epigenetic information is information stored in various cell structures but not in DNA sequences — plays a critical role in forming animal "body assemblies" during embryological development. Epigenetic studies examine heritable phenotype changes that do not involve alterations in the DNA sequence. It most often involves changes that affect gene activity and expression or the turning off and on of the genes. There are two types of structures within the cell that provide epigenetic or contextual information that influences gene activity besides noncoding DNA. (Interestingly, the noncoding DNA accounts for over 98 percent of the total DNA or genome, and coding of the DNA as genes consists of about 1–2 percent!)

Within the cell's nucleus, our twenty-three pairs of chromosomes contain histones and methyl (CH_4) groups. Histones are proteins around which DNA can wind for compaction and gene regulation. (NOTE: This complex is also called "heterochromatin.") Histone modification occurs when the binding of epigenetic factors to histone "tails" alters the extent to which DNA is wrapped around histones and the availability of genes in the DNA to be activated. In addition, methyl groups can also be added to DNA at various sites to affect gene regulation. "DNA methylation is what occurs when methyl groups, an epigenetic factor found in some dietary sources, can 'tag' DNA, and activate or repress genes."[308]

The sources of epigenetic information within the cells are (a) cytoskeletal arrays, which are internal skeletons that are made up of several different kinds of filaments and are located around the cell's nucleus — they help to distribute essential proteins used during their development at specific locations within the cell's cytoplasm (e.g., a fluid-like substance between the nucleus and cell membrane), (b) centrosomes are microscopic organelles that sit next to the nucleus — these microtubule arrays give a cell its 3D shape and provide internal tracks for the directed transport of organelles and essential molecules to and from the nucleus, and (c) cell membranes have ion channels or openings that allow electrical particles to pass in both directions so that the cells can communicate efficiently. This epigenetic information is stored in the arrangement of sugar molecules on the exterior surface of the cell membrane. These sugar molecules "surpass" amino acids and nucleotides in information-storing capacity since they can assume positions that can attach to lipid molecules in the membrane itself or to proteins embedded in the membrane. The precisely arranged sugar molecules on the surface of cells represent another source of information independent of that stored in DNA base sequences.[309]

Evolutionary biologist James Valentine has noted that "one useful way of comparing the degrees of complexity is to assess the number of cell types in different organisms."[310]

> Biological complexity scale is measured in the number of cell types of different organisms. Cellular grade: (a) protists = one, (b) sponges = five, and (c) cnidarians = ten; Tissue grade: (d) flatworms = twenty; and Organ grade: (e) echinoderms = forty, (f) arthropods = fifty, and (g) chordates = sixty cell types.[311]

> Though a single-celled eukaryote has many specialized internal structures, such as a nucleus and various organelles, it still, obviously, represents just a single type of cell. More complex animals require more cell types to perform their more diverse functions. Arthropods and mollusks, for example, have dozens of specific tissues and organs, each of which requires "functionally dedicated" or specialized cell types. These new cell types, in turn, require many new and specialized proteins; thus, building novel cell types typically requires building novel proteins, which requires assembly instructions for building proteins — that is, genetic information. Thus, an increase in the number of cell types imply an increase in the amount of genetic information.[312]

> One way to estimate the amount of new genetic information that appeared with the Cambrian animals is to measure the size of the genomes of modern representatives of the Cambrian groups and compare that to the

amount of information in simpler forms of life. Molecular biologists have estimated that a minimally complex single-celled organism would require between 318,000 and 562,000 base pairs of DNA to produce the proteins necessary to maintain life.[313]

More complex single cells might require upwards of a million base pairs of DNA. Yet, assembling the proteins necessary to sustain a complex arthropod such as a trilobite would need orders of magnitude more protein-coding instructions. By comparison, the genome size of a modern arthropod, the fruit fly Drosophila melanogaster, is approximately 140 million base pairs.[314]

Thus, transitions from a single cell to colonies of cells to complex animals represent significant — and in principle measurable — increases in genetic information. During the Cambrian period, a veritable carnival of novel biological forms arose. But because the new biological form requires new cell types, proteins, and genetic information, the Cambrian explosion of animal life also generated an explosion of genetic information unparalleled in the previous history of life.[315]

Of course, the fossil record does show an overall increase in complexity of organisms from the Precambrian (specifically the Ediacaran) times, as Darwin expected. But the problems posed by the Burgess Shale discoveries are not the increase in complexity but the "sudden quantum leap" in complexity. The jump from the simpler Precambrian organisms to the radically different forms appears to occur far too suddenly to be readily explained by the gradual activity of natural selection and random variations. As an example, instead, unique organisms, such as the bizarre arthropod Opabinia with its fifteen articulated body segments, twenty-eight gills, thirty flipper-like swimming lobes, long trunk-like proboscis, intricate nervous system, and five separate

eyes, appear fully formed in the Cambrian strata along with representatives of other fundamentally different body plans and design of
equal complexity.[316] Paleontologists called these significant and abrupt
changes in the forms of life (i.e., new body plans or phyla) a "disparity."

Paleontologists Douglas Erwin, James Valentine, and Jack
Sepkoski note in their study of skeletonized marine invertebrates that

> the (*Cambrian*) fossil record suggests that the major
> pulse of diversification of phyla occurs before that of
> classes, classes before that of orders, orders before that of
> families…The higher taxa (or levels of the classification
> system) do not seem to have diverged through an accu-
> mulation of lower taxa.[317]

In other words, instead of a proliferation of species and other representatives of lower taxa level occurring first and then building the
disparity of higher taxa, the highest taxonomic differences, such as
those between phyla and classes, appear first (instantiated by relatively
few species-level representatives). Only later, in most recent strata,
does the fossil record document proliferation of representatives of
lower taxa: different orders, families, genera, and so on. Yet we would
not expect the neo-Darwinian mechanism of natural selection acting
on random genetic mutations to produce the top-down pattern that
we observe in the history of life following the Cambrian explosion.

Some Questions to Think About!

Based upon the origin of the Cambrian animals requiring vast
amounts of new functional or specified information, what produced
this information explosion? Is it plausible to think that natural selection working on random mutations in DNA could produce the precise
arrangements of DNA bases necessary to generate the protein building

blocks of new cell types and novel life forms? How difficult would it be for (beneficial) random mutations to generate, or stumble upon, the genetically meaningful or functional sequences needed to supply natural selection with the raw material — the genetic information and variations — it needed to produce new proteins, organs, and life forms of life?

Summary

After nearly 3 billion years of only various single-celled organisms surviving through "hostile" environmental conditions on land, in the oceans, and in the atmosphere, how did multicellular organisms suddenly appear slightly over half a billion years ago? They appeared in the Precambrian or Ediacaran biological periods. They were enabled by the right conditions, such as major increases in atmospheric oxygen and extensive biomass (of dead organisms) to support new life requirements. According to most scientists, most of these "enigmatic" organisms went extinct and seemed to have only a tiny contribution to the Cambrian explosion of animal life. Evolutionists have proposed various evolutionary "missing link" theories, such as the "artifact" and "deep-divergent hypotheses," to account for this sudden Cambrian era increase in new phyla (e.g., completely new body plans and designs with integrated systems working together). Most paleontologists have dismissed these hypotheses due to the lack of evidence. As an alternative, the Christian concepts of "common design" and "direct intervention" are used by God to generate this increase in complexity of relatively "simple" to complex to advanced life forms. Creation or creationism of initiating and forming life is worth considering!

This sudden increase in major phyla occurred in what paleontologists call the "Cambrian explosion," perhaps within a 5-to-6-million-year time frame. These two hypotheses or explanations seem to explain away this sudden increase in advanced life; however, they tend to be problematic. They are inconsistent or incongruent with the fossil record and seem unsupportable by modern genetic discoveries. In addition, these explanations do not support the evolutionary concepts of Darwinism or neo-Darwinism, which propose gradual changes through the mechanism of natural selection acting on beneficial mutations and other mechanisms, ultimately leading to a common or universal ancestor. In other words, this "bottoms-up approach" that forms Darwin's evolutionary "tree of life" appears to be in "*direct conflict*" with the findings of the fossil remains in the Cambrian fauna, which demonstrates a "top-down approach" of Linnaeus' classification system!

Also, the sudden appearance of more advanced animals from the Paleozoic, Mesozoic, and Cenozoic eras, as seen from their fossil remains, was discussed. This apparent sudden appearance of animals during these periods is even more impressive and consistent with the sudden appearance of animals in the Cambrian period. The question is, "*how*" did this occur? Philosopher of science Steven C. Meyer offers another explanation, "The origin and subsequent development of complete body plans and designs require vast amounts of new functional or specified information." He concludes that this can only come from an intelligent designer or agent. Christians believe this Creator is the God of the Bible.

Through numerous discoveries and lab experiments, scientists have shown that genetics and epigenetics function directly to determine an organism's anatomical, physiological, and behavioral traits.

The bottom line is that scientific discoveries *do not* support biological evolution. The main findings for this conclusion come from the "Cambrian explosion." Complete body forms that suddenly arise in the fossil remains imply the intervention of a biblical God. This sudden increase in complexity is also observed in the post-Cambrian period fossils.

The following chapter describes, in some detail, our search for connections or pathways between animals and humans, which are also sometimes classified as "hominids" by paleontologists. These terms have generated much controversy and confusion, especially within the debates between evolutionists and creationists.

CHAPTER 9:

Discounting the Evolutionary Pathway to Humanity!

Initial studies have shown that approximately 96 to 98 percent[318] of a chimp's genome is identical to the human genome. Does this mean we are descended from apes? Likewise, many believe Neanderthals are our closest relatives. Many of these illustrations are depicted in natural museums, magazines, and textbooks. What are the implications to these "man-made" drawings and reproductions?

Introduction

This high degree of genetic similarity to most scientists, particularly evolutionary scientists, means that "humans" share a common ancestor with the great apes, such as the chimps. However, they are not saying that humans necessarily come from apes like chimps but that they share a common ancestor![319] In addition, through mitochondrial DNA (mtDNA) molecular clock and argon-argon radioisotope analyses, this common ancestor (but yet unknown or discovered) is estimated to have occurred around 8 to 9 million years ago and then took almost another million years to split into the "great ape" (*Gorillini*) lineage and the "hominid" (*Hominini*) lineages.[320] This "African great ape" lineage comprises the gorillas, bonobos, and chimpanzees. The "Hominid lineage" is composed of the following genera: Ardipithecus, Australopithecus, and the Homo groups.[321] See Figure 16 for an illustration of the proposed split between hominids and the Gorillini, or great apes, around 7 to 8 million years ago and a perspective of the divergence of hominids leading to Homo *sapiens*.

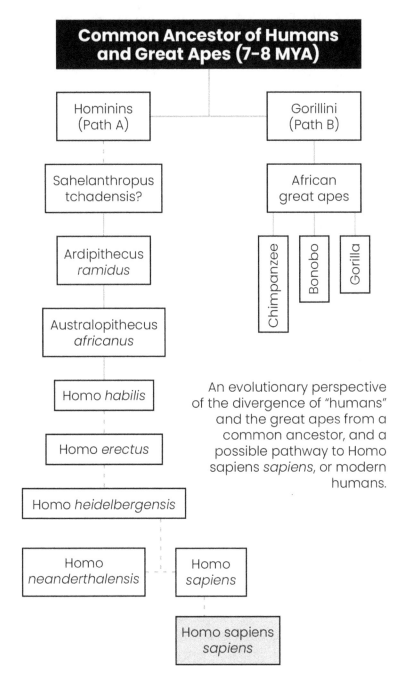

Figure 16: Early Human Phylogeny

NOTE: The Paranthropus group is not shown in this illustration since not all scientists accept it as part of this lineage. Also, the Sahelanthropus tchadensis, or "hope for life," was discovered in Chad (Africa) in 2001 and dates to about 6 to 7 million years old. Some scientists, see them as the earliest hominid and others do not. They walked erect, possessed a brain size close to a chimpanzee, lived in the woodlands and green savannas. He was called the "Tumai Man." They had a complete skull, along with a partial jawbone and some teeth.[322]

The Smithsonian Institute has illustrated these hominid genera as major branches of a "hominid Tree of Life."[323] This evolutionary hominid tree depicts individual species within each genus or group with associated timelines from their dated fossils (and unique species). However, there are important evolutionary implications to this tree:

1. The ends of the twigs identify the individual species within each genus, such as those species within the Ardipithecus, Australopithecus, Paranthropus, and Homo groups. The connections of the hominid twigs to the associated genus branches are through a most recent common ancestor (MRCA). In most cases, this MRCA is not known or found in the fossils.

2. Each primary genus branch ties into the main trunk at different divergent points over unknown spans of time. Again, the connections from the branches to the main trunk are through different MRCAs. These MRCAs are not known or found in the fossils.

3. All of the branches connect to the main trunk, which is then presumed to feed into the primate, mammal,

chordate, and animal "eukaryote" trees composed of protists, fungi, plants, and animals through different MRCAs. These MRCAs are not known or found in the fossils.

4. These eukaryote trees combine with two other trees (domains): "Eubacteria" (i.e., cyanobacteria and carbon-eating bacteria) and "Archaea" (i.e., salt, heat, and cold-loving "extremophile" microbes) trees. These three trees ultimately connect, through different MRCAs, to a last universal common ancestor, or LUCA (i.e., single-celled microorganisms), that can survive and reproduce. Therefore, the above scenario seems to imply that they can eventually relate to Darwin's initial and somewhat simple "Tree of Life" concept.

Because there is much *uncertainty* in the unknown MRCAs, much "faith" is needed by evolutionists to believe in this natural tree, which corresponds with Darwin's simple "Tree of Life." This conclusion implies that this detailed "Tree of Life" is like a "bush rather than a tree" because of the numerous diversity of subspecies, species, genera, families, orders, classes, phyla, and kingdoms according to Linnaeus' classification system. Figure 17 summarizes the evolutionary progression of modern man to the LUCA. The MRCAs are assumed to connect each classification level to the next level.

LUCA to Modern Man

Inverted Evolutionary "Tree of Life" Emphasizing Homo Group, Species, and Subspecies

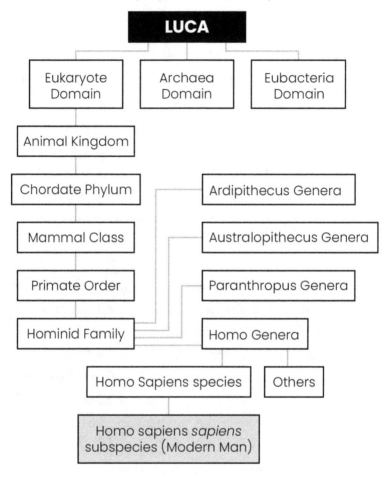

Figure 17: Inverted "Tree of Life" — LUCA to Modern Man

NOTE: The LUCA is considered a primitive or primordial single cell with reproductive and survival traits. Evolutionists identify this LUCA as a prokaryote, which has no nucleus, limited DNA, and few organisms within its single cell. After these single cells combine and multiply, they eventually evolve (*somehow*) into Eukaryotes, which have a nucleus for DNA and more organelles in the cell for more functions. Eventually, three distinct domains form - Eubacteria, Archaea, and Eukaryote. Specifically, modern taxonomy has placed anatomically modern humans or "Homo sapiens *sapiens*" as a species within the following structure: The first and most common (i.e., with similar traits) group at the top level is called the Domain and successive sublevels of Kingdom (Animals can move on their own.), Phylum (Chordates have a backbone.), Class (Mammals have fur or hair and milk glands.), Order (Primates have a collar bone and grasping fingers.), Family (Hominids have a flat face and 3D vision.), Genus (Homo group is sometimes called by anthropologists and other historian scientists as "Humans," which have an upright posture and a large brain), and finally, Species (such as Homo sapiens *sapiens* or anatomically modern humans having a high forehead and a thin skull).[324]

(However, Linnaeus did not discuss "breeds" as successive micro-evolutionary changes within a species, such as the wolf species evolving into subspecies of dog breeds.)

Evolutionary Perspective

"Evolutionary biologists maintain that ('human') evolution is both a fact and a theory. That it occurred is the fact. How it occurred is the theory. These biologists actively debate evolution's mechanism, but they insist the debate does not mean that the fact of Evolution is uncertain."[325]

Evolutionary biologists, paleontologists, geneticists, archeologists, and other historical scientists employ the following two primary methods to determine the pathway for the origins and evolution of "humans":

- The hominid fossil and associated archeological records and
- Hominid genetic comparisons.

The Hominid Fossil and Associated Archeological Records — an Introduction

The hominid fossil record (should) provides the chief means to determine whether humans evolved... It acts as a proxy for the natural history of primates. If humans evolved from an apelike ancestor, the fossil record must display telltale patterns and features... It should be rooted in a single knuckle-walking apelike primate that existed 6 and 5 million years ago... It should appear in a branching, treelike pattern from this ancestral form, a clear evolutionary pathway from this supposed ancestor to modern humans should be evident...and it should document the gradual emergence of the anatomical and behavioral traits that define humanity, such as the ability to walk erect (a.k.a. bipedalism), large brain size and structure, and advanced culture. Furthermore, transitional forms that connect Australopithecines to primitive Homo specimens (such as Homo *erectus* and Neanderthals) and then to modern humans (a.k.a. Homo sapiens *sapiens*) should be readily discerned in the fossil record.[326]

In addition, the archeological records should provide artifacts co-deposited with fossils and provide clues into the behavior and cognitive ability of hominids and humans.

These artifacts result from reason, symbolic thought, technological inventiveness, and artistic, musical, and religious expression. These artifacts include: ropes, bone spear points, fishhooks and harpoons, sculptures, paintings, jewelry and other personal items of personal adornment, musical instruments, clothing, burial practices, and grave goods. They help to establish the proposed gradual increase in culture and technology in the hominid fossil record.[327]

Significant Features of Early or Ancient "Humans" or Very Early "Hominid"

Evolutionary biologists (and others such as paleoanthropologists) consider bipedalism and brain size and structure to be humanity's two most significant anatomical features. For these scientists, understanding the emergence and development of bipedalism and brain size equates to knowledge about the origin of humankind.[328]

Evaluation of Bipedalism

Paleoanthropologists believe any transition from a "knuckle-walking quadruped" to an "upright biped" would involve extensive anatomical changes such as the relocating of the foramen magnum, restructuring of the inner ear bones, introducing of the spinal curvature, restructuring of the rib cage, reshaping of the pelvis, altering the lower limbs, enlarging joint surfaces of the knee and other joints, restructuring of the feet and hands, and the reorganizing of the body's musculature. Dramatical anatomical changes must occur in a coordinated, integrated, and simultaneous fashion to transform knuckle-walking quadrupeds into bipedal primates. (*However*) Fossil evidence shows that bipedalism *did not* emerge gradually, as expected from an evolutionary framework. Rather, this defining trait for humanity appeared suddenly and with the hominid's first appearance.[329]

A recent statistical analysis of over 200 pelvic bones from apes, extinct hominids, and modern humans reveals a historical pattern that amplifies the challenge facing an evolutionist's explanation of bipedalism's natural history. Instead of gradually changing over time, bipedalism endured through two long periods without change. The first period lasted roughly 5 million years; the second — about 2 million years. The fossil record indicated that the transition from one form of locomotion to another occurred rapidly. Australopithecines manifested facultative (or optional) bipedalism. The Homo genus has always possessed obligatory (or non-optional) bipedalism. Although Australopithecines existed for nearly three million years, facultative bipedalism did not gradually change into an obligatory (mandatory) form. Instead, it remained static throughout the Australopithecine's existence. With the appearance of the Homo genus, a distinct new form of bipedalism (obligatory) suddenly appeared in the fossil record... and remained static for nearly two million years. Interestingly, Homo *erectus* and Neanderthals possessed an identical form of obligatory bipedalism but distinct from that seen in (*other*) human beings. Again, a new form of bipedalism suddenly broke forth with the arrival of humanity.[330]

Evolutionary biologists have yet to agree on the selective pressures that might have produced bipedalism in primates. Neither have they demonstrated the evolutionary mechanism that brought these anatomical and physiological characteristics. To date, the most cited evolutionary pressure to explain this transformation remains the loss of a woodland habitat throughout East Africa.[331]

Evaluation of Brain Size and Structure

Paleontologists focus on brain size and structure because a large brain can support human intelligence and contain special (mental) abilities for people to develop and use symbolic communication, speech, and tools, all of which are foundational for establishing and maintaining human cultures and civilizations and structured to support consciousness and self-awareness. The evidence shows that brain size and its architecture are "discontinuous" or that abrupt changes occur over a narrow window of time rather than a gradual increase (as predicted by evolutionary theories). Surveys of the hominid brain size measurements show a different pattern. For each hominid species, brain size remains relatively constant throughout the time it existed. The "discontinuous" jump in brain size occurs as new hominid species successively appear in the fossil record.

For example, the (average) brain size of the Australopithecines, which existed from about 4.2 to 1.9 MYA, was about 400 cc (i.e., cc = cubic centimeter). Brain size for those specimens assigned to Homo *habilis*, existing between 2.5 and 1.8 MYA, jumped to between 650 and 800 cc. Homo *erectus/ergaster* (about 1.8 million to 500,000 years ago) had a brain size that was larger still, ranging between 850 and 1,000 cc. The Neanderthal's brain size was 1,000 to 1,400 cc. By comparison, modern human brains range in size between 1,000 and 1,500 cc. These numbers show the general pattern of discontinuous leaps in brain size, not gradual increases.[332]

Hominid Genetic Comparisons

Molecular anthropologists scrutinize variations (e.g., from mutations occurring throughout history) in DNA sequences among people who reside or originate in different geographical locations worldwide. These variations reveal essential clues about humanity's beginning. These mutations are typically unique for populations that have been isolated for some time. This uniqueness allows them to identify DNA sequences (and hence population groups) from the same ancestral sequence (and, therefore, populations). The researchers say these sequences coalesce. Once ancestral sequences and populations have been identified, repeating this process throughout the gene genealogy leads backward to the ultimate ancestor and population. They refer to this basic sequence and population as the MRCA (or most recent common ancestor). They employ various genetic techniques to study the origin of humankind, such as genetic or nuclear DNA sequence diversity, molecular clock analyses of mitochondrial DNA (mtDNA), and Y chromosome DNA sequence comparisons.

Evaluations of Mitochondrial and Y Chromosomal DNA Genetic Markers

Mitochondrial DNA (mtDNA) analysis is a popular method among biologists interested in constructing gene trees and determining origin dates. It produces genealogies that trace humanity's maternal lineage; therefore, this type of DNA is inherited exclusively from one's mother. (NOTE: This type of DNA is only found in the mitochondria organelle, which is located outside the nucleus but inside the cell's cytoplasm and wall or membrane.) They use "molecular clocks" to date humanity's origin. However, some factors confuse the calibration (i.e., accuracy) of these mtDNA molecular clocks that detect mutations between two species. For example:

> Since the 1980s, numerous and various comprehensive studies and analyses of mtDNA have been performed by biochemists and other scientists. However, there are many factors that (have) complicated the use of mtDNA molecular clocks to date humanity's origin. Individuals may have up to three types of mtDNA. These multiple types vary from tissue to tissue and increase with age; sometimes this condition results from mutations in the egg's cell and other times in the body's cells after fertilization; mutation rates may differ from region to region within mtDNA, and the level of radioactivity in the environment

also impacts mitochondrial DNA mutation rates and molecular clock analysis. These factors confuse the calibration of mtDNA clocks. Age-accelerated mutation rates render genetic diversity artificially high.[333]

> NOTE: Since the 1980s, there have been significant advances in molecular anthropology to allow for greater accuracy when estimating dates.

Advances in molecular anthropology allow for greater accuracy when estimating the recent date for "mitochondrial Eve" (e.g., known as the initial or single biblical female ancestor of all humans where theologians believe she lived in the "Garden of Eden" somewhere in East Africa or the Mediterranean areas).[334] Here are some of their findings:

- A 2009 study by Phillip Endicott questioned the assumptions used to establish the mtDNA mutation rate, which relied on humans and chimps sharing a common evolutionary ancestor, some 6 MYA. The "mutation rate" that produced these results contradicted the date for events in human history derived from fossil and archeological records. They determined a new mutation rate for mtDNA by considering these factors and used the widely agreed-upon dates from the fossil and archeological records to calibrate the mtDNA molecular clock. Their date for "mitochondrial Eve" came in close to 108,000 years ago.[335]
- A 2013 study described a calibration of the mtDNA clock over a larger time frame without making assumptions. Scientists calibrated the mtDNA clock using genomes recovered through ancient DNA analysis from

the fossil remains of ten humans that lived over about 40,000 years ago. These remains were confidently dated using carbon-14 isotopic dating methods. Using this calibration, these researchers concluded that "mitochondrial Eve" lived about 157,000 +/- 40,000 years ago.[336]

- A related UK study employed a similar approach using a database of 350 complete genome sequences of mtDNA recovered from well-dated ancient human remains and contemporary individuals. It is estimated that "mitochondrial Eve" lived about 157,000 +/- 30,000 years ago.[337]

Y chromosomal DNA analysis serves as a counterpart to the mtDNA analysis. This technique traces humanity's origin through the paternal side because it passes exclusively from father to son. It offers a much larger DNA sequence in which to detect mutations. (NOTE: mtDNA is limited to about 16,000 nucleotide base pairs.) In addition, it does not suffer from mtDNA factors or complications. Later studies used many expansive regions of the Y chromosome. Scientists have also revised the date for "Y chromosomal Adam" (i.e., the initial or single biblical male ancestor of all humans where theologians believe he lived in the "Garden of Eden" somewhere in East Africa or the Mediterranean). Based on the best and most recent analysis of Y chromosomal variants, the date for "Y chromosomal Adam" is between 100,000 and 200,000 years ago.[338]

Creationists believe these two genetic markers are used to characterize humanity's origin, and they will trace back to a single set of individuals. Here are some of these studies:

A study conducted in 2011 and three more in 2013 made use of a larger portion of the Y chromosome and rare Y chromosome variants to estimate respective dates of "Y chromosomal Adam" at: (1) 142,000 +/- 16,000 years ago; (2) 101,000 to 115,000 years ago; (3) 120,000 to 156,000 years ago; and (4) 180,000 to 200,00 years ago. These four studies align with the best, most recent date for "mitochondrial Eve."[339]

However, the concept of "mitochondrial Eve" (a.k.a. biblical Eve) and "Y chromosomal Adam" (a.k.a. biblical Adam) is *rejected* by evolutionists. They contend that it arose from a population of several thousand of many Eves and Adams that existed. "Mitochondrial Eve" and "Y chromosomal Adam" were the "lucky" ones whose lineages just happened to survive, and their mitochondrial and Y chromosomal lines were lost over time. Evolutionary biologists argue that these Eves and Adams were not the same individuals as "mitochondrial Eve" and "Y chromosomal Adam." They rationalize that this claim is based on the nature of the mechanism driving evolutionary change and, more substantially, on estimates of the human ancestral population sizes based on genetic diversity. Most scientific community members assume that biological evolution is a fact. That is, it is a given that the evolutionary paradigm provides sufficient explanation for life's origin, history, and diversity. Most biologists begin their study of human origins, if humanity evolved from a preexisting lineage of hominids. In that case, our origins must have started with a population, not two individuals, because, according to the tenets of neo-Darwinism, evolutionary transformations are at a population level, not an individual-level phenomenon. As a result of this presupposition, when studies in molecular anthropology trace the origin of all humanity back to single ancestral sequences for mitochondrial DNA and Y chromosomal DNA, it is assumed that "mitochondrial Eve" and "Y chromosomal Adam" have been members of a population, not two individuals.[340]

> Now that researchers have used better estimates of the mutation rate for mtDNA, looked at larger regions of the Y chromosome, and included rare Y chromosome variants, the dates for mitochondrial Eve and Y

chromosome Adam converge around 150,000 years ago. Added support for this conclusion comes from a study in which researchers determined that the last ancestor of all human males lived between 120,000 and 156,000 years ago, and the ancestor of all human females lived between 99,000 and 148,000 years ago… From a scientific standpoint, the revised dates are gratifying because they both align with estimates of humanity's origin from the fossil record (between 100,000 and 200,00 years ago) and also comport fairly well with the archeological record. History places the first evidence for symbolism, which we (creationists) take as a reflection of God's image in humans between 70,000 and 80,000 years ago (and arguably as far back as 160,000 years).[341]

Original Population Size Analysis

Next, regarding original population size, there seems to be significant controversy over the applicability of the modeling studies. On the one hand, for many scientists, the genetic diversity observed among human population groups powerfully supports the argument that humanity began as a population. Mathematical models make it possible to estimate the effective population size of any ancestral group from the genetic diversity of present-day populations if the mutation rate is known. These studies indicate that humans stemmed from a small population on the order of a few hundred to a few thousand.[342]

On the other hand, validating these population-size estimates requires that a sample of a known value and location be analyzed. Three studies involving mouflon sheep, Przewalski's horse, and gray whales show when the original population size was known, genetic diversity that measured generations later was much more significant than expected based on the models.[343] Consequently, these models were used to estimate the effective sizes of humanity's ancestral population. From the measure of the genetic diversity at any point in time, they would have overestimated the original population size to be much larger than two individuals.... To be fair, the sheep study does not necessarily invalidate the more sophisticated models used to characterize humanity's initial population size, but it gives some pause for thought. Therefore, "RTB Creationists, such as Hugh Ross and Fazale Rana, maintain that the methods used to generate these population-size estimates have not been adequately validated."[344]

Comparative Genetic Divergent Assumptions and Analyses between Hominids

Anthropologists maintain genetic relatedness can also be used to determine how long ago two primates diverged from a common ancestor. The basis for this assertion hinges on some important assumptions. Along with the understood supposition that evolution accounts for the origins and diversity of life's major groups, evolutionary biologists assume that mutations cause genetic differences among organisms. They also believe these mutations to the genetic material occur at a roughly "*constant rate*" over long periods of time. If these assumptions are correct, then organisms that share an ancestor in the recent past will display fewer genetic differences. On the other hand, organisms that share ancestors in the more distant past will have accrued more mutations and display greater genetic disparity. If mutation rates are known, then the divergence time can be readily calculated once the genetic difference between two organisms is determined.[345] For example, molecular clock studies show that DNA-DNA hybridization comparison places the timing of the human-chimp split between 7.7 and 5.7 million years ago.[346] Mitochondrial DNA analysis places the human-chimp common ancestor at around 5 MYA, and DNA analysis of nuclear DNA sequences typically places the divergence time at between 6 and 4.5 MYA.[347]

Specifically, molecular anthropologists and biologists base these genetic discoveries and comparisons on random mutations as a primary source of DNA sequence variation. These molecular anthropologists use a technique called "genetic (or DNA sequence) diversity."[348] (Remember, we are talking about the changes in the nucleotide bases of A, T, G, and C contained within the DNA biomolecule.) Genetic diversity techniques assume that these DNA sequence variations accrue at a constant rate, turning the DNA sequence differences into a molecular clock. When they know the mutation rate (or the change in the number of nucleotide base substitutions per year), they can estimate the coalescence time — the time since the DNA sequences (and hence populations) diverged from the shared ancestral sequence (or population), which is also known as the MRCA. In addition, molecular clock analyses estimate the timing of humanity's origin and spread around the globe. This methodology measures the average number of sequence differences between various people groups for a particular DNA segment. Scientists determine the average genetic difference by making pair-wise comparisons of all the individual DNA sequences that comprise the same.[349]

Early "Human" Phylogeny

However, there is considerable disagreement as to the actual ("human") pathway since the fossil record of these very early (e.g., "ancient") hominids is very limited to portions or fragments of the skull, jaw, teeth, and arm and leg bones. In contrast, the later remains of species (e.g., "archaic") are much more complete. Also, molecular biologists do not use molecular genetic analysis since DNA from a small number of fossils is generally not available to examine within these extinct species. In addition, there is still some controversy over the first three extinct or "archaic" subspecies (i.e., Homo sapiens *idaltu*, Homo sapiens *denisova*, and Homo sapiens *neanderthalensis*) as to where they fit into the Homo genus. For example, some scientists consider them to be categized into a separate genus, such as Homo *neanderthalensis*. See Figure 16, with the "dashed" lines indicating various pathways.

> NOTE: In particular, paleontologists typically inter-pret hominids in the fossil record within an evolu-tionary framework. They view hominids that existed between 7 to 2 MYA as transitional evolutionary forms (a.k.a. "intermediate" or "missing links") that gave rise to the Homo genus. Most think Ardipithe-cus *ramidus* gave rise to Australopithecus *anamne-sis*, which yielded Australopithecus. *afarensis*. Some paleoanthropologists think A. *afarensis* then evolved to produce A. *africanus*. They suggest this hominid produced Homo (H) *habilis*. Others believe that A. *afarensis* was the ancestral species for H. *habilis*. Some paleoanthropologists regard Kenyanthropus as H. *rudolfensis's* direct ancestor. Almost all paleoanthropol-ogists agree that Paranthropus represents an evolu-tionary side branch. Again, these (historical) scien-tists are *not clear* whether A. *afarensis* or A. *africanus* produced the Paranthropus. Most paleoanthropolo-gists say H. *habilis* gave rise to H. *ergaster*. However, this is where agreement ends.[350]

Nevertheless, using mtDNA and Y chromosomal DNA data analyses, evolutionary paleoanthropologists have derived three primary explanations or perspectives for humanity's origins and subsequent dispersal (migration) patterns starting with the Homo *erectus* origi-nating in Africa some 1.8 MYA.[351] See Figure 18.

The multiregional evolution (or regional continuity) hypothesis suggests that "anatomically modern human"' or Homo sapiens *sapiens* (or Homo sapiens) evolved from early humans (such as the Homo *erectus*) throughout Europe, Asia, Africa, and Oceania. Substantial natural selection and gene flow or migration occurred on the borders of each of the regions, accounting for the physical similarities of anatomically modern humans in each area. (NOTE: As indicated in Figure 16, other evolutionary scientists believe "modern humans" came from H. *heidelbergensis* and H. *ergaster*.)

The "Out of Africa" (a.k.a. complete replacement) hypothesis suggests that "anatomically modern humans" exclusively arose in Africa within the last 200,000 years and then migrated from Africa, completely replacing populations (i.e., from preexisting various "archaic" hominids) in Europe, Asia, and Oceania (except Africa). During this replacement, there was no gene flow between modern and archaic humans.

The intermediate African assimilation hypothesis suggests that modern Homo sapiens *sapiens* evolved in Africa like the "Out of Africa" model. From there, they migrated to Europe and Asia, replacing archaic populations inhabiting those regions. However, unlike the "Out of Africa" replacement model, this model proposes that gene flow did occur between anatomically "modern human" and "archaic" Neanderthals and Denisovans. This model has recently become more popular because the genome sequencing of Upper Paleolithic skeletons found in 2014 and 2015 has shown Homo sapiens *sapiens* carry "archaic" (e.g., Neanderthal and Denisovan) genes that are greater than the trivial amounts (that) the "Out of Africa" hypothesis allows through interbreeding and simultaneously less than what the multiregional hypothesis predicts.[352]

THREE "HUMAN" MIGRATION HYPOTHESES		
MULTI-REGIONAL *Regional Continuity Model*	Homo *erectus* migration out of Africa to Europe, Asia, and Oceania (~1.8 MYA)	Independent multiple origins or shared multi-regional evolution with continuous gene flow between continental populations to produce all races
OUT-OF-AFRICA *Replacement Model*	Homo *erectus* migration out of Africa to Europe, Asia, and Oceania (~1.8 MYA)	Second migration of early African modern humans replaced all archaic populations (~100k YA). No interbreeding or gene flow. All races produced.
OUT-OF-AFRICA *Assimilation Model*	Homo *erectus* migration out of Africa to Europe, Asia, and Oceania (~1.8 MYA)	Second migration of early African modern humans replaced all archaic populations (~100k YA). Minor interbreeding or gene flow. All races produced.

Figure 18: Comparisons between the Multiregional, "Out of Africa," and Assimilation Hypotheses

Humanity's Origin, Location, and Migration

Scientific data indicates that humanity's origin locates in Africa (or, at least, in populations currently living in Africa). African people are the most genetically diverse and compose the earliest branches of all "human" gene trees... The latest work has striven to incorporate the complex structure of African subpopulations into the analysis of human genetic variability. Based on these studies, mtDNA gene trees place humanity's origin in the southern and eastern parts of Africa, Y chromosomal DNA variation puts it in north-central Africa, and studies using nuclear DNA sequences place it in South-West Africa.[353]

Evolutionary biologists argue these disparate results indicate that humanity arose from several populations that coalesced over time into modern humans. It is presumed that mtDNA, Y chromosomal DNA, and nuclear DNA represent different genetic loci, each with its own history. These results line up with the notion that the various genetic markers trace an origin to many Eves and Adams, according to evolutionary scientists.[354]

Analysis of Humanity's Origin, Location, and Migration

However, there are concerns about this conclusion when using genetic data to locate humanity's origin. Specifically, they assume that the current location of population groups represents their location throughout human history. This assumption remains questionable because numerous groups have migrated thousands of miles throughout history.

Recent studies attempting to account for the substructure of African populations were conducted independently using different modeling techniques. The lack of uniformity in this new research could account for the disparate results. Genetic drift (e.g., gene spread over a population) also raises problems, particularly for mtDNA and Y chromosomal DNA genetic markers when population sizes are small.

Finally, scientists must reconcile humanity's passage through a recent (*perhaps 100,000 years ago*) "*genetic bottleneck*" with our origins. These scientists believe a "genetic bottleneck" would cause a limited genetic diversity around the world, which creates an appearance that humanity arose from a small population. This study was from distinct populations in widely separated regions of Africa that coalesced before the bottleneck.[355]

NOTE: A "genetic bottleneck" is a sharp reduction in the size of a population due to environmental events such as famines, earthquakes, floods, fires, disease, droughts, or human activities such as genocide and human population planning.[356]

In addition, Quentin Atkinson, a scientist from the University of Auckland in New Zealand, used linguistic analysis of languages to trace humanity's origin. When people began to migrate around the world, a small group left the site of humanity's genesis. Serial fracturing of the migrating population occurred, generating the "serial founder effect." Atkinson analyzed 504 languages and discovered that African languages displayed the most significant number of phonemes — the sounds of language, such as vowels, consonants, and tones. (e.g., African populations are the most genetically diverse and thought to be the oldest people groups.) He also determined that the languages of people groups in South America and Oceania possessed the fewest number of phenomes. (These people are believed to be the youngest.) Atkinson also noticed a cline (e.g., a gradual decrease) in phonemes as the languages moved away from Africa and into Europe and Asia.[357]

Therefore, evolutionary biologists argue that these disparate results indicate that humanity arose from several populations (around 200,000 years ago) that coalesced over time into modern humans about 70,000 to 80,000 years ago. In addition, the global migration journey of modern humans started some 60,000 to 70,000 years ago out of Africa using all the above analysis methods. They migrated to Europe around 35,000 to 45,000 years ago, to Australia around 50,000 years ago, to China and Asia around 35,000 to 45,000 years ago, to North America some 15,000 to 20,000 years ago, and to South America some 12,000 to 15,000 years ago.[358] See Figure 19 for one perspective on the migration pattern and dates for the spread of modern humans worldwide.

MIGRATION PATTERN OF MODERN HUMANS FROM AN EVOLUTIONARY PERSPECTIVE	
Migration from Africa to Middle East	Africa 110,000 - 200,000 YA to Middle East 50,000 - 70,000 YA
Migration from Middle East to Europe and South East Asia/ Oceania	Middle East 50,000 - 70,000 YA to Europe 35,000 - 45,000 YA Middle East 50,000 - 70,000 YA to South East Asia and Oceania 50,000 YA
Migration from South East Asia to Central to Pacific Asia	South East Asia Minor 50,000 YA to Central/Pacific Asia 35,000 - 45,000 YA
Migration from North Asia to North American Continent	North East Asia 35,000 - 45,000 YA to North America 15,000 - 20,000 YA
Migration from North America to Latin and South America	North America 15,000 - 20,000 YA to Latin/South America 12,000 - 15,000 YA

Figure 19: Migration Pattern of Modern Humans from an Evolutionary Perspective

The Emergence of Sophisticated Behavior of Humanity

Without question, hominids living as long ago as 2 million years ago employed tools and possessed a "culture." Still, their crude technology and simple lifestyle remained static for hundreds of thousands of years. When new modes of technology and culture began in the archeological record, the advances represented relatively small steps upwards, followed by long periods of stasis. The hominids used remarkably unsophisticated technology even as recently as 100,000 years ago.[359]

However, based on recent and numerous archeological finds, researchers have independently dated the artifacts from the South African caves (Blombos, Sibudu, Pinnacle Point, and Diepkloof Rock Shelter) to be between 70,000 and 80,000 years old. These discoveries reflect the activities of humans endowed with the capacity for "symbolism." The findings at these sites include red ocher with engravings, engraved ostrich eggs, jewelry beads, heat-and-pressure-treated stones (which allows for easier flaking), adhesives, and bedding made from evergreens with insect-repellent properties.[360] They were measured using the luminescence dating method, which measures the amount of light emitted from mineral grains when they are heated in a controlled manner or stimulated by light. The emitted light estimates the age of bones or artifacts sandwiched between the rock layers that house the mineral grains.[361]

In addition, early Southeast Asian cave art affirmed the early appearance of symbolism. In 2014, an international team of scientists redated the Sulawesi (an Indonesian island) cave art to 35,000 to 40,000 years old. They used a new technique that measured the age of calcite deposits overlaying the cave art. These deposits form when water runs over the walls of a cave and leaves behind a calcite film. Trace amounts of radioactive uranium and thorium isotopes associated with the calcite can be used to date the mineral deposit, providing a minimum age for the artwork. In addition, a second independent study dated rock art throughout China, Indonesia, Thailand, Cambodia, and Malaysia found these specimens to be over 40,000 years old. These two studies indicate that modern humans possessed the capacity to produce art when they migrated into Asia about 50,000 to 60,000 years ago... The Southeast Asia cave art is of the same quality and (roughly) the same age as cave art found in Spain, France, and Germany. Such a parallel suggests that humans possessed the capacity for symbolic expression before they began global migration, pushing the origin of modern human behavior at least 60,000 years ago. Anthropologist Christopher Stringer of the Natural History Museum in London commented on the Southeast Asia art redating by saying, "It is a *really important* find; it enabled us to get away from this Eurocentric view of a creative explosion that was special to Europe and did not develop in other parts of the work until much later..." The basis for this art was there 60,000 years ago; it may even have been there in Africa before 60,000 years ago, and it spread with modern humans.[362] In light of Stringer's assessment, it is worth noting that researchers estimate that humans began migrating out of Africa about 72,000 years ago. They arrived at this date by using a mtDNA molecular clock calibrated with mtDNA isolated from the ancient remains of modern humans.[363]

In addition, molecular anthropologists have discovered the FOXP2 human master regulatory language gene that originated ~100,000 years ago. Language derives from complex networks of gene interactions (which developmental biologists Eric Davidson and Roy Britten called "development gene regulatory networks" or dGRNs) that dynamically vary through the course of human development. The FOXP2 represents only one of these genes. Symbolism is the closest proxy to the origin of language.[364]

Sociocultural "Big Bang" of Humanity

This special "Eurocentric" view of a creative explosion around 40,000 to 50,000 years ago, which Stringer has alluded to, dominated many of the researchers' perspectives during the early 2000s regarding the differences between earlier and later hominids. However, as new art, marine shell jewelry, stone tools, and other artifacts were found (with fossil remains) principally in cave sites in South Africa, Algeria, Ethiopia, Israel, and other locations, this "big bang" date (which exemplifies human behavior) has moved to at least 70,000 to 80,000 years ago and even earlier based upon more precise dating methods such as the thermal luminescence, mtDNA, and Y chromosomal techniques. Nevertheless, these observations during the early 2000s are still relevant today as they give more insight into the details of their findings and subsequent perspectives. Here are some of their thoughts:

> A "quantum leap" occurred in tool inventories, manufacturing techniques, and usages. This new technology (called Late Stone Age, Mode IV, or Late or Upper Paleolithic Period) includes a wide range of sophisticated implements made by complex manufacturing techniques. In addition to employing stone, the first "humans" used ivory, bone, and wood. They transported the raw materials for tool production in significant distances…the first humans made projectile points, awls, punches, fishhooks, harpoons, and needles with eyes. They lived in solidly built dwellings and made fireplaces and hearths bordered with stones for heat retention. Compared to the earlier hominids, the first humans behaved in sophisticated ways that reflected superior cognitive abilities and technical inventiveness. A much more significant proportion of older individuals made jewelry and other items for personal adornment. This behavior demonstrates advanced mental capacity, artistic expression, marks of symbolic language, decorations, communication, group membership, social identity, and gender.[365] They found musical instruments, such as an ivory flute, dated to between 30,000 and 37,000 years old in southern Germany.[366] Artistic and lyrical expression was not part of the earlier hominid's life. This behavior is unique to humans and coincides exclusively with human remains. Perhaps one of the most critical advances in prehistoric

archeology in recent years is the recognition that artistic (including musical) expression did not gradually emerge but exploded onto the scene simultaneously with humanity's appearance about 40,000 years ago. Archeologists and anthropologists refer to this surge of human culture as "the big bang of art."[367]

In addition, evolutionary biologists and anthropologists (for the most part) agree that

a sharp difference exists between the culture and technology of humankind and those observed for hominids existing between 250,000 and 50,000 years ago (*such as the Neanderthals*). Frequently scientists refer to these quanta changes in behavior as the "dawn of human culture," the "human revolution," a "creative explosion," the "great leap forward," or the "sociocultural big bang."[368] They struggle to make sense of it — some argue that the social structure of modern humans was much different than the one displayed by earlier hominids. According to this view, the newer social structure required re-ordering and the communication of complex ideas, leading to the "creative explosion" seen in the archeological record. Others assert that the invention of new technology catalyzed a cascade of advances that precluded the sociocultural big bang.[369]

Anthropologists and archeologists can readily distinguish between humans and hominids in the fossil record based not only on morphology but also on behavior. Hominids possessed some low level of culture and technology, but these were relatively simplistic and remained stagnant for long periods of time; then, around 40,000 years ago (about the time humanity appears throughout the fossil record), advanced human culture exploded onto the scene. The culture and technology displayed by the earliest human beings indicate that they possessed 1) advanced cognitive ability, 2) the capacity for symbolic thought, 3) a powerful imagination, 4) superior craftsmanship, 5) inventiveness and superior adaptability, 6) a driving desire for artistic and musical expression, and 7) ritual behaviors and religious activity. Theologians generally consider all these characteristics as defining features of God's image in humans. None of the hominids that preceded humans in the fossil record displayed these unique behaviors. Nor did they live in complex societies with tight social cohesion.[370]

Clothing also appears to be a practice associated exclusively with humans. Archeologists lack direct evidence for clothes because skins and furs do not survive long. The recovery of ivory needles (with eyes) from sites that date to around 40,000 years ago, however, can be considered indirect evidence of sewing because these devices were needed to manufacture wearing apparel... (NOTE: The origin of body lice coincides with the origin of clothes, and based on the genetic variation of a global sample of such like, it appears that these lice originated around 72,000 years +/- 42,000 years ago and more recently about 100,000 years ago.)[371]

The earliest humans had at least some religious motivations when they produced cave and figurative art. If so, the spiritual expression dates to at least 30,000 years ago. Of course, this interpretation of cave art and figurines in the archeological record may not be valid. Frequently, archeologists examine grave sites, looking for evidence of burial practices as signs of ritual behavior.[372]

Some findings suggest that Neanderthals and other archaic hominids have buried their dead. However, these burial practices appear non-ritualistic and relatively simple. The Neanderthals dug shallow graves that contained few, if any, artifacts. Human burial practices contrast sharply.[373] Early burials involved a profusion of grave goods (special items and body ornaments), providing strong evidence for ritualistic beliefs. These articles suggest that humanity had a sense of an afterlife. Currently, archeologists lack a rigorous date for the onset of religious expression. This human behavior is much more challenging to identify and interpret than art, music, or jewelry use. However, it is safe to say that spiritual activity dates to at least 28,000 years ago. Ritual burials and possible religious expression (through art) appear unique to human beings.[374]

In addition, these molecular geneticists investigate humanity's origin (and migration worldwide) by studying the association of the timing, location, and spread of disease-causing microbes or parasites (i.e., tapeworms, malaria, bacteria, lice). They believe that the time and place for these parasites started and their spread around the world mirrors the timing, location, and spread of humanity. Therefore, the worldwide genetic variation of these infectious agents can be used in the same way molecular anthropologists see a human genetic variation to gain an understanding of humanity's past.[375]

Separating Modern Humans from Chimps and Neanderthals

Modern Human versus Chimpanzee Differences

Evolutionary scientists have assumed the chimp is our "closest living relative." By that assumption, gene comparisons have been studied extensively in both genomes. These scientists studied their similarities and differences in their DNA. These genes, which "code" for proteins, are crucial for all living anatomical, physiological, and behavioral traits and characteristics. These initial studies revealed a high correlation percentage (e.g., ~98 percent). However, when researchers made unbiased comparisons of larger regions of these two genomes (including the noncoding DNA, which is about 98 percent of the genomes that turn genes on and off), significant differences began to emerge. Much of the chimp's DNA did not align with the sequences in the human genome database, according to studies performed by the Chimpanzee Genome Project Team and the Max Planck Institute. Specifically, 15,000 of the 65,000 DNA fragments did not align with any sequences in the human genome database. They appeared as unique regions.[376] In addition, researchers compared over 10,000 regions and found that for two-thirds that did align, about one-third did not. These and other studies are based upon nuclear DNA-to-DNA, gene-to-gene, and chromosome-to-chromosome comparisons.[377]

As more data is collected and analyzed, here are some specific results from recent studies that show significant differences:

- *Nuclear DNA-to-DNA comparisons* show a chimp's genome (i.e., a genome represents all the nuclear DNA comprised of the A, T, C, and G nucleotide bases) sequencing significantly differs from humans by about 6.4 percent or 212 million nucleotide base pair differences. (NOTE: Chimps have an estimated 3,309,577,922 base pairs versus 3,096,649,726 base pairs in humans.)[378]
- When insertion and deletions (a.k.a. indels) of single nucleotide substitutions are considered, as mentioned before, early studies showed a 98 percent DNA similarity between chimps and humans. More recent studies show they are reduced to about 96 percent.[379] Finally, a 2018 study shows that the DNA similarity could be at

84.4 percent or about a 360 million base pair difference between the two.[380]

- There is approximately a 1.23 percent difference in single base pair (i.e., DNA letters or bases such as A, T, G, and C) substitutions (i.e., A instead of G), which relate to insertions (added bases) and deletions (missing bases) within the two genome sequences. This relates to 40 to 45 million bases in humans missing from the chimps and about the same number present in chimps that are absent from man that are not one-to-one aligned or exact matches. This puts the total number of DNA differences at about 125 million.[381]

- *Gene-to-gene comparisons* show that protein-coding gene regions of humans are (on average) only about 86 to 87 percent like chimps. (NOTE: These regions are called exons and produce, via the transcription process, many different individual messenger RNA [mtRNA] variants that are due to gene expression regulations. There are about 28,000 to 30,000 genes in humans.)[382]

- Roughly 10 percent of genes examined showed significant differences in gene expression levels between chimps and humans.[383]

- Due to these gene expression differences, here are some examples: Humans have an accelerated rate of cognitive brain activity, higher gene expression patterns or levels of the cerebellum, caudate nucleus, and cerebral cortex regions.[384] A different shape of the FOXP2 gene that is responsible for brain development for language capability is caused by two different amino acids (out of fifteen needed for this gene) between humans and chimps.[385] The spontaneous emergence of the abnormal spindle-like microcephaly (ASPM) gene causes an expansion of the cerebral cortex that leads to the ability to reason abstractly[386] and an increased level of gene expression of the induced pluripotent stem cells (iPSCs) in 1,375 in human genes and 1,050 different genes in chimps that significantly affect early embryonic development and form different cell types like stem cells.[387]

- Humans have 689 genes that chimps lack, and chimps have eighty-six genes that humans lack. Such differences mean that 6 percent of the gene complement is different between humans and chimps, irrespective of the individual DNA base pairs, and thus, affects an organism's phenotype or how traits are physically expressed in the environment.[388]

- *Chromosome-to-chromosome comparisons* show humans have much shorter DNA base pair sequences (about 10,000) at the end of each chromosome (a.k.a. telomeres are protective caps) versus about 23,000 for chimps.[389]

- Humans have twenty-three to twenty-four pairs of chromosomes for chimps. This is because portions of two small chimp chromosomes (called 2A and 2B) look somewhat like human chromosome 2. This difference in the number of chromosomes equates to about 88 percent similarity between humans, depending on the chromosome. Overall, the genomes of humans and chimps were only about 88 percent similar, according to the recently revised versions of the BLASTN algorithm calculations.[390] While eighteen pairs of chromosomes are virtually identical, chromosomes 4, 9, and 12 show evidence of being "remodeled" or, in other words, the genes and markers on these chromosomes are not in the same order.[391]

Gene expression patterns are arguably more significant than the DNA sequences' similarities or differences alone, particularly when influencing brain tissue activity. They act as a switch that tells the genes when to turn on or off. They are largely made up of noncoding DNA (such as indels), which represent over 98 percent of the genome. (NOTE: In other terms, only 1 to 2 percent of the genome is made up of genes that code for proteins.) In addition, epigenetic parts of the cell also contribute to genetic expression and activity. Also, the environment plays into this scenario in terms of how our bodies "read" a DNA (i.e., gene) sequence. Therefore, within a particular environment, genomes of humans and chimps contribute to the anatomical, physical, spiritual, and behavioral differences. The chimp has a much smaller internal brain, a quadruped bone skeletal structure, and other major parts of their physiology to compensate for their open surroundings. Humans have a much larger internal brain, bipedal bone skeletal structure, and other features and traits that are unique and special. They have the cognitive and intellectual abilities to express their thoughts abstractly in speech, writing, and music, as well as develop other complicated systems of expression and communication that contribute to advanced civilizations. This is why humans stand above all other types of creatures. Chimps do not do anything close. The bottom line is that for even an 84 to 95 percent similarity between humans and chimps,

evolutionary theory has a difficult enough time explaining how only 2% of the three billion bases could have evolved (*changed*) in the 3-6 million years since they believe chimps and humans shared a common ancestor? They (*evolutionists*) want to avoid the task of explaining how 15 or 20% of the three billion bases evolved in such a short time! Natural processes cannot create 369 million letters (*i.e.*, *DNA bases*) of precisely coded information in a billion years, let alone a few million years.[392]

Human versus Neanderthal Differences

Evolutionary scientists have assumed the "Neanderthals" to be our "closest" extinct or archaic relatives. This assumption is based upon the genetic comparative study between modern humans and Neanderthals conducted in 2010. This National Institute of Health (NIH) genome study shows:

> Neanderthal DNA to be 99.7% identical to present-day human DNA. The comparison produced a catalog of genetic differences that allowed the researchers to identify features unique to modern humans. In many regions of the Neanderthal genome, they found, are more like those of the chimpanzee than present-day humans. In addition, their analysis suggested that up to 2% of the DNA in the genome of present-day people outside of Africa originated in Neanderthals or their ancestors. Neanderthals appear to have re-encountered (*i.e.*, *interbred*) anatomically modern humans in the Fertile Cresent of the Middle East about 60,000 years ago. As modern humans migrated out of the Middle East and dispersed across the globe, they carried Neanderthal DNA with them (*as well as perhaps with the Denisovans in Asia and Native America?*).[393]

By contrast, this study implies a very small percentage difference (i.e., 0.3 percent) between the two species. Given this implication, why are there different anatomical, physiological, behavioral, and even spiritual features? For example, although anatomically similar in many ways, Neanderthals and humans exhibit significant morphological differences. In some instances, Neanderthals display a unique combination of features unknown in any other hominid.[394] Compared to human beings, Neanderthals displayed:

- An extraordinarily long face
- A pronounced midface projection
- A poorly developed chin
- A highly developed brow ridge
- Large, round-eye sockets
- Cavernous sinuses
- Large front teeth
- A retromolar cap
- An occipital bun
- A brain flatter and small in front and more bulged in the back and sides
- A flatter skull
- An elongated foramen magnum (opening in the skull for the spinal cord)
- A higher larynx
- Thicker bones
- A more compact body with a barrel chest and shorter limbs
- Smaller hyoid and the hypoglossal canal for crude communication skills
- A smaller parietal lobe, which plays a vital role in language, math reasoning, sense of self-identity, and religious experience
- Limited symbolic thought or sophisticated behavioral patterns, as seen in cave paintings, jewelry, etc.
- Larger brain size, but brain-size to body-mass ratio was smaller (a.k.a. encephalization quotient).[395]

Perhaps genetic and environmental differences can help to explain some of these differences. Significant genetic differences were found when comparing their fossil remains and artifacts. Some of these differences are predominantly observed in the FOXP2 regulatory genes for language, the melanocortin one receptor (MC1R) genes for regulation of skin and hair pigment production, the leptin receptor (LEPR) genes for adaptation to cold, the basonuclin zinc finger protein 2 (BNC2) genes for keratin in skin pigmentation, and in general, different genes for skull morphology, rib-cage structure, skin and hair features, metabolism, and cognitive development.[396] These genetic disparities help to account for some of the critical anatomical, physiological, and behavioral differences between modern humans and Neanderthal. Generally, the researchers concluded that these genes must have merged independently in humans and Neanderthals.[397] Specifically, a 2014 analysis of the high-quality "Altai" Neanderthal genome revealed that the Neanderthal's FOXP2 gene is distinct from the one found in humans.[398]

In addition, there were different methylation patterns (the methyl group attaches to DNA in the chromosomes) in about 2,000 regions between these two genomes. These map patterns influence brain development, neurological and psychiatric disorders, and immune and cardiovascular systems. They are part of epigenetics and are influenced by the environment.[399]

Finally, the question that is often asked is: Are Neanderthals and modern humans distinct species, or did present-day humans evolve from Neanderthals?

> No scientist doubts that Neanderthals and humans are distinct species. The anatomical, genetic, and developmental differences between humans and Neanderthals justifies viewing them as distinct species. However, from a Christian perspective, it is still possible to view humans

and Neanderthals as distinct products of God's creative activity. On this view, the ability to interbreed reflects common design, not common descent.[400]

Even though there are some similarities between chimps, Neanderthals, and modern humans, there are still significant differences between them, especially in the gene expression levels (which turn genes on and off at different times). Therefore, many scientists and nonscientists consider humans a "unique" species when comparing their anatomical, physiological, behavioral, archeological, and, most importantly, genetic differences. Connections between them were observed to be *"problematic"* because significant changes were made relatively quickly. In addition, multiple, simultaneous, and integrated positive selections of predominately beneficial mutations (rare in the first place) of genes to generate new species is not realistically possible without divine intervention either by an Intelligent Designer/Agent or a Creator — supernatural "God." The biblical perspective makes these changes possible and believable!

Summary and Conclusions

Most paleontologists, molecular geneticists, and anthropologists interpret hominids in the fossil record within an evolutionary framework. They view hominids from 7 to 2 MYA as "transitional forms" or "intermediate and missing links" that gave rise to the Homo genus. Modern humans are classified as Homo sapiens *sapiens* or Homo sapiens within the family called "hominids." This distinction is due to their "unique" morphological (anatomical, physiological, and genetic) structures and behavioral characteristics or traits. Creationists often use Homo sapiens *sapiens* or modern humans to distinguish the Homo sapiens subspecies from the: Homo sapiens *idealtu*, Homo sapiens *denisova*, and Homo sapiens *neanderthalensis* "archaic" species.

According to evolutionary scientists, the Homo *erectus* species has been replaced by the Homo *heidelbergensis* species that evolved into the Homo *neanderthalensis* and Homo *sapiens* species. Many evolutionary paleoanthropologists and other historical scientists use the term "humans" to describe all hominids. This usage tends to create confusion between other scientists and the public. This evolutionary hominid "Tree of Life" shows some uncertainty of hominids going from the Ardipithecus, Australopithecus, and Paranthropus to the Homo groupings or genera. Also, these paleontologists do not seem to have a clear understanding of the biology of the early ("ancient") hominids (7 to 2 MYA) since their DNA (from a few numbers of fossils) is challenging to find, analyze, and compare against later (or archaic) hominids or "humans."

Scientific investigations demonstrate that while paleontologists have discovered a menagerie of hominids, scientists have *failed* to establish the necessary evolutionary connections (e.g., MRCAs) with a high degree of certainty. Without these connections, human evolution cannot be declared a fact. Instead of solidifying evolutionary hypotheses about human origins, each new hominid generates further turmoil.[401] Early human phylogeny depicts this situation with "dashed" lines. Paleontologists cannot adequately account for the evolutionary emergence of bipedalism or brain size, generally considered to be humanity's two most significant anatomical characteristics. Bipedalism appeared rather suddenly and concurrently with the hominid's first appearance. Instead of gradually increasing in the fossil record, hominid brain size shows discontinuous jumps as new hominid species successfully enter the fossil record (over a narrow "geological and biological" window of time). These sudden steps were relatively small from hominid to hominid until modern humans appeared. With human's advent, brain size dramatically increases.[402]

Molecular clock analyses use several assumptions to construct a hominid "Tree of Life" to determine the migration pattern of "humans" from the three migration patterns or dispersal hypotheses. Most scientists believe that the intermediate African assimilation hypothesis best represents the migration pattern of modern humans. This hypothesis is based on DNA interbreeding analyses between modern humans, Neanderthals, and Denisovans. According to evolutionary theories, modern humans first coalesced or merged into one ("relatively small") group or population and then left Africa about 72,000 years ago and migrated around the world where they either replaced the existing hominid populations or assimilated (e.g., interbred) with Neanderthals and Denisovans according to DNA comparison analyses. Scientists have determined that anatomically, modern humans originated in different parts of Africa as seen by ancient or old-world fossil remains (primarily in dating skulls and measuring their brain sizes or capacities). However, there is some question about how they are related since they moved around and with the "genetic bottleneck" restraint or limitation.

Early modern humans evolved around 200,000 years ago in Africa, according to most evolutionists today. They assert that modern humans are probably descendants of H. *heidelbergensis* and H. *erectus*. Evolutionary scientists believe that modern humans came from small African populations of "Eves" and "Adams" that began around 150,000 years ago. Some creationists think that this was the (mitochondrial) biblical "Eve" and the (Y chromosomal) biblical "Adam" that God divinely created to produce modern humans, while others (namely, creation scientists) believe they were created much later (perhaps 6,000 to 10,000 years ago).

According to geneticists, the FOXP2 human "master regulatory language gene" originated ~100,000 years ago. The language gene derives from complex networks of gene interactions that dynamically vary throughout human development. The FOXP2 gene represents only one of these genes. Symbolism is the closest proxy to the origin of language and relates to archeological artifacts.

Archeological artifacts were dated approximately 70,000 to 80,000 years ago. Still, most findings start around 40,000 to 50,000 years ago during the Upper Paleolithic period and show a major cultural and technological explosion (e.g., "the sociocultural big bang"). "Just-right" timing for humanity to exist and reproduce seems to demand precise conditions and timing considerations for their existence and survival.

Evolutionists debate about what is included in the genera/species Homo sapiens. Some of these questions include: Is the Neanderthal species in a separate genus or part of the Homo sapiens? What genera are included as "humans"? Are all primates that walk erect called "humans?" What is the pathway or phylogeny from early (ancient) "humans" to modern man? What are the selective pressures that might produce bipedalism in primates (e.g., from four-legged or quadruped)? What is the most accurate human dispersal or migration "Out of Africa" pattern?

Creationists and neo-creationists (e.g., Intelligent Design) proponents have *doubts* over hominids going from quadrupedal to bipedalism over a relatively short (geological) time; more than one "Eve" and "Adam" coming from preexisting populations as the evolutionists theorize; the lack of an agreed-upon evolutionary pathway(s) connecting hominids to "modern humans"; the inaccuracy of molecular clock analyses in estimating the time of humanity's origin and their spread around the globe. RTB creationists believe that "mitochondrial Eve" and "Y chromosomal Adam" lived at the same time, approximately 150,000 years ago. They believe these two individuals lived in the North Eastern Africa or Eastern Mediterranean area, which generally agrees with the ongoing scientific fossil and genetic studies. They do not see any contradiction with the biblical interpretation.

Even though there are some similarities between chimps, Neanderthals, and modern humans, there are still significant differences between them. Therefore, many scientists and nonscientists consider modern humans a "unique" and "special" species in several ways. This conclusion was based on comparing their anatomical, physiological, behavioral, archeological, and, probably the most critical, genetic differences. Scientists explained these scientific findings through evolutionary theories and associated mechanisms. When they made these comparisons, they observed connections between these species to be "*problematic,*" especially when significant changes in their makeup were made in a relatively short period of time (perhaps 5 to 6 million years).

Given these factors, scientists and nonscientists, who are biblical creationists, believe these multiple, simultaneous, and integrated changes are virtually *impossible* without divine intervention. From a biblical perspective, an Intelligent Designer/Agent, or a Creator "God," makes these changes possible and believable from a "common design" perspective. From a common design perspective, it is very possible and even probable that He engineered our genome to make it unique and special. Astronomer Sir Fred Hoyle once said,

> A commonsense interpretation of the facts suggests that a super intellect has monkeyed with physics, as well as chemistry and biology and there is no blind forces worth speaking about nature.[403]

Psalm 139:13–14 says, "For you created my inmost being; you knit me together in my mother's womb. I praise you because I am fearfully and wonderfully made; your works are wonderful; I know that full well." The NKJV of this passage says it a little differently. That their hearts may be encouraged, being knit together in love, to reach all the riches and full assurance of understanding and the knowledge of God's mystery, which is Christ.

Additionally, Colossians 2:2 says, "My purpose is that they may be encouraged in heart and united in love, so that they may have full riches of complete understanding, in order that they may know the mystery of God, namely, Christ."

Because these differences from validated scientific discoveries cannot adequately explain the evolutionary pathways from modern humans to archaic and ancient hominids and back to chimpanzees and an "unknown" common ancestor, the biblical creation story is not only relevant but makes more sense today than ever before, especially in our doubting and secular "woke" culture.

One last thought regarding the evolutionary chain of life or the "ascent to man" illustrations that have left an everlasting impression on each of us.

The progression called the "ascent of man" was first illustrated in Professor Clark Howell's book, *Early Man*, in the 1968 and 1973 editions. It traces human evolution in fifteen pictures from Pliopithecus (chimp) to Proconsul, Dryopithecus, Oreopithecus, Ramapithecus, A. *africanus*, A. *robustus*, Advanced Australopithecus, H. *erectus*, Early H. *sapiens*, Solo man, Rhodesian man, Neanderthal man, Cro-Magnon man, then to modern man.

This "ascent-of-man" series resembles a baby first learning to walk, from crawling to fully upright walking. The 'branching bush' tree diagram of evolution, which pictures evolution as a tree with putative humans branching off the trunk, has today succeeded the straight-line "marching parade" concept of human evolution. This fact is a tacit admission that anthropologists have known for many years that the parade was wrong. However, since then, Neanderthals are no longer considered part of our evolutionary lineage, but another branch of the human family tree, where both Neanderthals and modern humans are today assumed to have evolved from Homo *erectus* (or H. *heidelbergensis*). Also, many of the proto-apes were not bipedal, yet shown as biped (i.e., were quadrupedal) and shown walking, not standing, even balancing on one foot in the air, unlike the quadrupedal "knuckle-walking" gait. Also, size of illustrations was greatly distorted going from short to tall and progressively less hairy, clothed with flesh . The Dryopithecus is shown as stooped and is only known from a "few jaws and teeth." In 1965, a Ramapthithecus skull convinced evolutionists that it had no part in human evolution. Also, the Solo man was known by two shin bones and some fragments of skull and A. robustus, both which are now interpreted as "an evolutionary dead end in man's ancestry." Thus, the visual image has effectively "sold" the concept of human evolution even though the book revealed that the parade was fictious.[404]

Therefore, this parade implies that evolution from our putative ape-like ancestor called Pliopithecus (chimp) to modern humans was very straightforward, showing hereditary changes progressively moving forward along a single line from our apelike ancestor to modern humans. Archaeologist G. Burenhult shows four different human evolution trees. Each of these trees shows several offshoots or side branches.[405]

From a complete progression perspective, the common version shows a fish in water, then a fish crawling out with small legs evolving into a four-legged animal, and lastly, a set of primates like the old parade leading to human. A *Newsweek* article pictured the parade as the "old view" and, next to it, showed the new view, a complex bush that is very different than the now-famous progression... biblical creationist Russell Miller recommends that "it would be best to scrap the (progression) illustration altogether."[406] The progressions that show an ape to an African, then to a Caucasian, or an ape to a Neanderthal to modern man, are very inaccurate, grossly distorted (except for modern man), or a fish to a bird, then to a dog, a monkey, and an African or some other "primitive human" and last to a Caucasian, often appearing Nordic or Scandinavian. These drawings are not only false, but they are also clearly racist, as is obvious when we compare the drawings to photographs of the animal or race they are supposed to represent. Most of the drawings depict African-looking males as primitive humans evolving into modern humans of lighter skin and hair.[407]

The racism discussed above still exists in our society. One study showed that "Americans of various races still unconsciously dehumanize their black fellow citizens by associating them with apes," an association no doubt reinforced by the common progression drawings.[408]

The next chapter integrates confirmed scientific evidence within the six creation days of Genesis chapter 1. Creation events make it especially possible to conceive or believe in relation to scientific findings, especially using the "dialog" compatibility model, which is the *fourth* perspective.

CHAPTER 10:

Genesis and Science Compatibility Consideration?

Since evolution alone is unlikely, the question becomes, "Is the Genesis account of creation compatible with scientific discoveries?" And if so, "Can these separate domains overlap or be compatible in some way regarding our origins?"

Historically, several compatible and incompatible models between science (predominately based on reason) and religion (predominately based on faith) were developed to address this issue.

In terms of incompatible models, the "conflict thesis," which is a contentious or hostile model between these disciplines, has been *rejected* by most contemporary scientific historians. "Historically, studies have shown that Christianity (and other religions) have often encouraged scientific endeavors, while at other times the two have co-existed without tension or attempts at harmonization."[409]

In addition, the "independence model," as the other modern incompatible view, is taught in many US public school science classes and is supported by the National Academy of Science. "Science and religion deal with fundamentally separate aspects of human experience, so when each stay within its domain, they co-exist peacefully."[410] This is also called the "nonoverlapping magisterial" or NOMA concept of separate realms of science and religion and was developed by evolutionist Stephen Jay Gould. Science tries to document the natural world's authentic character and develop theories that coordinate and explain these facts. On the other hand, religion operates in the equally important but utterly different realm of human purposes, meanings, and values — subjects that the factual domain of science might illuminate but never resolve... The net, or magisterium, of science covers the empirical realm: What is the universe made of (fact), and why does it work this way (theory)? The magisterium of religion extends over questions of ultimate meaning and moral value. These two "magisterial" do not overlap.[411]

From a "compatible" standpoint, the "cooperative mode" attempts to integrate or harmonize religious or theological perspectives with scientific events as the norm so that they can coexist peacefully. Proponents of this view prefer to avoid any differences between these two areas and attribute any clashes between them from extremists of both disciplines over a very few topics. From a faith versus reason perspective, this model is considered a "strong" compatible model.

Lastly, there is the "dialog or weak compatible model." This model is preferred by the author. From this perspective, there is an overlap between these two domains regarding our origins. Recognizing the possibility of this overlap provides the opportunity for individuals and groups to engage in productive discussions and useful conclusions that correspond to their beliefs. As science probes the universe, she encounters problems and questions that are philosophical in character and therefore cannot be resolved scientifically but that can be illuminated by a theological perspective... By the same token...world religions make various and conflicting claims about the origin and nature of the universe and humanity, and they cannot all be true. Science and religion are thus like two circles that intersect or partially overlap. It is in the area of intersection that the dialog takes place.[412]

In one respect, science and religion are different ways of knowing about something or someone. However, just because they are different, it does not mean that one discipline cannot explain (to some degree) the other discipline. This is especially true regarding the study of our origins. Science and the "hard and soft" scientific disciplines primarily know or discover things through the rigorous and systematic process of validating empirical data or evidence. This process uses the scientific method of reasoning, which is based on the rules of science. Religion, on the other hand, approaches morality, metaphysics, and the identification of the Creator (e.g., God) from a biblical (e.g., Genesis) perspective. These beliefs are primarily based upon faith, divine revelations, and miracles found in the Word of "God" and inspired by the "Holy Spirit." Even though general/natural revelation of nature can be observed from both scientific and religious perspectives, only special revelation provides the insight into "who" provided creation and "why" it was done. Figure 20 illustrates the intersection between these two domains for the discussion or dialog regarding our origins and answers the question, "How did we get here?"

Science and Religion "Dialog" on Our Origins

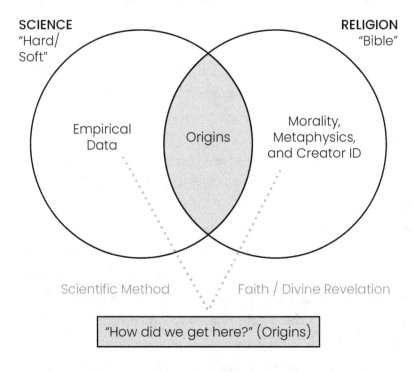

Figure 20: Science and Religion Dialog on Our Origins

If we use the dialog approach, there are six ways in which science and religion are allies and are relevant or relate to each other:

1. Religion furnishes the conceptual framework in which science can flourish. This "shell" can provide the "space" for pertinent (e.g., biblically sound) modern scientific discoveries that were not available until recent times.

2. Modern science is the child of European civilization… due to the unique contribution of the Christian faith to Western culture. Science can both falsify and verify claims of religions. When religions make claims about

the natural world, they intersect the domains of science and are, in effect, making predictions that scientific investigations can either verify or falsify.

3. Science encounters metaphysical problems that religion can help solve. Science has an insatiable thirst for an explanation, but eventually, science reaches the limits of its explanatory ability.

4. Religion can help adjudicate between scientific theories, particularly in cases in which two conflicting theories are empirically equivalent so that one cannot decide between them based upon on the evidence, metaphysical concerns, including the religious concerns, that come into play.

5. Religion can augment the explanatory power of science. One of the pillars of the current scientific view of the world is the evolution of the gradual rise of biological activity from more primitive life forms. The current "neo-Darwinian synthesis" or "modern synthesis" mechanisms of random mutation and natural selection work far too slowly to produce unaided and conscious life.

6. Science can establish a premise in an argument for a conclusion having religious significance, such as the purpose of life.[413]

The Christian "Reasons to Believe" ministry offers a "unique" Genesis approach or possible compatibility scenario between science and Genesis. They demonstrate the Genesis "days of creation" account can ("*approximately*") coexist with many modern scientific explanations. The RTB scientists and theologians constantly adjust their creation model based on new scientific discoveries only if these findings agree or are compatible with the Genesis creation account from the Bible. These scientific explanations are based upon the discoveries from leading historical and current scientists such as cosmologists, astrophysicists, planetary geologists, chemists, biologists, geneticists, paleontologists, and anthropologists. "What we (*RTB*) find out is that the biblical sequence of creation events aligns with the scientific findings for the sequence of the origins, the formation of the earth, and the beginning of life."[414]

> NOTE: Progressive creationists, such as RTB, believe that the sun, moon, and stars became visible on the fourth day, whereas strict, literal, or very conservative Christian creationists (such as CS) believe the stars and other heavenly bodies were created on the fourth day vice the first day.

The following approach slightly modifies and expands this RTB scenario. It incorporates a general scientific explanation for each biblical creation day. Figure 21 illustrates and summarizes this "inclusive" biblical perspective, which is based on the "dialog-compatible model." This is the "*fourth perspective.*"

SCIENTIFIC EVENTS "FOLDED" INTO THE SIX BIBLICAL CREATION DAYS		
Day 1	Genesis 1:1-2	"Big Bang" to start everything. The beginning and expansion of the universe (~13.8 BYA to now)
Days 1 and 2	+ Genesis 1:3-8	Continued formation and development of our galaxy, solar system, and Earth. Earth's atmosphere changes. (~13.2 to 4.6 BYA)
Days 3 and 4	Genesis 1:9-19	Development of Earth supports plant and primitave life. Evaporation causes a greenhouse effect. (~4.6 to 3.8 BYA)

SCIENTIFIC EVENTS "FOLDED" INTO THE SIX BIBLICAL CREATION DAYS		
Days 5 and 6	Genesis 1:20-25	Explosion of multicellular and early simple life. Complex air, land, and marine life appear. (~3.8 BYA to 543 MYA)
Day 6	Genesis 1:26-31	Appearance of advanced animals (hominids), early modern "humans," and biblical humans (~543 MYA to now)

Figure 21: Scientific Events "Folded" into Six Biblical Creation Days

Specifically, the scientific explanation for each "creation day" is expanded to include the major validated scientific eras and their significant events.

> NOTE: The following scientific eras and events are from a "cause-and-effect" time perspective. They are further described in detail in Hugh Ross' book *Improbable Planet: How Earth Became Humanity's Home.* Here, a short description and "flow" of these events is provided for each era.[415] They are illustrated in figures 24 to 28. They provide the scientific explanations for the "starting" and "shaping" of the universe, Earth, and life itself. Also, the initial chronology of the universe, as in the first creation day. This chronology is also detailed in the "Chronology of the Universe" (Wikipedia),[416] while the other creation days are detailed in the "History of Earth" (Wikipedia).[417]

Creation Day 1

God created the heavens and the earth.

— Genesis 1:1–2

A "Big Bang" to Start Everything — the Beginning and Initial Expansion of the Universe

Cosmologists, astrophysicists, and other historical scientists break down these "big bang" events into nine categories (with associated estimated times) for a better understanding or explanation of how the universe "unfolded" into its current but nevertheless still ever-changing conditions after the beginning or at time equal to zero (T=0).

> NOTE: The symbol ~ indicates an approximation. Again, "BYA" means billions of years ago, and "MYA" means millions of years ago. In addition, the events for each day are briefly described in the "cause-and-effect" diagrams. Finally, some of the days are combined to reflect specific scientific events. They are slightly adjusted from the RTB sequences.

- Plank and quantum gravity era (up to perhaps at ~$T=10^{-43}$ of a second after T=0?) **(NOTE: This means a decimal point and then forty-three zeros after it!)**
- Grand unification era (~$T=10^{-43}$ to ~10^{-36} of a second)
- Electroweak era including an inflationary period (~$T=10^{-36}$ to ~10^{-10} of a second)
- Elementary particle era and quantum fluctuation period (~$T=10^{-10}$ to ~ 0.001 of a second)

- Nucleosynthesis era (~T=0.001 of a second to roughly ~T=3 or 4 minutes)
- Photon era (~T=3 to 4 minutes to less than ~380,000/400,000 years)
- Cosmic dark ages and the recombination era (~T=380,000/400,000 years to ~150 million years)
- Reionization era (~T=150 million years to ~1 billion years)
- Galaxy formation and evolution era (~T=1 to ~10/12.8 billion years)

Figure 22 illustrates these periods with associated main scientific events within each era. This diagram summarizes the formation and development of the universe. It traces the changes in the cosmos to its earliest known moments. Except for the very beginning or T=0 to ~T=10^{-43} of a second (a.k.a. plank and quantum periods), this evidence was corroborated by independent scientific discoveries. Data were measured and verified from the different land and satellite telescope images.

In particular, the cosmic microwave background (CMB) radiation findings (e.g., afterglow light pattern) were primarily from NASA's Cosmic Background Explorer (COBE) and WMAP satellites and later from the European Space Agency's (ESA) Planck satellite and now the James Webb space telescope.

CAUSES AND EFFECTS FOR THE BEGINNING AND DEVELOPMENT OF THE UNIVERSE	
Causes	Effects
Big Bang "Explosion" *Space expands.* *Quantum gravity dominates.*	· Lambda CMD Hot Big Bang Theory and predictions · Initial state or condition of a "Cosmic Ball" or "Singularity" · T = 0 (or Beginning)

CAUSES AND EFFECTS FOR THE BEGINNING AND DEVELOPMENT OF THE UNIVERSE	
Causes	Effects
Hyper Expansion & Cooling *Separation of forces and dimensions.*	· Sea of subatomic (quantum) particles and fields form in space and time · Relativity starts to dominate · To T = 10^{-36} seconds
Expansion & Cooling *Nucleosynthesis*	· Quantum fluctuations in Quark-Gluon Plasma "Soup" · Protons and neutrons form · To T = .001 second
Expansion & Cooling *Recombination of ionized particles.* *Decoupling of photons.*	· Positive-charged nuclei and negative-charged electrons form · Hydrogen fuses into helium + trace amounts... (20 seconds) · To T = 3 minutes
Expansion & Cooling *Reionization*	· Neutral atoms form · Gravity-Matter dominates after 47,000 years onward · CMB observed · Cosmic Dark Ages start (no photons released) · To 380,000 years
Expansion & Cooling *Star/Galaxy separation*	· First large-scaled structures form (early stars, galaxies, etc.) · Dark Ages end (1B years) · To 1B years
Present *Universe as it appears today*	· Stellar evolution: additional star, galaxy, planet life-cycles · Heavy elements form · Dark energy dominates after 7/8B years · To 13.8B years

Figure 22: Causes and Effects for the Beginning and Development of the Universe

Based upon figure 22's events, figure 23 summarizes a "big bang" timeline for our universe's beginning, formation, and development, which is necessary to support early primitive or primordial life on Earth.

"Big Bang" Eras and Events Timeline

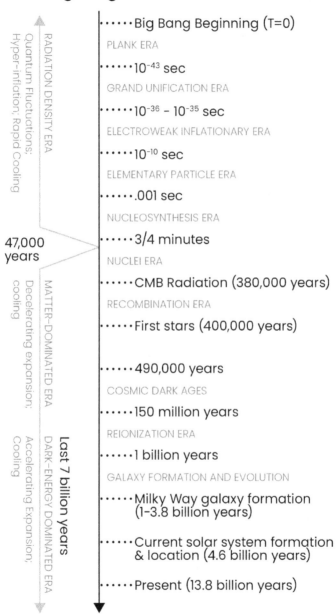

Figure 23: "Big Bang" Eras and Events Time Line

(NOTE: Dates are approximate and time line not drawn to scale.)

However, what triggered the scientific "big bang" to form or evolve the universe and everything in it?

Astrophysicist Paul Sutter has said, "In the beginning, there was a question mark. All else followed. The end." He went on to say that from his article entitled "What Triggered the Big Bang? It's Complicated":

> The "Big Bang" Theory is a cosmological scientific model of the history of the Universe tracing evolution and the cosmos to its earliest moments. It is supported by extensive evidence. The evidence started with Edwin Hubble's note that every galaxy is, on average, flying away from every other galaxy. The Universe is expanding and today it is different from how it was yesterday, and it will be different tomorrow. And if you notice every day that the Universe is getting bigger, you can make a tremendous leap of logic to conclude that, long ago, the Universe was... smaller.[418]

The history of the "big bang" theory began with the "big bang's" development from observations and theoretical considerations. Much of the theoretical work in cosmology now involves extensions and refinements to the basic "big bang" model. The theory itself was originally formalized by Belgian Catholic priest, theoretical physicist, mathematician, astronomer, and professor of physics, Georges Lemaître. Hubble's law of the expansion of the universe provided foundational support for the theory. In 1931, he proposed in his "hypothesis of the primeval atom" that the universe began with the "explosion" of the "primeval atom" — what was later called the "big bang."[419]

To expand upon this "deductive" theory, NASA uses the "Lambda cold dark matter hot big bang model," which is generally accepted as the standard model today by most scientists.

> NOTE: The "Lambda" term contains the cosmological constant for dark energy, the most Dominant component in the Universe, and the "Cold Dark Matter" (CDM) term contains the second most Dominant component in the Universe. It is the simplest model that provides a reasonably good account (*evidence*) of the following properties or entities of the Universe: 1) existence and structure of the Cosmic Microwave Background (CMB) radiation, 2) abundance of hydrogen (including deuterium), helium, and lithium, 3) large-scale distribution of galaxies, and 4) an accelerated expansion of the Universe observed in the light from distant galaxies.[420]

In summary, in Genesis creation day 1, "God" created the heavens and the earth... Most historical scientists and all evolutionary scientists believe the universe started and expanded naturally via the "big bang." Although the universe is still changing (e.g., stars are born and die; planets, moons, and other space objects form), the emphasis shifts from what is happening in outer space to the earth itself. Nevertheless, there are still changes to the universe during all the remaining days of creation. On the other hand, creationists call these events from a "creation big bang" perspective because God was involved from the very beginning to form His creation.

Creation Days 1 (continued) and 2

Light appeared.

— Genesis 1:3–5

Water separated from water calling the expanse sky.

— summarized version of Genesis 1:6–8

Continued Formation and Development of Our Galaxy, Solar System, and Earth — Earth's Atmosphere Changes

Cosmologists, astrophysicists, and other historical scientists have broken down this era into the following nine major events and conditions for the formation of our Milky Way galaxy (MWG), solar system (planets, moons, asteroids, etc.), and early (relatively simple) life to be supported on Earth (see figure 24 for these key events.):

- Location and formation of our solar system within the Milky Way galaxy (starting at ~T=13.2 BYA)
- Movement and formation of our solar system (~T=13.2 to 4.6 BYA)
- Formation of our planets (~T=4.5 BYA)
- Moon-forming event (30 to 50 MYA after formation of Earth)
- Late veneer event (50 to 100 MYA after moon-forming event)
- Late heavy bombardment period (~T=3.9 to 3.8 BYA)
- Arrival of early (primitive or primordial) life (starting at ~T=3.9 to 3.7 BYA)
- Launch of plate tectonics and its contribution to early life (starting at ~T=3.8 BYA)
- Formation of continents and oceans and its contributions to support early life (~T=3.8 to 3.0 BYA)

CAUSE-AND-EFFECT RELATIONSHIPS OF EVENTS NECESSARY TO SUPPORT EARLY LIFE ON EARTH	
Causes	Effects
Formation of the Solar System	· Dust and gas coalesced from supernova to form sun and disk · Originated closer to MWG center than present location (Hadean Era)
Movement of the Solar System	· Surfed outward along MWG's spiral arms · Located in Galactic Habitable Zone, just inside corotation distance and 2 arms
Formation of Planets	· Core Accretion Scenario forming rocky and gas planets · Nice Movement Model resulting in current configuration · Grand Tack Event · 1:2 Orbital Resonance · Jumping Jupiter
Moon-Forming Event	· Mars-sized object collided with Earth, changing Earth's atmosphere, crust, mantle, tilt, rotation, magnetic field, etc. · Moon coalesced from ejected dust and gas
Late Veneer Event	· Planetesimals impacted Earth, affecting orbit, etc. · Added key mass, elements, water, and organic matter on Earth.
Late Heavy Bombardment	· Gravitational Disturbance caused massive shower of asteroids and comets to pelt the inner Solar System · Changed Earth's matle, core, oceans, atmo-sphere, etc.

CAUSE-AND-EFFECT RELATIONSHIPS OF EVENTS NECESSARY TO SUPPORT EARLY LIFE ON EARTH	
Causes	Effects
Arrival of Early Life	· Temperatures cooled · Simple organisms formed and survived harsh conditions · Contributions from plate tectonics and the formation of continents and oceans

Figure 24: Cause-and-Effect Relationships of Events Necessary to Support Life on Earth

In summary, the remaining part of day 1 and all of day 2 continue with the formation and final development of our MWG and solar system including its planets and moons (as well as other space objects). Now, with the formation of our star (e.g., Sun), Earth, and a single moon, an observer on Earth could detect for the first time the appearance of light that penetrated the darkness, the cycle of day and night, and the separation of the atmospheres to form the sky. This scientific interpretation basically agrees with the Genesis account. Science describes the formation of the troposphere, the atmospheric layer above the ocean where clouds form and humidity reside, as distinct from the stratosphere, mesosphere, and ionosphere lying above. This interpretation receives confirmation in Psalm 148 (a psalm reflecting on Genesis 1), which distinguishes the "highest heavens" from the "waters above the skies" and declares that God "set them in place."

Creation Days 3 and 4

"Let water under the sky to be gathered in one place and let dry ground appear"; God creates plants and trees.

— summarized version of Genesis 1:9–13

Sun, moon, and stars are now visible.

— summarized version of Genesis 1:14–19

Development of the Earth Supports Plant and Primitive Life — Evaporation Causes a Greenhouse Effect

Astrophysicists, geoscientists, and planetary scientists continue to further break down major events that support advanced life on Earth after the late heavy bombardment (LHB) period. Numerous oxygen and mass extinctions and mass speciation events on Earth provide the necessary elements and conditions for advanced life in the sea and on land.

- Great oxygenation event or GOE (~T=3.8 to 2.45 BYA)
- Slushball "ice" event (~T=2.45 to 2.32 BYA)
- Loma Gundi and Shunga ("ice") events (~T=2.32 to 2.0 BYA)
- Boring billion period (~T=2.0 to 1.0 BYA to perhaps 750 MYA)
- Cryogenian era (~T=750 to 580 MYA)
- Neoproterozoic oxygenation event or NOE (~T=750 to 580 MYA)
- First and second Avalon explosion eras (~T=635 to 543 MYA)

As a summary of these areas, figure 25 illustrates and summarizes the scientific events on Earth that led to simple and then advanced new animal and plant life.

CAUSE-AND-EFFECT RELATIONSHIPS FOR SIMPLE/ADVANCED LIFE ON EARTH	
Causes	Effects
Great Oxygenation Event (GOE)	· Major jump in atmospheric oxygen level (3.8 - 2.45 BYA) generated major glaciation events and a slush-ball (~2.45 - 2.32 BYA) · Simple unicellular organisms only · Deposition to minerals
Loma Gundi Event	· Major plate tectonics buried bio and mineral deposits (~2.2 - 2.056 BYA) · Climate warms
Shunga Event	· Transferred deposits into petroleum, kerogen, bitumen, natural gas, etc. (~2 BYA) · Crash in Oxygen
Boring Billions	· Slush-ball event · Geochemical cycles, ecology, oxygen, temperature, and tectonic activity remained mostly the same (~750 - 580 MYA) · Biomass/Biodiversity
Formation of 5 Supercontinents leaving Pangaea	· Intense nutrient delivery to continental shelves and shallow seas via erosion; boosted plate tectonics (~2.7 - 0.25 BYA) · Biological Soil Crust (BSC) microorganism colonies everywhere

CAUSE–AND–EFFECT RELATIONSHIPS FOR SIMPLE/ADVANCED LIFE ON EARTH	
Causes	Effects
Cryogenian Era (CE) & Neoproterozoic Oxygenation Event (NOE)	· CE had 3 glaciation events (~750 - 580 MYA) · NOE was 2nd oxygen boost right after CE · New plant species
1st and 2nd Avalon; Cambrian Biological Explosions	· Large-bodied sea-floor fossils found (~575 MYA) · Mass extinctions · More advanced animals found (~560 - 542 MYA)

Figure 25: Cause-and-Effect Relationships for Simple/ Advanced Life on Earth

In summary, day 2 exposed the ground as the water receded; days 3 and 4 formed a cloudy atmosphere, and all that evaporation on the earth had a giant greenhouse effect, so God created plants, which needed this kind of perfect growing climate. (NOTE: God did not create the sun, moon, and stars on day 4 — as some literal or strict Creationists believe; it happened on day 1. Also, other space objects became apparent for the first time from the perspective of an observer on the earth as the atmosphere went from transcalent to transparent.)

Creation Days 5 and 6

God created marine creatures as well as winged birds.

— summarized version of Genesis 1:20–23

God created land animals.

— summarized version of Genesis 1:24–25

Explosion of Multicellular and Animal Life — Advanced Air, Land, and Marine Life Appear

Numerous fossils and traces of fossils have been discovered, especially during the Cambrian and post-Cambrian periods, by paleontologists, archeologists, and other historical scientists. These findings indicate a significant "jump" in sophistication with a "sudden" and "dramatic" increase in the structure and functionality of numerous complex and advanced organisms. Paleontologist Kevin Peterson characterized this significant "pow" as an apparent quantum leap in organismal and ecological complexity within "a geological blink of an eye."[421] Through radioisotope dating methods, scientists have determined that these changes occurred over a relatively brief period of geological time (perhaps less than 5–6 million years in some cases). As previously mentioned, what is rather unexpected for geologists and paleontologists to find is that these changes have occurred after a little less than 3 billion years of "stasis" of relatively no change from single-celled microorganisms.

After nearly 3 billion years of only various single-celled organisms surviving through "hostile" conditions on land, in the oceans, and in the atmosphere, multicellular organisms seemed to suddenly appear in a little over a half a billion years ago. They appeared in the Precambrian or Ediacaran biological period and were enabled by the right conditions, such as major increases in atmospheric oxygen and extensive biomass (e.g., of dead organisms) to support new life requirements. Most of these "enigmatic" organisms went extinct and seemed to have only a relatively small contribution to the Cambrian explosion of animal life, according to most scientists.

Based upon these scientific findings, new plant and animal multi-cellular life forms seem to "suddenly" appear on Earth! They are found in the following periods:

- Additionally, just after the second Avalon geological era, the Ediacaran biota (multicellular organisms) existed from ~635 to 543 MYA.
- The Cambrian geological era then occurred from ~543 to 485 MYA, when the "biological big bang" occurred. During this era, Cambrian biota (organisms with complete body designs, plans, and systems integrated together to function as a whole) appeared rather suddenly. This sudden explosion of these advanced organisms occurred around 543 MYA.
- The post-Cambrian biological period was from ~485 MYA to the present. Three major geological eras are summarized by scientists that record mass extinction and mass speciation events with their approximate dates. Again, these advanced forms appeared suddenly. Numerous fossils were found, and they were placed in the Paleozoic, Mesozoic, and Cenozoic periods.[422]

Figure 26 illustrates and summarizes these additional events and their cause-and-effect relationships within the Paleozoic, Mesozoic, and Cenozoic eras and periods after the sudden Cambrian explosion of major new animal body plans and phyla containing skeletons. It also shows the different animals that existed during these eras and periods.

CAUSE-AND-EFFECT RELATIONSHIPS BETWEEN EVENTS IN THE PALEOZOIC, MESOZOIC, AND CENOZOIC ERAS	
Causes	Effects
Cambrian Explosion	· Sudden appearance of many animal body plan/ phyla containing skeletons (~543 - 542 MYA)
Paleozoic Era (~542 - 251 MYA)	*Ordovician-Silurian Transition* (~444 MYA) · Jawed and bony fish, arthropods (invertebrate animals with exoskeletons, segmented bodies, & jointed appendages), & vascular land plants *Lau Event* (~424 MYA) · Extinction of 2/3 of fish taxa *Devonian Period* (~420 - 359 MYA) · New plant and fish species, trees, and insects appeared *Devonian-Carboniferous Transition* (~359 MYA) · Major extinction of 50% genera *Carboniferous Mass Extinction Event* (~359 - 305 MYA) · Amphibians were dominant; vast forests grew · Large stores of limestone & petroleum produced · Climate change (from warm & humid to cold & dry) led to glaciations, drop in sea level, and destruction of carboniferous rainforests · Reptile species introduced (305 MYA) *Permian-Triassic Mass Extinction* (~252.3 MYA) · 90-96% of marine species wiped out · 70% of land species wiped out

CAUSE-AND-EFFECT RELATIONSHIPS BETWEEN EVENTS IN THE PALEOZOIC, MESOZOIC, AND CENOZOIC ERAS	
Causes	Effects
Mesozoic Era (~252 - 66 MYA)	*Triassic Recovery Period* (~252 - 201 MYA) · Dinosaurs and mamals first appeared *Triassic-Jurassic Mass Extinction Event* or TJEE (~201 MYA) · 1/2 of all species on Earth extinguished by wild-fires and volcanic ash *Jurasic Recovery after TJEE* · Mass speciation of large theropod dinosaurs appeared *Jurassic-Cretaceous Radiations & Bio Deposits* (~201 - 66 MYA) · Breakup of Pangea expanded coastlines, continental shelves, and shallow seas · Weather changed to humid · Temperatures increased · Rainforests replaced deserts · Conifers become dominant · Dinosaurs become dominant on land · Fish and marine reptiles dominate oceans/seas · First birds, mammals, and lizards appeared (~144 - 66 MYA)

CAUSE-AND-EFFECT RELATIONSHIPS BETWEEN EVENTS IN THE PALEOZOIC, MESOZOIC, AND CENOZOIC ERAS	
Causes	Effects
Cenozoic Period (~66 - 0 MYA)	*Cretaceous–Paleogene Extinction Event* (~66 MYA) · At least 75% of Earth's species went extince · Paleogene Recovery Era of mass speciation (~66 - 25 MYA) · Rise of Tibetan Plate (~50 MYA) · Antarctica split off from Australia (~40 MYA) and from tip of South America (~23 MYA) · Appearance of angiosperms (plants with flat leaves and seeds embedded in fruit) and new grass species, new advanced birds and large-bodied mammals, & diverse insects *Neogene Continental Alignment* (~23 - 2.59 MYA) · Continents migrated to current positions; affected climate and optimized landmasses *Quaternary Period* (~2.588 - 0 MYA) · Massive sheets of ice cyclically advanced and retreated over much of northern hemisphere, setting up the conditions for human life · Earth still in 'ice age' — 5% of total land area · Continents occupy 29% of Earth's surface area · Isthmus of Panama land bridge formed (~3 MYA) · Greenland moved northward

Figure 26: Cause-and-Effect Relationships Between Events in the Paleozoic, Mesozoic, and Cenozoic Eras

In summary, scientists believe water creatures (fresh or salt) usually include mollusks, crustaceans, fish, first mammals (whales, porpoises, etc.), and amphibians. It may also include reptiles, such as the dinosaurs from 250 to 65 million years ago. Additionally, all kinds of birds (and other flying creatures) were created. Many of these animal species were radically different from any previously mentioned. These living ("soulish") creatures could be described as capable of expressing yearnings, emotions, passions, and will, is implied. Day 3 provided the vegetation for water and air for the animals to live on the earth. Scientists believe that three specific kinds of land animals appear: livestock, creatures that move along the ground, and wild animals.

Creation Day 6 (continued)

So, God created man in his own image.

— Genesis 1:26–31

Appearance of "Advanced" Animals (Hominids) and Modern "Humans"

According to evolutionary geologists, chemists, biologists, paleontologists, and anthropologists, the first hominid or "human" life began around seven to eight million years ago in one or more places in Africa. Most paleoanthropologists provide the following types and dates for these hominids, as previously mentioned. They consider them as the "missing links" or "transitional intermediates" that "evolved" into anatomically modern humans or Homo sapiens *sapiens*.

Ardipithecus group (~5.6 to 4.4 MYA) — evolutionary scientists believe these earliest "humans" are our closest link to other primates (except possibly for the Sahelanthropus *tchadensis*). They evolved in Africa and took the first step toward walking upright.

> NOTE: A species called Sahelanthropus *tchadensis* or "hope for life" was discovered in Chad (Africa) in 2001 and dates to about 6 to 7 million years in age and is considered, by some scientists, as the earliest

hominid. It walked erect, possessed a brain size close to a chimpanzee, and lived in both the woodlands and green savannas. It was called the "Tumai man" and had a complete skull, along with a partial jawbone and some teeth.[423]

Australopithecus group (~4.2 to 1.9 MYA) — species in this group of early "humans" walked upright on a regular basis, but they still climbed trees.

Paranthropus group (~2.6 to 0.6 MYA) — same as the Australopithecus group, except they had large teeth and powerful jaws, which enabled them to feed on a variety of foods.

Homo group (~2.4 MYA to present) — like modern humans, other subspecies in this group had large brains and used tools. Most of the fossils and associated artifacts come from this group. Members of this group are believed to be the first to expand beyond Africa.

Within the Homo *sapiens* genera, some paleoanthropologists have identified at least four potentially distinct (sub) species. However, where they came from has three different views:

Since the 1970s, Homo *heidelbergensis* assumed the central role in human evolutionary scenarios, representing a key transitional intermediate linking H. *erectus* to modern humans and Neanderthals. Some anthropologists believe the "Heidelberg Man" is the common ancestor that gave rise to two separate lineages leading to 1) modern humans, 2) Neanderthals, and 3) the Denisovans. Others think that H. *heidelbergensis* led to Neanderthals and the Denisovans, with H. *antecessor* serving as the common ancestor to the modern human and Neandertal-Denisovan branches of the human evolutionary tree.[424]

The four distinct subspecies are the:

- Homo sapiens *idaltu* fossils were from three crania dated 154,000 and 160,000 years ago, which were found in a South African cave in 2010 and one of the first Homo sapiens subspecies.[425]
- Homo sapiens *denisova* (e.g., Denisovans) fossils were from a female finger bone dated at 40,000 and 50,000 years ago. They also found molar teeth from three males dated 30,000 to 100,00 years ago. Also, a partial leg or arm bone fragment from a male dated 90,000 years ago — all found in a Siberian cave in 2010. These now-extinct humans lived as far back as 200,000 years ago.[426]
- Homo sapiens *neanderthalensis* (e.g., Neanderthals) fossils were from a nearly complete specimen dated between 40,000 and 250,000 to 400,000 years ago, which was first found in the Neander Valley in a West German cave in 1856. The Neanderthal genome has been completely sequenced, and studies are being conducted to compare them with modern humans as well as the interbreeding between these two species.
- Homo sapiens *sapiens* or modern humans (or just Homo *sapiens* by most scientists). The human genome has been completely sequenced, and research continues to study how their DNA, genes, chromosomes, epigenetics, and the environment affect the development of individuals.

NOTE: Most of these naturalistic scientists see the above groups from an evolutionary perspective and see the progression of life go or evolve from simple to complex. However, even though there are some progressive creation scientists who basically agree with these findings, they disagree with *how* they occurred. That is, they believe that God intervened in this progression rather than just exclusively occurring naturally over time. From a biblical perspective, where creation breaks or splits between "animals" and "humans" is extremely important and relevant to the philosophical worldview belief of God or no God, as it applies to each person's life journey. According to Genesis day 6, the "creatures that move along the ground" could include "pre-Adamic" or before "Adam" animals such as the Neanderthals and others from the Homo group and, therefore, distinct from anatomically modern humans from this same "human-structured" classification system (based on the traditional Linnaeus hierarchy).

In summary, God created humans in His image on day 6. Days 3 and 4 provided the "right" atmosphere, soil, and vegetation (plants and trees), and days 5 and 6 provided food for sea, land, and air animals and humans to survive and reproduce on Earth.

Summary

Scientists agree with the biblical account of creation in two primary ways. First, there must be the necessary conditions for life to begin and survive on Earth. Second, there is a logical and chronological order or sequence for the development of life — from very simple single-celled life to very advanced or complex animals to ultimately human life, from structural (morphological) and physiological perspectives.

PART 3:

"A Time to Reflect on Our Beliefs"

CHAPTER 11:

An Integrated Origins Perspective — A "Big" Picture Summary

Introduction

The purpose of this chapter is to bring together all the significant areas discussed in the previous chapters and illustrate them from a "big" picture perspective. The approach combines the historical and philosophical views.

The historical view describes the compatibility and incompatibility models between science and religion. The cooperative (or integrative) and the dialog (or intersection) perspectives comprise some level (or lack of) compatibility between these two domains. The incompatibility models describe the conflict (or hostile) thesis and independent (or separate) perspectives between these domains. Which model one chooses factors into an ongoing "tension" between the role of science and/or religion (and correspondingly, reason and faith) and how they "factor" into our understanding of our origins. Also, these perspectives are relevant to the understanding of the role of evolution and creation and their implications regarding our belief in "God" as the Creator. The PEW Research Institute addressed this situation.

The philosophical view tends to be much more complicated. This perspective starts with the assumption of "tension" between science and religion. The new Pew Research Center findings show that most Americans (59%) say, in general, that science often conflicts with religion, although a sizeable minority of adults (38%) consider science and religion to be mostly compatible. Those most inclined to see religion and science as generally in conflict are those who, themselves, have no religious affiliation or are not religiously observant. At the same time, however, most adults (68%) say there is no conflict between their personal religious beliefs and science. Among the three-in-ten adults who say their own religious beliefs conflict with science, the most common area of conflict centers around teachings about the creation of the universe and evolution.[427]

Science is an inquiry process and attempts to understand empirical evidence obtained from the laws of nature (a.k.a. naturalism). Scientific disciplines observe and measure only natural events and phenomena. The evidence or discoveries obtained by various scientific disciplines is from the scientific method of reasoning. However, many scientists recognize that faith indirectly affects this overall inquiry process in coming to their validated conclusions.

Regarding religion, the practice of one's faith is from different religious disciplines and associated theological doctrines. Faith involves a personal or individual journey. This journey considers a belief in a biblical single God or multiple gods as the Creator(s) of everything. Supernaturalism incorporated these concepts. These divine or supernatural occurrences use authoritative doctrines and texts, such as the Bible and personal experiences, to reveal what is believed to be the real "truth" to our reality. Also, most religious individuals and organizations recognize that reason plays, at least, an indirect role in establishing a rational and believable faith and, ultimately, a purpose for our existence in this world.

The position taken by the author is that both domains must be considered in searching for knowledge and "truth" regarding our origins! By considering both religion and science from an integrated perspective, one's existing beliefs have the possibility of either being changed or enhanced (but hopefully not ignored as to their relevance). The formulas *Faith + Evidence = Belief (Claim)*, *Beliefs + Desires = Actions*, and *Knowledge = Properly Justified Beliefs* are very relevant in the understanding of both domains.

More specifically, this integrated approach is relevant in discussing and deciding on different evolution and creation models as explanations for our origins. The main evolution explanations have progressed over time from classical Darwinism to neo-Darwinism to modern synthesis and to the proposed extended evolutionary synthesis concepts. In response to these evolutionary explanations, the main creation categories include creation science, (neo-creation) intelligent design, and the Reasons to Believe concepts. Historically and practically, they were generally organized to respond to these evolutionary concepts.

Finally, the author believes these beliefs can influence and are usually incorporated into one's philosophy of life. These beliefs ultimately determine one's worldview or purpose in life. The worldview positions regarding whether God or gods exist or are involved in the creative process include the religious (theological) or ideological forms of theism, deism, agnosticism, atheism, secular humanism, and wokeism.

> NOTE: However, the reverse is also true. That is, one's worldview can and does influence beliefs in how we approach the concepts of evolution and/or creation.

As illustrated in figure 27, this consolidated approach and *fifth* perspective combines philosophical and historical processes to better understand our origins. Each block is summarized below.

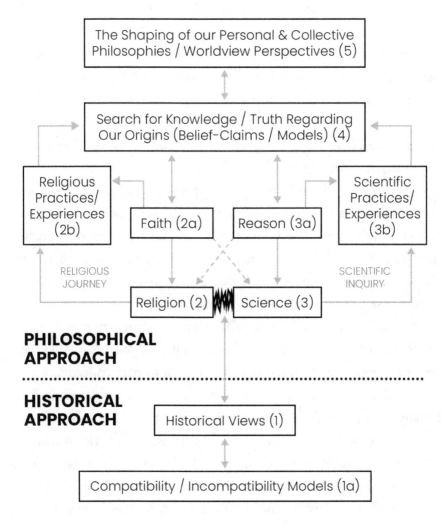

Figure 27: "Big" Picture Perspective of Our Origins

Historical Approach Summary
(Block 1)

The *historical views* provide an overall foundation for understanding complex and often controversial relationships between "man-organized" initiated activities, beliefs, characteristics, and concepts in the domains of the religion and science. The "tension" between science and religion has existed from the very beginning of human (written) history but never so much as initiated with the onset of modern scientific findings and conclusions starting with the modern era in the late 1700s and early 1800s in the "West." This modern era of natural science is often associated with the introduction of the Darwinian biological theory of evolution in the mid-1800s, attributed to naturalist Charles Darwin. Two models represent the intellectual historical discussion and relationship between religion and science: compatibility and incompatibility perspectives.

These intellectual historical views or models were discussed in some detail. Again, these models were initially developed by the theologian, priest, and physicist John Polkinghorne. Discussion of the models contained the debate over the compatibility and/or incompatibility between religion and science. These models are directly related to our origins, as discussed in chapter 2, "Survey of Five Origins Questions and Possible Answers."

Compatibility and/or Incompatibility
Views/Models (Block 1a)

For a quick review, two models consider science and religion to be compatible (to some degree), and two consider science and religion incompatible. These models distinguish between reason and faith and their impact on science and religion.

Compatibility Models

The *cooperative or integrative model* shows that even though the interactions between the influences of science, theology, politics, and social and economic concerns are complex, the productive engagement between science and religion throughout history should be duly stressed as the norm. These proponents advocate strong compatibility or organic connection between reason and faith. Additionally, perhaps even parity with articles of faith being philosophically demonstrated by deductive reasoning from widely shared theological premises or inductive reasoning from common experiences.

The *dialog model* comprises an overlapping community of interested and involved scientists, priests, clergymen, theologians, and engaged nonprofessionals. These proponents advocate weak compatibility between reason and faith, though both maintain distinct realms of evaluation and cogency. (NOTE: This model was used in chapter 10, where validated scientific discoveries were "folded" into the Genesis religious account of the six "days of creation." It is amazing to see how God could biblically describe the overall creation framework and foundation for His Hebrew people in ancient times but resonate with modern "Western" society and culture from a scientific perspective! This "inclusive" feature provides us with a basis to understand the involvement of both religion [e.g., creation] and science [e.g., evolution] regarding our origins.)

How Are Science and Religion Similar or Compatible?[428]

Here are some of the key similarities between science and religion. They both have historical traditions that exhibit development over time and places for personal insight and communal discernment; analytic and synthetic reasoning can be found in both; they continue to be formative elements shaping an increasingly global human community, serve to jeopardize and contribute to the common good, and involve interpretations of belief claims (science over controversial findings and religion over the proper understanding and meaning of scriptural passages) and community acceptance.

Incompatibility Models

Most contemporary historians now reject the *conflict thesis model.* These proponents implied (and fabricated) a perceived "warfare" or genuine rivalry between reasoning (via the scientific method) and faith (via religious revelation).

Today, the *independence model* (or NOMA Model) is taught in many science classes in US public schools. These proponents advocate an incompatibility that is distinctly compartmentalized between reason (aimed at empirical truth) and faith (aimed at divine truth).

How Are Science and Religion Different or Incompatible?[429]

Here are some of the key differences between science and religion. Science: provides explanations, not proof; depends on deliberate, explicit, and formal testing (of the natural world) and explanations for how the world is, the processes that led to its present state and its possible future; validates numerous independent observations and measurements by repeating well-confirmed scientific explanations; serves the scientific community as a reliable theory until new evidence is discovered, which may confirm the current understanding or revise or replace the answers; demonstrates a theory in science is the highest form of scientific explanation, not just a "mere" opinion.

On the other hand, religion may draw upon scientific explanations, in part, as a reliable way of knowing what the world is like, about which they seek to discern its ultimate meaning through a supernatural cause (this view is vital when scientific evidence is lacking or problematic); test the religious understandings of the world as incidental, implicit, and informal during the life of the religious community; draw insights from personal insight and traditional authority (i.e., authoritative texts); and include traditions of rational reflection.

Philosophical Approach Summary (Blocks 2–5)

The philosophical approach provides a "bridge" between the religious and scientific concepts for a better understanding of our origins. Philosophy unifies seemingly complex and irreconcilable concepts. The assumption was that by obtaining a more complete and balanced treatment of the beliefs behind the concepts of creation and evolution, we would be able to discover reasonable or rational answers to our philosophical questions. And by doing so, we could consider and perhaps incorporate these belief claims into our personal and collective philosophies regarding our origins. Because "when our real-life situations are filtered through the grid of our philosophy, this becomes our worldview."[430] These processes are represented by a:

- religious journey (2, 2a, and 2b) and
- scientific inquiry (3, 3a, and 3b).

Both processes are circular such that they are changeable or malleable (as seen historically) and are not only significantly influenced by each other but also by the historical views/debates just previously mentioned in the historical approach.

Search for Knowledge/Truth Regarding Our Origins (Belief Claims/Models) (Block 4)

Both processes contribute to our search for knowledge and, ultimately, "truth" regarding understanding our origins. This endeavor identifies some significant belief claims championed by religious believers and/or scientists. Initially, these belief claims were consolidated into religious/

theological or scientific perspectives. The religious/theological belief claims incorporate faith/divine revelation, and the scientific claims use pure reason (with no bias). These belief claims have helped consolidate our perspectives regarding the evolution and creation concepts.

Four main evolutionary models or concepts were presented:

- Classical Darwinism (CD)
- Neo-Darwinism (ND)
- Modern synthesis (MS) — a.k.a. neo-Darwinian synthesis
- Extended evolutionary synthesis or EES (proposed but not entirely accepted by the scientific community)

In addition, and perhaps in response to these and other evolutionary models, three main "Western" creation models or concepts were presented (which are advocated by current and active organizations, respectively, that believe in the biblical God or an intelligent designer as the Creator):

- Creation science (CS)
- Intelligent design (ID) (NOTE: ID considers themselves more from a scientific perspective, but the US courts have ruled that they are religious) — also, some call them "neo-creationists"
- Reasons to Believe (RTB) Ministry

The Shaping of Our Personal and Collective Philosophies/Worldview Perspectives (Block 5)

These belief claim concepts, as represented by the above models or explanations, significantly contribute to the impact of our personal and collective philosophies. Often, they influence our worldview philosophical and theological perspectives. There are four dominant worldview perspectives or positions that factor into our everyday life experiences that also relate to "God":

A theistic position is where one believes in the supernatural (such as the biblical monotheistic "God") as the creator of the universe, Earth, life, and ultimately humanity. He is constantly involved in his creation. (NOTE: Polytheistic gods are also recognized as a possible but unrealistic explanation for creation. As documented in their scriptures and other holy or ancient texts, multiple gods do "terrible" things to each other to "create" our world.)

A deistic position is where one believes there is a "God" (not necessarily the biblical God) who created everything but who stands apart and does not deign to intervene or interfere in any way with creation (a.k.a. "watchmaker principle"). God exclusively uses naturalistic principles to evolve one form or state into progressive or advanced stages.

An atheistic position is where one believes only in the natural occurrences as initiating and contributing to the evolutionary formation and progression of everything in nature. Therefore, these individuals believe there is no Creator "God," and evolutionary principles are used exclusively.

An agnostic position is where one believes that the supernatural (such as "God") is not able to be comprehended and, therefore, is not needed or unnecessary for nature to occur and change. They tend to support evolution over creation.

Author's Disclaimer

I believe all these processes, debates, and influences are vitally necessary for us to better understand and appreciate the complexity in our origins. This "big" picture view proposes an integrated approach for future refinement and teaching. Admittedly, it is somewhat generic or simplistic but is intended to summarize and consolidate the main perspectives and ultimately form a story consistent with the previous chapters. Ultimately, any review of our origins through creation and evolution concepts comes down to whether one believes in "God" or gods or not!

A Religious Journey Summary

At the outset of the discussion of a religious journey, the reader must understand or realize that this endeavor is uniquely and ultimately a human or individual discovery process. This journey is heavily influenced by existing belief systems embodied within many different religious groups. In addition, it seems we all must go through a personal journey, whether we are scientists or nonscientists. Even if we consider ourselves as irreligious (e.g., agnostic) or nonreligious (e.g., atheistic), we consciously (either directly or indirectly) address the area of a supernatural being(s) as the possibility or the potential cause and progression of creation at some time in our lives. I believe this sense of curiosity is imbedded or "wired" into each of us. The Bible says that God created us in His image and likeness (Genesis 1:26–27) and that He has placed eternity in our hearts (Ecclesiastes 3:11). This means that we have an innate desire to know God and to seek Him out. The Bible also tells us that God is not far from any one of us and that if we seek Him with all our hearts, we will find Him (Acts 17:27; Jeremiah 29:13).

This human activity begins as mythologies that form into religions through revelations by religious leaders or prophets. Whether we believe it or not, each of us is on a personal journey to try to make some sense and purpose out of our existence. The following religious (simplified) process helps us gain additional insight into how our beliefs about creation and evolution form, maintain, and even change. This religious process is composed of the following main components:

- Historical views (previously discussed in block 1a)
- Religious concepts (block 2)

- Faith as the primary/direct factor (block 2a) and reason as the secondary/indirect factor (block 3b)
- Religious practices/experiences/conclusions (block 2c)
- Theological/Philosophical belief claims (block 4)
- The shaping of personal and collective philosophies/worldview perspectives (block 5)

What Are the Religious Concepts? (Block 2)

Religions are cultural phenomena comprised of social (e.g., human) institutions and traditional practices, sacred texts and stories, and sacred places that identify and convey or contribute to an understanding of an individual's ultimate meaning or purpose. There are similarities between all religions. They are usually identified by a founder and sacred or holy people associated with a particular religion; are defined by major churches or groups (a.k.a. faiths), denominations, or divisions; usually have holy and authoritative texts; use faith or a particular set of core beliefs; usually contain a reason for our (human) predicament and a solution for overcoming it; involve practices usually in the form of rituals, holy events, and places; contain a specific theology or understanding of "God" or gods; have specific creation and flood accounts, which usually started as oral myths or stories; and contain many mystical beliefs, movements, or groups outside the mainstream.

Religion (and its associated philosophy and theology) is considered a set of traditional beliefs followed by individuals who may be part of a larger group or community. These beliefs include the religious or traditional faiths of Judaism, Christianity, Islam, Hinduism, Buddhism, Chinese folk and Native American traditions, and others. A predominant feature of religion uses the principle of "faith" historically based upon some divine revelation and contained in some holy and authoritative text(s). The texts and doctrines of these faiths are considered authoritative because they are directly received from God (e.g., God's inspired Word) and/or based upon the teachings of the founders or influential leaders from various religions and associated, theological, and philosophical perspectives. They include but are not limited to the Jewish/Hebrew (Old) Testament Bible (i.e., Torah) and the Talmud, Christian Old and New Testament Bible, Muslim Qur'an and Hadith, Hindu Vedas, Upanishads, and Bhagavad Gita, and Buddhist Tripitaka.

> NOTE: There is no specific Chinese traditional/folk unified doctrinal statement or concise creed regarding our origins.

In addition, they may also be a personal conviction not tied to a particular religious tradition or culture, such as the New Age movement of spiritualism and current forms of secular humanism such as wokism.

Religions are diverse. They are generally defined by their texts, doctrines, and leaders. Most religions identify the ultimate with some form of deity (or spirits, such as the Native Americans), but not all do (such as Buddhism, which recognizes the ultimate reality as Brahman). They deal with the spiritual realm and focus on the supernatural perspective. The two main spiritual, biblical orientations from the Belgic Confession of Faith are:

- General revelation embodies God's creation or the natural revealing or understanding and observation of nature. From a philosophical and theological perspective, a natural revelation was communicated by God through so-called "natural" phenomena of His creative works.

- Special revelation documents God's words (such as documented in the Bible) and our insight into God's theological character. From a philosophical and theological perspective, a supernatural revelation was communicated by God through divine intervention (i.e., dreams, visions, works, miracles, testimonies, etc.)

Religions lead to a personal and communal practice of one's faith. This practice is done in many ways as observed by faithful practices usually directed or commanded by the authoritative texts and the governing bodies or individuals within that traditional religious body. Reason plays a role (often undermined because of its indirect and sometimes subtle nature of influence) that affects religion. Arguably, the principle of logic or reasonableness of the faiths is often noted or indicated by the concept of a "justified or rational religious faith." Here are some views of how reason seems to play a role. Reason is systematic and logical nature of scriptures (e.g., it makes sense), consistency of scriptures (e.g., passages do not generally contradict each other), practical nature of scriptures (can be readily applied), and philosophical and theological arguments that seem to make logical sense.

What Is Faith? (Block 2a)

Faith, and in particular, religious faith, involves a stance toward some claim that is not, at least, presently demonstrated by reason; it is a kind of attitude of trust or assent ordinarily understood to involve an act of will or a commitment; it is some kind of implicit or explicit reference to a transcendent source on the part of the believer. In a general sense, properly used faith refers to a particular type of subset of beliefs. Faith is the basis for believing in a particular religion, consistently applied to the practices of religions that constitute life experiences needed to formulate belief claims, which are consolidated into models (such as the CS, ID, and RTB explanations and models).

Scripturally, there are several passages that talk about the power of faith. In particular, Hebrews 11:1 says, "Now faith is being sure of what we hope for and certain of what we do not see." Romans 10:17 says, "Consequently, faith comes from hearing the message, and the message is heard from the word of Christ." Hebrews 11:6 says, "And without faith it is impossible to please God, because anyone who come to Him must believe that He exists and that He rewards those who earnestly seek Him."

What Are Religious Practices, Experiences, and Conclusions? (Block 2b)

Religious practices use spiritual traditions employing one's faith or conviction that decree or reenforce their religion to be true. Therefore, it represents a reality to them that governs their behavior and lifestyle. Religious practices are observances and experiences that flow from a religious commitment to synagogue, church, mosque, and other places of worship, works of charity and giving, moral self-discipline, observance of holy days and events, participation in ceremonial and traditional rituals, and obedience to their laws or doctrines.

Belief Claims and Models (Block 4)

These "Western" creation accounts or views were summarized by:

- *Young earth* (universe) *creationists* (YEC) interpret the Bible literally or strictly and are mainly represented by YEC strict or literal concepts. According to them, the Bible is a sacred text that provides an inerrant account of how the universe and all life came into existence. These proponents believe in literal six twenty-four-hour days for creation some 6,000 to 10,000 years ago, when animals were created as distinct "kinds." In addition, human beings were created through a direct act of divine intervention in the order of nature and made in God's image. They believe in a universal flood geology concept. Many conservative Christian religions advocate the creation science (CS) concept. The Institute for Creation Research advocates the CS position. This position is the most recognized position that is criticized by evolutionary scientists in creation versus evolution debates. The US courts have ruled that CS cannot be taught in public science classes because it teaches religion and, therefore, violates the First Amendment to the US Constitution.

- *Old earth* (universe) *creationists* (OEC) interpret the Bible more progressively and are mainly represented by the day-age, gap, and Reasons to Believe (RTB) concepts. According to them, the Bible, as a sacred text, is an infallible account of why the universe and all life came into existence (just like the CS position). However, they accept the "days" of creation as symbolic or figurative as "God's days." Therefore, in actual "human" days, they could represent very long periods (e.g., perhaps billions of years for each day of creation). While many aspects of nature may be the consequence of direct acts of divine creation, at the very least, these proponents hold that the very beginning of the universe and the origin of humankind are the consequences of distinct acts of divine intervention in the order of nature. In particular, the RTB concepts stress the "careful and diligent" compatibility of the Christian religion with science. The RTB's mission is to demonstrate that "sound reason and scientific research — including the latest discoveries — consistently support, rather than erode, confidence in the truth of the Bible and faith in the personal, transcendent God as revealed in both Scripture and nature."[431] More liberal or progressive Christian religions advocate the OEC concepts, such as through the RTB organization and ministry.

- *Scientific design believers* are often represented by the intelligent design (ID) concept. They propose that features of the natural world (such as the divine manipulation of DNA and the "fine-tuning" of the universe and Earth) for which no natural explanations exist can be shown analytically (i.e., mathematically or statistically) and are the result of a designing or intelligent agent as the cause. These proponents do not specify who the designer or intelligent agent is. Still, the logic of the proponent's argument requires the designer to be beyond nature or, in other words, supernatural. The ID concept is advocated by some Christian and non-Christian religions, such as the Eastern religions of Hinduism and Buddhism. Sometimes, ID individuals are referred to as "neo-creationists." The Seattle Discovery Institute advocates the ID position. Likewise, the US courts have ruled that ID is a religion and cannot be taught in public science classes because it violates the First Amendment to the US Constitution regarding the "Church v. State Separation" interpretation.

- *Theistic evolutionists* (TE) have a spectrum of beliefs. Many TE believe that the sacred text (e.g., Bible) provides an infallible account of why the universe and all life came into existence. Still, for the most part, the diversity of nature, from stars to planets to living organisms, including the human body, is a consequence of the divine using processes of evolution to create indirectly. However, other proponents assert that the very beginning of the universe, the origin of life, and the origin of what is distinctive about humankind (e.g., souls) are the consequence of direct acts of divine intervention in the order of nature. Also, some deists believe that "God" created everything (matter, energy, time, laws, etc.) in the beginning and then let evolution take over completely to form everything, including humans (e.g., watchmaker principle).

- *Evolutionary theists* (ET) believe that sacred texts (not necessarily the Bible and, therefore, this is a theological position), while giving witness to the ultimate divine source of all of nature, in no way specify the means of creation. These proponents assert that the divine creates only indirectly through evolutionary processes without any intervention in the order of nature.

How Do "Eastern" and "Western" Individuals Incorporate Evolution into Their Religious Worldviews?

While the concepts of creation and evolution seem opposite, religious believers often include evolutionary ideas in their religious worldviews.

"Eastern" (sub-Asian or Indian, Asian, and Oceanic areas) religious worldviews, such as the polytheistic and pantheistic traditions of Hinduism, Buddhism, Confucianism, etc., do not assume an all-powerful creator "God." They see the world as interconnected and dynamic and tend to engage scientific accounts of evolution (and creation) with little difficulty.

"Western" (initially from the Mediterranean area) religious worldviews, such as monotheistic traditions of Judaism, Christianity, Islam, etc., affirm a Creator "God" concerning the world has a central place and vital role in creation. In principle, they are all considered "creationists." They believe that the order of nature exists because a reality beyond nature, commonly called "God," is the ultimate cause of all existence. Many accept that "God" created the material world primarily using specific creative processes (e.g., YEC and OEC positions). Some are committed to a few specific acts of innovative divine intervention, such as the beginning of the universe and the origins of life/humankind (e.g., TE positions). Some hold that a "God" creates entirely using evolutionary processes without any intervention, even in the case of humans (e.g., ET position).

The Shaping of Personal and Collective Philosophies/Worldview Perspectives (Block 5)

In attempting to understand our origins and, ultimately, the impact of this understanding on our personal views about the meaning of life, the processes, as outlined earlier, involve embracing two aspects in the spiritual or supernatural realm of reality.

First, embracing the spiritual realm includes the overriding philosophical concept of supernaturalism and special or direct revelation alone. From an "Abrahamic" religious belief perspective (and forms or denominations of Judaism, Christianity, and Islam), individuals believing in creation alone are considered theists, while others believing in some form of creation and evolution are regarded as evolutionary theists (ET) or theistic evolutionists (TE). On the other hand, individuals believing in the "Dharmic, Asian, and Oceanic" religious belief perspectives (forms of Hinduism, Buddhism, etc.) take the position of creation alone and are theists, while others believing in some form of creation and evolution are ET/TE. In addition, some individuals may not have a clear view or care about the subject of our origins (e.g.,

Buddhists). They could be considered an atheist, agnostic, or theist from a "Western" perspective.

Second, in embracing the spiritual realm, the overriding philosophical concept of supernaturalism, general, natural, and special revelation, and "hard and soft" scientific findings are considered. Individuals believing in creation could be considered a theist, or individuals believing in some form of creation and evolution could be regarded as or tend to be evolutionary theists or in the multiple beliefs within theistic evolution. Many conservative and evolutionary scientists take the position of deism, which is generally considered within the TE concept.

A Scientific Inquiry Summary

Likewise, the reader should also understand the importance of the scientific process in gaining a better insight into the understanding of our origins. Unlike an individual's religious journey, the scientific inquiry process, while accomplished by individuals or groups of scientists, recognizes the validity of their findings and discoveries is contingent upon the general acceptance of the scientific community. Historically, this situation is regarded as a fact. How it happened is considered a theory. This circular scientific (simplified) inquiry process is composed of the following main components:

- Historical views (discussed above in block 1a)
- Scientific concepts (block 3)
- Reason as a primary/direct factor (block 3a) and faith as a secondary/indirect factor (block 2a)
- Scientific practices/evidence/conclusions (block 3b)
- Scientific belief claims (block 4)
- The shaping of personal and collective philosophies/worldview perspectives (block 5)

What Are the Scientific Concepts? (3)

As mentioned earlier, it seems easier to say what science does or does not do rather than what it is. Nevertheless, a very simplistic definition is science is a particular way of understanding or making sense of the natural world by developing explanations for the structures, processes, functions, and history of nature. This way is accomplished through the following means:

Science uses a systematic and self-correcting process (called "methodological naturalism") to seek and produce logical, accurate, reliable, and well-tested conclusions (or scientific knowledge) through repeated experimentations, observations, and (often) measurements of natural phenomena. This approach is also called the "scientific method."

Science investigates the occurrence of natural phenomena through various content "hard and soft" disciplines in which their experiments, observations, discoveries, and findings are conducted or made in the lab and/or field environment by scientists from universities, industry, and governments. Again, "hard" sciences, such as physics, astronomy, and chemistry, are characteristically "simple" in nature because the observations or occurrences can be predicted mathematically (i.e., equations or formulas). "Soft" sciences, such as basic biology and paleontology, are generally more "complex" because there are too many variables to be quantified into equations and are usually less predictable. However, both are needed to explain our origins. (NOTE: Some traditional "soft" sciences are now, arguably, considered "harder," such as molecular genetics. Geneticists use various "tools" to analyze DNA, population migration, gene flow, and other patterns between and among species. Also, the use of radiometric isotope methods, such as carbon dating, can give paleoanthropologists approximate ages of different species.)

Science attempts to obtain (and often does obtain) a broad consensus of agreement from the scientific community in regards to the most likely (best) interpretation of the individual lab/field findings or discoveries, subject to numerous peer reviews, criticisms, and "ruthless" independent verification and validation testing.

Science seeks a "consilience of inductions" (inductions from different areas of science explained by the same principles or laws) and "converging lines of evidence" (investigations in various areas of science that dovetail to produce mutually reinforcing results). William Whewell first proposed these concepts.

Several initial ideas and assumptions "fall out" from this description of what science is. Here are the major ones that have a connection with "reason" (block 3a) and "faith" (block 2a):

All science is based on or guided by natural or physical laws of nature. This conclusion means that for the practice of science (block 3b) to occur, certain assumptions, conditions, and boundaries must first be defined and understood.

The laws of science are practical conclusions reached by the scientific method (block 3a); they are intended to be neither laden with "ontological" commitments nor statements of logical absolutes. (NOTE: Ontological arguments conclude that God exists and is derived from sources other than observation of the world — e.g., from logic or reason alone.)

In summary, several points are deduced regarding scientific or natural laws.

- First, natural laws (as expressed via principles, statements, mathematical equations, or constants) are discovered through logical reasoning using the scientific method (block 3a).
- Second, natural laws contain certain assumptions or preconditions (regularities, universalities, or absolutes

are the same everywhere in the universe) of observable natural phenomena to do science. Science assumes a single vast system in which knowledge gained from studying one part of the universe applies to other regions. This regularity requires a certain amount of faith or belief that the natural laws apply everywhere in time and space (block 2a).

- Third, natural laws do not consider the supernatural or spiritual aspects and, therefore, are neutral in considering cause, purpose, or meaning.
- Fourth, natural laws are subject to change or modification, but rarely are they replaced. They are authoritative and considered a fact under certain conditions but not dogmatic because they can be questioned or revised as new evidence is found or discovered (e.g., the falsification principle).
- Fifth, natural laws provide the "engine" or basis to guide the practice of science (block 3b).

Reason (Block 3a)

Science is shaped by logic and imagination (or creativity). All scientific inquiries must conform to the principles of logical reasoning — that is, to test the validity of arguments by specific criteria of inference, demonstration, and common sense.[432] There are essential reasoning criteria for determining what science is: logical and rational and makes well-defined claims; hypotheses are falsifiable, as in testable; experiments are repeatable; science requires that peers examine claims in the same field, views unexplained gaps in theories with suspicion, requires evidence and causation in reviewing it, requires objectivity (or open-mindedness), does not accept anecdotal (of an account not necessarily accurate or reliable because based on personal reports rather than facts or research) evidence as proof, insists that extraordinary claims require extraordinary evidence, and believes absence of evidence is not evidence of absence.

The scientific method is used throughout the scientific inquiry process to accomplish these reasoning criteria. The scientific process is defined as follows. The scientist observes the natural world, asks a question, proposes a causal explanation to the question (a.k.a. hypothesis — which may be tentative initially and may be changed based on the outcome of rigorous testing), tests the hypothesis by making further observations or conducting experiments, verifies and validates the results of such testing by either confirming or contradicting or falsifying the hypothesis, reaches a conclusion(s) based on the results, and if it is contradicted or falsified, the hypothesis is discarded, and a new one is generated until the outcomes/results can be successfully repeated and verified (e.g., this method proves that the results are always the same and can be readily predicted by independent testing).

Scientific Practices/Evidences/Conclusions (Block 3b)

The practice of science is evidence-based. Science demands solid evidence that must be verifiable, measurable, and valid (i.e., accurate empirical data at every stage of the scientific process). Measurements can gather this evidence only by our senses or the extensions of our senses (via instruments). Progression is from a hypothesis to a theory using testable scientific laws. (Only a few scientific facts are natural laws, and many hypotheses are tested to generate a theory.) The concept of testability of the empirical world of natural phenomena is critical in understanding how hypotheses become accepted as scientific knowledge. The concept uses the following:[433]

The epistemic (natural) method states that even if an authority makes a claim (e.g., hypothesis) that seems to be rational, it must be open to testing. Only a rational argument combined with evidence can finally justify a scientific theory. Specifically, this method employs science, producing repeatable naturalistic explanations for observable phenomena. As a "ground rule" of modern science, it requires scientists to seek explanations in the real (physical) world based upon what can be observed (directly or indirectly through instruments), tested, replicated, and verified. The scientific community tests the results, which is driven by a peer review process that cultivates creativity, curiosity, and skepticism and ensures that no one can have the final say.

Scientific naturalism is powerful because of its empirical ruthlessness. Naturalism sees the world as a self-contained system of matter and energy that operates by unbroken natural law...everything in the world happens by chance and necessity with no reference to God, and it shows no sign of His presence. This view leads to philosophical naturalism and methodological naturalism. Philosophical naturalism relies on the belief that no ultimate or supreme being (e.g., God) or multiple beings (e.g., gods) are responsible for the creation of the universe. Methodological naturalism observes and tests natural phenomena to form theories and provide predictions. This perspective (also) leads to various forms of evolution and subsequent evolutionary biological theories (i.e., covered in the CD, ND, MS, and EES explanations). Today, most scientists and the scientific community support the explanation within MS.

Belief Claims/Models (Block 4) — Previously Discussed

These evolutionary accounts or views, in which most scientists and most of the scientific community tend to believe and follow in their explanations, are summarized by:

- *Classical Darwinism (CD) concepts* — CD includes the basic theory of evolution, common descent (including humans), speciation, gradualism, and natural selection.

This interpretation observes and describes life from a species-level perspective.

- *Neo-Darwinism (ND) concepts* — ND includes the basic theory of evolution, common descent, Mendelian genetics, and very early molecular genetics, which were influenced explicitly by natural selection. This interpretation also observes and describes life from a species-level perspective but initially looks at the influences of genes.

- *Modern synthesis (MS) concepts* — MS includes neo-Darwinism, speciation, gradualism, natural selection, population genetics, and intermediate molecular genetics. This interpretation observes and describes life from a molecular or DNA/gene and a population perspective.

- *Extended evolutionary synthesis (EES) concepts* (proposed but not approved) — EES includes modern synthesis plus molecular genetics, sociobiology, evolutionary biology, evolutionary psychology, and other concepts. This interpretation observes and describes life from an organism's perspective and considers the influences or changes due to the DNA, genes, epigenetics, and environmental factors.

NOTE: These evolutionary concepts are not officially advocated by any organization, as the creation concepts are. Creationists vigorously attempt to address and "counter" selected evolutionary principles.

The Shaping of Personal and Collective Philosophies/Worldview from Physical Perspective (Block 5)

In attempting to understand our origins and, ultimately, the impact of this understanding on our personal views about the meaning of life, the process, as outlined earlier, involves embracing the physical realm or the philosophical view of naturalism of reality. Applying the scientific approach of philosophical and methodological naturalism and the combined "hard and soft" scientific disciplines, most scientists and others tend to explain nature through the evolutionary process. These individuals tend to believe in the atheistic, deistic, or agnostic perspectives or worldviews.

Summary

This "big" picture (*fifth*) perspective shows the dynamic interaction of several concepts in our attempt to better understand our origins. Even though there is a "tension" or "struggle" to understand the relationships between the religious and scientific domains, humans seem to have a deep need to understand *why* (e.g., purpose) we are here. This chapter provides the concepts to answer that question. Specifically, figure 27 illustrates these dynamics in an integrated fashion.

The purpose of this conceptual and "operational" diagram is to "help" us to better inform us of the possibilities that "God" was and is supernaturally involved in the process of creation, even though He may have used natural or evolutionary means to evolve certain events/phenomena/objects into other forms or states. This belief supports the biblical account of creation. In addition, this figure helps us to understand that both religion and science concepts can help us to search for knowledge and seek the truth regarding our origins. In doing so, these belief claims have the potential to shape our philosophies and worldviews and, ultimately, our relationship with "God." The purpose of this chapter is to recognize our lifestyles are "*directly*" related to what we believe in terms of our understanding of our origins and, hopefully and prayerfully, in a Creator God!

Proverbs 3:5–6 says, "Trust in the Lord with all your heart; and lean not unto your own understanding; in all your ways acknowledge him, and he will make your paths straight." This verse is often interpreted as a call to trust in God's wisdom rather than relying on one's own understanding. It is a reminder that we should not be overconfident in our own abilities and should instead seek guidance from God.[434]

CHAPTER 12:

Chapter Conclusions

The following chapters capture key conclusions presented in this book. The reader is encouraged to return to the individual chapters to understand the basis for these conclusions.

Chapter 1: Our Miraculous Origins — Why Does Understanding It Matter?

A *biblical perspective* provides the most complete, reasonable, comprehensive, inclusive, and believable explanation for our origins.

In pursuing the understanding of our origins, "God" as the Creator of the universe and everything in it becomes relevant for our discussion and determines our direction or path.

Relying solely on scientific or naturalistic discoveries to explain an evolutionary pathway leading to humanity (modern humans) is problematic and unsubstantiated.

Students in US public schools have been limited to only the scientific and evolutionary explanations for understanding our origins due to US courts' interpretations of the First Amendment to our US Constitution regarding a "separation of church and state."

Understanding our origins from a creation (e.g., biblical God) perspective tells us why we were created and supplies a purpose for living and a hope for an eternal afterlife with God.

Today's "postmodern" and arguably "post-Christian" Western society is dominated by secular humanism and wokeism, which denies a supernatural view of the reality of God in our lives.

Secular humanism's impact on "Western" society limits our views or explanations of our origins to science, philosophical naturalism, and human ethics, which leaves out God and fosters atheism and agnosticism. Today, wokeism takes this belief further and is becoming a major factor in our culture. Wokeism is *incompatible with the biblical worldview* because it has different interpretations (e.g., perspectives) and leaves no room in the conversation for alternative views of addressing those social and political issues within our democratic process.

As a result, recent polls show a significant increase in Americans believing that we evolve by natural selection alone or with God guiding this natural process.

Modern scientific evidence has often "trumped" philosophical or logical and religious or faith claims. This situation leads to a "real controversy and dilemma" of many different beliefs about our origins.

The Christian worldview is heavily influenced by secular humanism and wokeism, which has led to materialism, hedonism, individualism, and politics as a religion.

Christians need to "be ready for an answer" to defend a rational faith in a biblical God as the Creator, especially when called upon.

Seeking God or something higher than ourselves is "wired" into all of us. Specifically, God's plan gives us the drive to search for meaning and purpose in our daily lives and the hope for eternal life. Science does not.

Chapter 2: Survey of Five Origin Questions and Possible Explanations

Different subjects, concepts, and explanations are needed to explore our various evolution and creation interpretations regarding our origins.

Examining whether one should consider "God" as a possible answer for the cause of our origins leads us to five logical or "cause-and-effect" questions.

Whether or not there was a "beginning" to our universe leads to several possibilities. Since science has determined and deduced a single beginning, as also declared in the book of Genesis, creationists and most scientists have dismissed other possibilities.

A cause is always required, either from a religious or scientific perspective. Only the "who" cause can be answered by religion or by faith, whereas the "how" can be answered by science. Since science speculates as to the real cause of our origins from exotic theories as to where we came from, only a real force is capable of causation, such as from a Creator "God." Random chance or unguided mindless processes are not the real causes or forces.

The process of the formation and development of the universe, Earth, and life is supernaturally explained by "big bang creation" accounts. Genesis reveals God commanding everything (time, matter, space, energy, laws, forces, constants, natural processes, etc.) into existence out of nothing. On the other hand, evolutionary scientists explain these ideas through the concept of random chance from the chaotic "big bang," which is further described by the events within stellar, chemical, and biological evolution theories.

The "age" of the universe is determined by deductions from scientific evidence, which has created much controversy, especially among Christian organizations. It has resulted in two basic interpretation camps — the "young earth (universe)" and "old earth (universe)" creationists.

The fifth question concerns whether there is a purpose for our lives. Only a spiritual explanation can answer the question of "why" we are here, leading to various theistic worldviews. The scientific, evolutionary, or naturalistic (physical) explanation does not give us any insight into this critical question and can lead to atheistic and agnostic worldviews.

Chapter 3:
The Biblical Creation Story

The account of creation in the book of Genesis and other related passages from the Old and New Testaments of the Bible is the foundation of the "inspired" Word of God.

From Moses, the presumed author of Genesis, six days of creation are declared by God with the beginning of the universe and light on day 1, sky and waters on day 2, land for plants and trees on day 3, stars, planets, moons, etc., visible on day 4, marine and air animals on day 5, and land animals and humans on day 6, and with God resting on day 7. In the first three days, God organized motionless spaces by separating one from another, and then God filled and ruled over those spaces in the second of three days.

God created man and women in His image to rule over all creatures and objects mentioned above.

God does not specify "how" He did it except by saying that He spoke everything into existence (fiat lux) and out of nothing (creation ex nihilo). This "simple" concept leaves room for us to try to figure out the "how" through validated scientific discoveries.

There are numerous objections to the biblical creation story, such as it is a myth, Moses did not write Genesis, Genesis chapters 1 and 2 tell a different story of creation, scientific evidence shows that there could not be six literal (twenty-four-hour) days for creation, and the biblical flood story was copied from ancient writings.

In response to these objections, first, the content of Genesis is significantly different and unique from earlier ancient writings, such as from the Babylonian creation myth of the *Enuma Elish*, where multiple gods played a "terrible" role in the creation vice a single monotheistic God of the Bible.

All efforts to undermine Moses as the author of Genesis and the following four books of the Bible, as a prophet of God, have failed. To date, no manuscript evidence for the "JEDP" model or any other ancient Jewish writings were discovered to counter Moses as the author of these five books of the Torah of the Hebrew Old Testament.

The differences between Genesis chapters 1 and 2 can be explained. Genesis 1 focuses more on physical creation issues — the what, where, how, and in what order or sequence of events. Genesis 2 zeros in on the why and lays out humanity's significant responsibilities in a step-by-step sequence.

Even though Genesis 1 specifies six "days of creation," they are interpreted differently. Some Christians believe God created everything literally in six twenty-four-hour days some 6,000 to 10,000 years ago. Others believe God's days of creation are symbolic and represent extended periods, perhaps millions to billions of years for each creation day based upon the Hebrew word *yom*. These Christians believe *yom* could be translated as a large span of time. Consequently, these different interpretations of this word tend to divide Christians into two camps — the "conservative" or "literal/strict" conservative creation scientists and the more "liberal or progressive" groups, such as the Reasons to Believe ministry.

The biblical Genesis flood story in chapters 6–9 is like the Mesopotamian or Sumerian poem, *Epic of Gilgamesh*, and the Sumerian *Eridu* Genesis. However, there are still significant differences between multiple gods versus a single God in charge of the universal or global flood.

Chapter 4: Creation Accounts

The concept of creation of our origins directly implies something or someone beyond the natural world. Biblically, this is a transcendent God who exists outside the universe He created. This concept is often represented by the theological concept of supernaturalism.

The theology of supernaturalism relies on the concept of theism, or the study of at least one "God" or divine being (or spirit or force) responsible for creating everything and providing significant meaning to us. This concept generally leads to various forms of creationism. Most creationists believe in some form of supernatural theism.

Theism acknowledges and worships the existence of one or more divinities or deities as the creator or creators that interact with the universe and yet transcend (e.g., are above and separate) his, her, or their creation. Out of its many religious beliefs, such as monotheism, deism, polytheism, and pantheism, only the monotheistic concept of a single (biblical) trinitarian or triune God (head) provides the "best" answer for His speaking our creation into existence.

The theological concepts of general and special revelation provide complete explanations for creation. Whereas general revelation of nature can apply to both evolution and creation explanations, only special/divine revelation can give insight into "who" that Creator is (e.g., God) and His supernatural characteristics, traits, and, therefore, ability to apply or execute His creative works via the revelations in the Bible.

The modern creation interpretations of Genesis, as mentioned earlier, consist of the progressive "old earth (universe) creationist's" (OEC) and the conservative "young earth (universe) creationist's" (YEC) perspectives or views.

The OEC proponents are the day-age theorists, theistic evolutionary creationists, intelligent (scientific) designer or "neo-creationists," gap theorists, and Reasons to Believe creationists. The common factor is that they all believe in an ancient (old) universe and Earth created by God as the Creator or Designer approximately 13.8 BYA.

The YEC proponents are essentially composed of creation scientists. They believe in a young universe and Earth approximately 6,000 to 10,000 years ago and a universal flood. Creation scientists primarily focus on the conditions of Earth to support life. They argue the earth "looks" or "appears" much older than it is and can be explained by Noah's global flood (a.k.a. flood geology). They reject many of the principles of modern science and most evolutionary conclusions, such as the "common descent" or "macroevolution" of humans and animals. This group is most often criticized by many scientists today.

Intelligent design scientists and philosophers support or focus on a scientific design interpretation (e.g., from DNA, in particular), which implies the earth, life, and humanity owe their existence to a purposeful (but unnamed) intelligent designer. They believe in the "common design" principle and stress the concepts of design inference, specified complexity, irreducible complexity, and fine-tuning.

Reasons to Believe scientists support a "creation big bang." They believe faith and reason and religion and science can be compatible, but science must not violate biblical scriptures. Their model collates biblical creation passages with scientific discoveries, especially when comparing Genesis' six "days of creation." They focus on God's supernatural beginning of the universe to His formation of all space objects, including Earth, which supports and sustains life. They believe God created human life, fully formed, in His image, and humans did not evolve from animals. They acknowledge some forms of evolution, such as "microevolution," but not common descent ("macroevolution") or the "universal common ancestor" (Darwin's "tree of life") concept. They believe God supernaturally used some forms of naturalism and evolution to "create" the universe and everything in it. Also, they believe in the common design and fine-tuning concepts.

Finally, even though there are philosophical arguments for the existence of God, such as Pascal's Wager, ontological, cosmological, teleological, moral, religious experience, and miracles to provide profound insight into the divine, each of us must decide for ourselves which path to take. Although reason may dominate scientific evolutionary thought and faith dominate religious and creation thought, both reason and faith "play" into each of these separate but related domains. This was demonstrated through the use of three "powerful" philosophical equations: Faith + Evidence = Belief (Claim), Beliefs + Desires = Actions, and Knowledge = Properly Justified True Belief.

Chapter 5: Science and the Evolutionary Path

Conclusions from scientific discoveries often lead to evolutionary interpretations and consequently form an evolutionary path of states, events, or occurrences.

In particular, the theory of biological evolution attempts to explain biological changes in the earth to support life primarily through the Darwinian mechanisms of natural selection and the related process of "common ancestry" or "descent with modification." This process is observed in Darwin's "tree of life" illustration.

Most scientists and the scientific community, in general, agree with these conclusions based on the scientific discoveries.

These scientific discoveries are solely based upon the philosophical concept of "naturalism," the use of the "scientific method" or "methodological naturalism," and exclude any participation or intervention in a "God" or gods in this process (a.k.a. "philosophical naturalism").

Science investigates natural phenomena through various scientific disciplines, tries to obtain a broad consensus of agreement of empirical data from many sources, and is evidence-based that must be observed, verified, tested, measured, replicated, and validated. Science can be falsified or corrected as new discoveries are made.

Science seeks a "consilience of induction" (inductions from different areas of science explained by the same principles or laws) and "converging lines of evidence" (investigations in various areas of science that dovetail to produce mutually reinforcing results).

NASA's "Lambda cold dark matter (CDM) hot big bang theory" describes the emergence or expansion of the universe and everything in it to support life from a scientific and evolutionary perspective.

The "theory of evolution" can be seen from a "big" picture perspective to involve stellar evolution (through NASA's big bang model), chemical evolution (through origins of life research), and biological evolution — the most discussed and controversial area — through the general concepts of "microevolution" and "macroevolution." These last two concepts form the basis for the most recognized theory of evolution, Charles Darwin's "principles of natural selection and common descent."

Based on these evolutionary theories, scientists and evolutionists have generated a timetable or scenario of events from the beginning of time (approximately 13.8 billion years ago — BYA) to the formation of the earth (about 4.5 BYA) to the first "simple" life (2.5 to 4.0 BYA) to first multicellular life (about 1.0 BYA) to eventually hominids or early or ancient "humans" (8 to less than 1 BYA) to modern humans (less than 200,000 years ago).

The "evolution of evolutionary explanations" has advanced from Darwin's first comprehensive theory of evolution in 1859 (called classical Darwinism or CD) to neo-Darwinism (ND), which lasted into the early 1930s, to modern synthesis (MS) from the 1930s to the present time. In 2007, the extended evolutionary synthesis or EES was proposed since it added additional discoveries post-MS. However, the scientific community has not accepted EES. They believe the concepts from EES can be and are incorporated into the latest version of the MS explanation.

These evolutionary theories "evolve" from species-centered (CD and ND) to gene-centered (MS) to organism-centered (EES) concepts.

All these evolutionary theories assume that naturally (randomly) selected beneficial (e.g., positive) gene mutations from the DNA biomolecule and given the right environmental conditions, species can survive, reproduce, and even change over time into another species (a.k.a. macroevolution).

Most creationists challenge "macroevolution" but not "microevolution" at the species or the genus level.

Chapter 6: Consolidation of Religious, Theological, Philosophical, and Scientific Paths

Our understanding of our origins falls into two major categories: supernaturalism, which implies creation accounts, and naturalism, which implies evolution theories/facts, as discussed previously.

Approaching our origins from a physical or material perspective leads to several concepts: Philosophical naturalism (e.g., implies no God) uses a purely physical perspective or path as our view of reality. Methodological naturalism uses the scientific method approach, which is interpreted by the "hard and soft" scientific disciplines, leading to evolutionary interpretations. This explanation is mainly believed by or identified with evolutionary atheists, evolutionary agnostics, secular humanists, or one having no perspective.

Approaching our origins from a spiritual perspective leads to two related paths.

In the first spiritual path, the view of reality is supernaturalism, which studies a Creator God through the religious/theological concepts of general or natural revelations. "Hard and soft" sciences interpret the discoveries differently. The evidence leads to explanations of creation or a mix of creation and evolution concepts. Theists believe in a strict view of creation, particularly monotheists, such as Christians. On the other hand, a blend of creation and some limited forms of evolution is believed by theistic evolutionists and evolutionary creationists, which also can be believed by Christians. In addition, deists "fall" into this path but rely on evolution as the means of change from one state or event into another.

In the second spiritual path, the view of reality is again supernatural, in which God is identified as the Creator through both general and special or direct revelation. These faith-based religious or theological belief claims are found in authoritative doctrines in the "Abrahamic" religion (such as the Bible or Qur'an) and the Dharmic, Asian, and Oceanic religions/philosophies. Again, explanations from the Abrahamic faiths are creation or a mix of creation and "limited" evolution with respect to individual perspectives believed by theists, theistic evolutionists, and evolutionary theists, who also can be Christians. Finally, the explanations from the Dharmic religions are more varied. Certain theists believe in creation explanations. Theistic evolutionists and evolutionary theists believe in evolutionary explanations with creation, while others are agnostics, such as New Age believers, or are atheists (e.g., Buddhism) from "Western" concepts or perspectives of creation and evolution.

Chapter 7: Evaluation of the Stellar and Chemical Theories of Evolution

Regarding our origins, one must examine the evidence in connecting scientific "facts" of the world as they are understood today into an evolutionary path. Understanding the "power or influence" of evolutionary mechanisms leads one to decide whether random chance or "mindless direction" can cause one thing or state to change into another by natural means alone.

Scientific discoveries provide scientists the ability to deduce that the beginning of the universe occurred roughly 13.8 BYA. They call this event the "big bang." However, scientific disciplines cannot explain how and where the initial conditions (e.g., possibly a highly fluctuating quantum plasma state that contains fundamental subatomic particles) came from or happened. Did they happen by random chance in the "big bang," or were they part of a "cause-and-effect" scenario that could imply a supernatural maker or designer (e.g., God) as the first cause as declared in Genesis 1?

It seems highly unlikely the initial explosive "big bang" event could evolve logically and sequentially or progressively into stars, planets, moons, etc., that are necessary to initiate and produce life ultimately on Earth. This undirected (e.g., mindless) or random scenario would inevitably lead to chaos and destruction without direction and control from a supreme being or supernatural God existing outside our universe. A more likely explanation is that the universe's beginning and expansion or unfolding started and developed from a well-thought-out, timed, directed set of events spoken or commanded by God. This explanation is often referred to as the "creation big bang" scenario and is contained in the "anthropic" and "Goldilocks" principles and is believed by most Christians.

Progressive Christians hold to the discovered and validated scientific events for a "creation big bang." They recognize the biblical God supernaturally caused many of these events to occur; however, He used natural processes under His initiation, direction, and control for the further development of the universe. Specifically, they focus on the conditions on Earth to support life and, ultimately, human life. This process is called the "Goldilocks principle."

Chemical and biological evolution principles were shown to be more problematic and highly unlikely to happen on their own.

Christians are skeptical that a primordial "soup" of inorganic chemicals colliding with one another could eventually form organic hydrocarbon compounds necessary for life, even given a "spark" to assist in the reaction. Also, they are highly doubtful that the evolutionary mechanism of natural selection of beneficial gene (DNA) mutations could change one type of an organism into another gradually since most mutations are harmful and eventually cause disease or death to an organism.

"Origins of life" researchers for chemical evolution have never found life coming from nonlife. This concept is called spontaneous generation. They considered two prominent positions: the "vitalist" position of living organisms containing immaterial "vital force or spirit" and the "reductionist" position of life explained solely or "reduced" by reference to the laws of physics and chemistry. Researchers have never found this immaterial vital or spiritual force that distinguishes life from nonlife nor any location on primordial Earth suitable for producing prebiotic molecules from assumed chemical compounds.

Miller-Urey's "spark-discharge" reductionist experiments attempted to duplicate Earth's early atmosphere and land to produce organic molecules. They were unable to validate the Oparin-Haldane hypothesis. Instead, they produced only a few amino acids but not enough heavy-rich hydrocarbon organic molecules to form amino acid chains (up to twenty essential amino acids are needed) to produce functional proteins to be transformed into the first living cell.

Researchers ran into the problem of "homochirality" or "handedness" (mirror images seen as right-handed and left-handed versions). Only left-handed (L-form) amino acids and right-handed (D-form) sugars are used to produce life. However, in nature, these molecules appear as a racemic (fifty-fifty) mixture. Further, no natural or lab method has been found to choose only these specific configurations to produce a protein or DNA biomolecule without some intervention.

Researchers such as Watson and Crick, who developed the "sequence hypothesis" or software digital "code," suggested the nucleotide bases or digits (A, T, C, and G) of the DNA molecule are organized into a specific arrangement (a.k.a. genes). They provide the instructions for arranging amino acids into chains (a.k.a. polypeptides). They produce the folding of multiple chains into a functional 3D protein. This complex process is highly regulated to make the right functional proteins. Specifically, this protein synthesis process involves several steps: splicing, transcription, translation, and folding to ensure a functional protein is made without mistakes to a very high degree of accuracy.

Philosopher of science Meyer suggested this highly specified and complex information in DNA does not reduce to or derive from physical and chemical forces by chance variation or lawlike deterministic processes of necessity. Therefore, the "chance hypothesis" and the following "self-organization or biochemical predestination theory" are in serious doubt, according to Meyer.

These natural or evolutionary mechanisms do not answer the origins-of-life question and come down to the "chicken-and-egg" dilemma. Does the chicken (DNA's nucleic acids like A, T, C, and G) direct the production of the egg (proteins), or are proteins needed to form parts of the DNA biomolecule? Which comes first — DNA or proteins?

Chapter 8: Evaluation of the Biological Theory of Evolution

Evolutionary biologists recognize the building of even the first protocell was quite complicated. The emergence of a primitive membrane that would enclose and protect DNA and a few other organelles is highly challenged by natural processes alone. The cell's membrane structure and associated functions are incredibly complex. Proteins are embedded in this two-layer membrane as well inside the cell. The proteins prevent harmful materials from coming in but allow in beneficial ones. Cell formation requires something besides an evolutionary mechanism to perform these complex discriminating functions.

Several scientists have addressed the unlikely evolutionary scenario for natural means to produce even the simplest life forms with a minimum of proteins. They computed the odds of this happening by chance or necessity alone. They have concluded that there is virtually no chance that undirected processes could form even a relatively small protein made up of a specified sequence. Therefore, the odds of developing a simple one-celled organism are also essentially "zero" unless this process is initiated, directed, and controlled by a higher intelligent designer (e.g., God).

From a biological evolution ("common descent theory") perspective, these proponents believe organic compounds combined and grew to form complex large biomolecules, such as DNA and RNA, over very long periods. They eventually started primitive protocells with membranes or walls to enclose and protect them from harsh environments around 3.5–3.8 BYA. These protists or prokaryotes (which had no nucleus for cell DNA), such as bacteria, grew and multiplied. A branch of them split off by integrating with a symbiotic partner to develop new energy production methods. They were called eukaryotes (had a nucleus for cell's DNA plus contained other organelles), such as blue-green algae. To date, this symbiotic partner is unknown.

It took almost 3 billion years of "stasis" to produce multicellular organisms composed of specialized cells cooperating with each other to ensure replication of their shared genes. This "Cambrian explosion" event suddenly made a variety of life forms, such as plants, insects, and animals. These life forms were fully formed. They had complete and integrated body plans, designs, and body types. These "sudden" changes, from essentially simple multicellular organisms to advanced organisms, over a relatively short geological time (5–6 million years), do not support the gradual changes through the evolutionary concepts of Darwinism, where beneficial mutations are selected to change one type of organism or species into another.

All evolutionary "missing link" theories dismiss these conclusions, such as the "artifact hypothesis" and the "deep-divergence hypothesis." Evolutionary biologists have conceded them. Any missing links or intermediate transitional forms from the previous Ediacaran or earlier biota were not found. A "common designer hypothesis" from an intelligent designer or agent that intervened in this progression of genetic information to explain this sudden increase in complexity seems to better answer this "explosion" of life from relatively simple to very advanced forms. Fossil evidence demonstrated this "explosion" of biota starting around 543 million years ago.

The sudden increase in post-Cambrian advanced large animals also demonstrates the necessity for an intelligent designer or Creator rather than through natural or evolutionary processes alone. Perhaps these periods demonstrate even a "bigger" biological explosion. The degree of complexity and rapid changes over a relatively "short" geological time of these organisms through the Paleozoic, Mesozoic, and Cenozoic periods are remarkable. These advances in complexity lead to Hominids and, ultimately, us.

Chapter 9: Discounting the Evolutionary Pathway to Humanity!

Based on genetic studies, evolutionary scientists say "humans" have a high degree of genetic similarity with chimps. Also, paleoanthropologists say "humans" share a common ancestor with chimps, some 8 MYA. Unfortunately, this common ancestor has never been found or validated. (NOTE: Part of the confusion is that these historical scientists often refer to all "hominids" as "humans.")

These scientists have constructed an evolutionary "tree of life" starting with the earliest hominids (humans), the Sahelanthropus, Ardipithecus, Australopithecus, Paranthropus, and finally, the Homo "genus" groups. Dates for these groups were determined through mitochondrial DNA (mtDNA) molecular clock and argon-argon radioisotope analyses. Nevertheless, fossils from these hominids indicated no "transitional" forms linking one genus to another had been found. If there were "transitional" "or intermediate" forms, they would exhibit characteristics of both groups, but none have been found so far. Therefore, they should not be considered "missing" links to humans. In addition, the exact evolutionary path is still unknown.

The hominid fossil and associated archeological records show one group did not evolve from another. Specifically, this conclusion is based upon the characteristics of bipedalism, brain size and structure (morphology), and genetic comparisons.

Transitioning a chimp from a "knuckle-walking" quadruped to an "upright" biped hominid did not occur slowly, as evolutionists believe, but suddenly. In analyzing many fossils, early hominids exhibited no change in locomotion for about 5 million years. Then, with the appearance of the Homo group, a distinct form of bipedalism suddenly appeared in the fossil record and then remained static for nearly 2 million years.

Examining brain size and structure of the hominids indicated major "discontinuous" leaps or gaps from hominid to hominid, not gradual increases as predicted by evolutionary theories. With the advent of humans, brain size dramatically increased.

The most significant differences between the hominids are in the genetic or genomic studies. Molecular anthropologists scrutinize variations (i.e., from DNA mutations) between these hominids. They employ various techniques to study the origins of humankind, such as genetic or DNA sequence diversity, molecular clock analyses of mitochondrial DNA (mtDNA), and Y chromosome DNA sequence comparisons.

The mtDNA analysis method tracks humanity's maternal lineage; therefore, this type of DNA is inherited exclusively from one's mother. However, even though progress has been made in this area to allow for greater accuracy, "molecular clocks" have several factors that confuse the calibration (i.e., accuracy) of these mtDNA molecular clocks. They range from three types of mtDNA individuals that vary with age, level of radioactivity in the environment, and mutation rates vary from region to region. However, mtDNA molecular clock techniques have recently improved to give a greater accuracy in age.

Nevertheless, mtDNA analyses estimate the "mitochondrial Eve" to have existed between 108,000 and 187,000 years ago, depending on the approach taken by these scientists.

The Y-chromosomal DNA analyses serve as a counterpart to the mtDNA analyses. It traces humanity's origin through the paternal side because it passes exclusively through the son from the father. It identifies the "Y-chromosomal Adam," and the different studies indicate that he was alive between 101,000 and 200,000 years ago. The RTB ministry believes "Y-chromosomal Adam" and "mitochondrial Eve" coexisted around 150,000 years ago.

Various mathematical modeling studies have produced conflicting results regarding the original population size. This situation is because the mutation rate is not known and is not constant. Therefore, these population-size estimates are not adequately validated. As a result, they may have overestimated the original population size to be much larger than two individuals. (NOTE: All these studies indicated the first humans stemmed from a small population of a few hundred to a few thousand.)

Anthropologists maintain genetic relatedness by determining how long ago two primates diverged from a common ancestor. However, these genetic diversity techniques assume a constant mutation (i.e., the average number of nucleotide bases substitutions per year) rate over long periods. If the mutation rate is constant, they can determine the coalescence time (since the DNA sequences and populations diverged from the shared ancestral sequence [population]). As mentioned, the mutation rates vary and often confuse the results or question their accuracy.

Paleontologists typically interpret hominids in the fossil record within an evolutionary framework. They believe hominids existed from 7 to 2 MYA and are transitional forms, intermediate or missing links that gave rise to the Homo (H) genus. There is a considerable disagreement as to the actual ("human") pathway or phylogeny since the fossil record of these very early (i.e., ancient or archaic) hominids is very limited to only a few fossil portions or fragments. There is still controversy over the "archaic" subspecies (i.e., H. sapiens *idaltu*, H. sapiens *denisova*, H. sapiens *neanderthalensis*, and H. sapiens *sapiens* or modern humans.) Most paleoanthropologists say H. *habilis* gave rise to H. *ergaster*, but this is where the agreement ends. Now, these scientists believe H. *heidelbergensis* gave rise to Neanderthals and anatomically modern humans.

Consequently, these (above) analyses gave rise to multiple explanations for humanity's origins and subsequent migration patterns worldwide. The "intermediate African assimilation hypothesis" is the explanation most agreed upon by these scientists. Most genetic analysts that study genomic (DNA) sequencing of Upper Paleolithic skeletons agree that hominids (H. *erectus*) began in at least one but probably multiple locations in Africa and then moved or dispersed to other parts of the world around 60,000 to 80,000 years ago (and perhaps more than one time out of Africa). DNA interbreeding analysis between modern humans with Neanderthals and Denisovans indicates these findings.

There are concerns or assumptions about using genetic data to locate humanity's origins, such as populations did not move or migrate throughout history, the same modeling techniques were used, and no "genetic or environmental bottlenecks" existed to limit the size of the population groups. All these conditions were found by studies to be false.

The emergence of sophisticated behavior of humanity began around 70,000 to 80,000 years ago. Findings from artifact discoveries (cave art, tools, jewelry, etc.) reflected the activities of "humans" endowed with the capacity for symbolism. The FOXP2 human "master regulatory language gene" is the closest proxy to the origin of symbolism. However, most of these findings were found around 40,000 to 50,000 years ago, showing a significant "quantum" cultural and technological explosion or leap (a.k.a. the "sociological big bang").

Question: Perhaps the biblical "Adam and Eve," representing the anatomically modern humans, could have existed between 40,000 and 10,000 years ago based on these findings and analyses, and previous humans could be considered as "pre-Adamites as explained by the RTB ministry?"

Separating modern humans from chimps and Neanderthals was discussed in detail.

Evolutionary scientists have assumed the chimp is our "closest living relative." By that assumption, gene comparisons have been studied extensively in both genomes. Genes "coding" for similar biological functions (e.g., proteins) gave a high correlation percentage. However, when researchers made unbiased comparisons of larger regions of these two genomes (a.k.a. noncoding or "junk" DNA), major and significant differences began to emerge. Much of the chimp's DNA did not align with the sequences in the human genome database, according to studies performed by the Chimpanzee Genome Project team. These and other studies are based upon Nuclear DNA-to-DNA, gene-to-gene, and chromosome-to-chromosome comparisons.

Additionally, evolutionary scientists have assumed the Neanderthals to be our "closest" extinct relatives. However, significant anatomical or morphological, genetic, and behavioral differences were observed when comparing their fossil remains and artifacts to modern humans.

Skull and skeletal comparisons show significant differences between Neanderthals and humans. Neanderthals displayed an extraordinarily long face, a pronounced midface projection, a poorly developed chin, a highly developed brow ridge, large round eye sockets, an extraordinarily long and wide nose, more prominent front teeth, a retromolar gap, an occipital foramen magnum, a higher larynx, thicker bones, a more compact body with a barrel chest and shorter limbs.

Neanderthals may have had a language based upon brain shape and architecture comparisons. Still, probably it was some crude form of communication, given a smaller hyoid and the hypoglossal canal. In addition, the Neanderthals had a smaller parietal lobe, which plays a vital role in language, math reasoning, sense of self-identity, and religious experience. Finally, they had limited symbolic thought or sophisticated behavioral patterns, as seen in cave paintings, jewelry, etc.

However, genomic comparisons between humans and Neanderthals indicate significant gene differences. These differences are predominantly observed in the FOXP2 regulatory genes of language, the MC1R genes for regulation of skin and hair pigment production, the LEPR genes for adaptation to cold, the BNC2 genes for keratin in skin pigmentation, and in general, different genes for skull morphology, rib cage structure, skin and hair features, metabolism, and cognitive development.

There were different methylation patterns (the methyl group attaches to DNA in the chromosomes) in about 2,000 regions between these two genomes. These map patterns influence brain development, neurological and psychiatric disorders, and immune and cardiovascular systems and are part of epigenetics.

Even though there are some similarities between chimps, Neanderthals, and modern humans, there are still significant differences between them, especially in the gene expression levels. Therefore, many scientists and nonscientists consider humans a "unique" species when comparing their anatomical, physiological, behavioral, archeological, and, most importantly, genetic differences. Connections between them were observed to be "problematic" because significant changes were made relatively quickly. In addition, multiple, simultaneous, and integrated positive selections of predominately beneficial mutations (rare in the first place) of genes to generate new species is not realistically possible without divine intervention either by an intelligent designer/ agent or a Creator supernatural "God." The biblical perspective makes these changes possible and believable!

Finally, the evolutionary chain of life or the "ascent of man" illustrations are quite "offensive" to many creationists because they trace modern humans back to apes and then to other hominids. In fact, many creationists consider this perspective as "racist." These drawings are not only "misleading and grossly distorted" but "false," according to these creationists.

Chapter 10: Genesis and Science Compatibility Consideration?

Could a correlation be made between the relatively "simple" symbolic explanations of the biblical six "days of creation" found in Genesis 1 and the current scientific findings? This chapter provides a potential or possible scenario where these validated scientific findings could be relatively "folded" into these biblical creation days.

The "dialog" compatibility model is preferred to discuss "how did we get here?" This model explores the intersection or overlap of the separate domains of science and religion. The "hard and soft" scientific disciplines produce the evidence or empirical data through the application of the scientific method. The Bible introduces us to the concepts of morality, metaphysics, and the identification of the Creator, which is believed and followed by faith and divine revelation.

This compatibility model was also used to fit these findings into "God" or "cosmic" days vice "human" days. Could a "God or cosmic twenty-four-hour day" translate into billions of Earth or human days? (NOTE: In more than one day, some scientific findings were found in this alternative model to the RTB model.)

On "day 1," Genesis 1:1–2 declares, "God Created the Heavens and Earth." Scientists attribute this to the "big bang" theory to start everything — the beginning and initial expansion of the universe. Nine categories are associated with this day: plank and quantum gravity era, grand unification era, electroweak era including an inflationary period, elementary particle era and quantum fluctuation period, nucleosynthesis era, photon era, cosmic dark ages, and recombination era, reionization era, and the galaxy formation and evolution era. (NOTE: Some of the earlier eras are speculation, while others are shown to be scientifically accurate and therefore possible.)

Genesis day 1 and day 2 are summarized as the universe's formation and development of our galaxy and solar system and now focus on the earth, where God separated water from water calling the expanse sky. Nine categories are associated with these two days: location and formation of our solar system within the Milky Way galaxy, movement and formation of our solar system, formation of our planets, Moon-forming event, late veneer event, late heavy bombardment period, arrival of early (primitive or primordial) life, launch of plate tectonics and its contribution to early life, and the formation of continents and oceans and their contributions to support early life.

Genesis days 3 and 4 are summarized as God letting waters under the sky gather in one place and letting dry ground appear. God creates plants and trees…in addition, on day 4, the sun, moon, and stars are now visible. (NOTE: Some Christians believe these space objects were formed on this day.) The development of the earth's atmosphere, land, and waters to support plant and primitive life, numerous mass extinctions, and mass speciation events on Earth provide the necessary elements and conditions (such as the "greenhouse effect and photosynthesis") for advanced life to occur. Seven categories are associated with these days: great oxygenation event, slushball "ice" event, Loma Gundi and Shunga "ice" events, boring billion period, Cryogenian era, Neoproterozoic oxygenation event, and the first and second Avalon explosion eras.

Genesis days 5 and 6 are summarized as God creating marine creatures as well as winged birds, and He created land animals and humans. There was an explosion of multicellular and animal life in the air, land, and water. During these days, three biological categories are the Ediacaran biota from the second Avalon geological era, the Cambrian biota from the Cambrian geological era, and the post-Cambrian biota associated with three geological eras: Paleozoic, Mesozoic, and Cenozoic eras and periods. Complete and advanced fossil "body plans, designs, and structures" were discovered during these eras.

Also, on Genesis day 6, God explicitly distinguishes between advanced animals, such as the hominids, and humans. The hominids include the Ardipithecus, Australopithecus, Paranthropus, and Homo (H) groups or genera. Within the Homo genera are the following subgroups or species: H. sapiens *idaltu*, H. sapiens *denisova*, H. sapiens *neanderthalensis* (arguably), and H sapiens *sapiens*, or anatomically modern humans. Each of them is a distinct species from modern humans. Biblically speaking, modern humans are created in God's image. Regarding artifacts found with Neanderthals, such as limited burial rites, crude tools, weapons, cloths, art, painting, and jewelry, indicate this possibility as well as limited communication and cognitive skills as seen from anatomical and genetic discoveries within their fossil remains, they were determined to be inferior to modern humans.

Chapter 11: An Integrated Origins Perspective — a "Big" Picture Summary

An integrated historical/philosophical approach provides the best way to summarize the concepts described in this book. Applying this approach to one's existing knowledge or belief can enable one to explore different perspectives regarding our origins.

Historically, the compatibility and noncomputability origin models have generated "tension" between religion and science and their associated components. The "dialog compatibility" model seems to be the most productive for discussion if one intends to consider some of the significant points within the scientific inquiry and the religious journey processes and any possible correlation or intersection between them.

Both perspectives are needed to understand our origins. Using only one approach without the other does not give us a complete picture of this complicated and controversial subject.

The scientific inquiry process is based upon independently verified and validated evidence. In practice, this process mainly uses deductive reasoning, derived from the scientific method, to make certain conclusions (usually evolutionary) about specific discoveries of how the universe and everything in it started and progressed over time. Here, we address those conclusions related to the question of our origins. However, faith in this overall process is also necessary, especially when attempting to connect one event to another. Scientific techniques and models are used to provide this linkage. In believing in natural processes alone, most of these historical scientists use evolutionary mechanisms to make these connections (such as used in natural selection and molecular clock analyses), as observed from the CD, ND, MS, and EES evolutionary periods and their associated explanations.

The religious journey employs faith and revelation, such as believing in the Bible as the inspired Word of God. This belief is especially relevant regarding the six "days of creation," as declared by Moses in the book of Genesis and other related biblical passages. In practice, individual and collective experiences and worship provide the basis for one's rational faith in God as the true Creator of everything. In particular, the Genesis account offers the linkage for each day of creation. Genesis provides the logical or chronological sequence of events for life to exist on Earth. Therefore, it is reasonable to conclude He had a "hand" in the overall creation process. Supernaturally, conservative and progressive creation Christian groups, such as the CS, ID (Christian individuals), and RTB organizations respectively, believe in God as the Creator or Intelligent Designer.

Philosophically and practically, consolidating these two distinct subjects provides additional clarity to these two complex and controversial subjects about our origins. As seen in chapter 10, "Genesis and Science Compatibility Consideration?" validated scientific discoveries can be relatively "fitted or folded" into Genesis' six "days of creation." They are separate but related areas or domains that can help to expand and explain our interpretations and perspectives regarding our origins.

By employing this integrated approach, we can better incorporate these belief claims into our personal and collective philosophies regarding our origins and other areas. They can influence worldviews such as atheism, agnosticism, theism, and deism.

This concept is extremely important because "when our real-life situations are filtered through the grid of our philosophy about our origins, this becomes our worldview."[435] Whether we take a naturalistic view of reality exclusively using scientific discoveries and evolutionary mechanisms or a strict supernaturalistic view of reality using religious (such as biblical) accounts of creation or some combination of the two, we eventually form or reinforce our position of a belief in "God" or no "God" in influencing our daily lives.

CHAPTER 13:

Final Thoughts and Observations

Understanding our origins is through the concepts of evolution and creation or creationism. Primarily, these concepts flow from a scientific and religious perspective. Science uses the philosophical principle of naturalism and answers the question, "How did it occur?" Religion uses the theological doctrine of supernaturalism and answers the question of "Who did it?" When approached logically, using the cause and effect law, both disciplines or domains can coexist and even support each other, under certain circumstances, to make sense of it all! However, when science and evolution cannot definitively answer all the questions about our origins, especially when needing significant assumptions to make their case, some of their unsupportable conclusions may be problematic or even difficult to accept! This situation allows us to consider religious or creation accounts more seriously and to examine how they interact with validated scientific discoveries. Creation explanations provide additional insight and even a more profound understanding of our purpose of "why" we are here and "what" we are supposed to do.

In answering these "why" and "what" questions regarding purpose, the biblical creation accounts are provocative, illuminating, and worthy of serious consideration. God divinely intervenes to create a universe and Earth to support all forms of life. He uses and adapts the common design principle as the prime mechanism to transform one species into more advanced genus/species forms, ultimately leading to human life. Probably, He uses some limited forms of evolution, but He is always in control and guides these natural processes to His purpose. In addition, only biblical beliefs give us purpose or meaning in our daily lives. Science and evolution do not address this area!

Taking the time to understand the dynamics behind this complex and often "hotly" debated and contested subject is essential in formulating our perspectives on life issues and perhaps ultimately impacting or influencing our worldview philosophy. This book recommends seeing this complex area through a "big" picture historical/philosophical "lens" approach. Looking at individual "stove-pipe" areas, such as mythology, religion/theology, philosophy, and science, is beneficial, but all come short in one way or another in our discovery process. Viewing our origins from an integrated and coordinated perspective may better assist you in your endeavor or quest for knowledge or "truth" or at least lead to a better or informed understanding of our origins. This decision is up to *you!*

In researching this controversial subject of creation and evolution, I have concluded that the biblical perspective provides the most complete, believable, and inclusive view of our origins. Even though the Genesis account of our origins is somewhat symbolic or figurative, it had to be. The story contained in the book of Genesis is for all humanity. It had to consider and be relevant to ancient or early Hebrew beliefs (e.g., civilizations) and all beliefs leading up to and including modern times. What we now know through validated scientific discoveries is entirely different from the past. The Genesis account gives us a blueprint in which to follow. The creation account is logical, in the correct order, and with the proper sequence (e.g., simple to complex) of events occurring at the right time to ultimately bring and establish anatomical modern humans on planet Earth to preside over all creatures as well as to protect our planet. The number of events necessary for this transformation to occur in the correct order is staggering and unimaginable without divine initiation and control to produce and sustain life ultimately!

In addition, notice how quickly (e.g., in Genesis 1) God moves from the heavens to events on Earth. Perhaps this is because He knew that most disputes would occur over the exclusive belief in (chemical and biological) evolution rather than His divine involvement in all creation. We now have many of the "tools," such as molecular or genetic analyses and radiometric isotope techniques, to investigate and refute many of these evolutionary principles. Evolutionists often lack "hard" empirical data to support their conclusions for an evolutionary pathway. Their "weak" explanations open the "door" to a more plausible reason for our origins: *God of the Bible as the Creator of the universe and everything in it.* Whether He used His unlimited supernatural powers to initiate and form every creation event or used them selectively in combination with natural events, we do not know. In Isaiah 55:8–9, it says that "'For my thoughts are not your thoughts, neither are your ways,' declares the Lord. 'As the heavens are higher than the earth, so are my thoughts higher than your thoughts.'" In other words, everything happens in the providence of God and is woven into the fabric of His perfect plan for those who love Him.

> The psalmist explains, how precious to me are your thoughts, God! How vast is the sum of them! (Psalm 139:17). God's thoughts and His ways do not always make sense to us, but we can rest in the knowledge that He is always good, and therefore, everything he does is good (Psalm 13:6: 100:5). Through divine providence God accomplishes His will. To ensure that His purposes are fulfilled, God governs the affairs of men and works through the natural order of things. The laws of nature are nothing more than God's work in the universe. The laws of nature have no inherent power; rather, they are

the principles that God set in place to govern how things normally work. They are only "laws" because God decreed them.[436]

These biblical quotes refer to the concept of divine providence.

Divine providence is the governance of God by which He, with wisdom and love, cares for and directs all things in the universe. The doctrine of divine providence asserts that God is in complete control of all things. He is sovereign over the universe, as a whole (Psalm 103:19), the physical world (Matthew 5:45), the affairs of nations (Psalm 66:7), human destiny (Galatians 1:15), human successes and failures (Luke 1:52), and the protection of His people (Psalm 4:8). This doctrine stands in direct opposition to the idea that the universe is governed by chance or fate.[437]

Only God knows how He specifically formed the universe and the "universe" within us. Science gives us mere and occasional glimpses of these details. I believe He delights when we discover them, giving Him credit and thanks for our lives!

The Bible declares that God did it in no uncertain terms. Scriptural words like God commanded, spoke, or announced the heavens and Earth into existence (fiat lux) out of nothing (creation ex nihilo) are simple and direct but definitive, consequential, and unapologetic. He used natural processes in His overall creative process besides supernatural events.

Nevertheless, there has arisen real controversy between strict or dogmatic evolutionists and creationists, who believe exclusively in their position. These "hardline" positions tend to leave little or no room for compromise or real, meaningful discussions. This "either/or" situation has caused much division, especially in the "West." Many creationists say that if you believe in evolution, you do not believe in God and are nonreligious (e.g., an atheist). At the other end of the spectrum, many evolutionists say that if you believe in creation, you believe in God, not science. Both claims are false, as I have demonstrated with my illustration of the physical and spiritual paths using the dialog compatibility model. Also, these paths illustrate intermediate individual positions. All these philosophical and theological worldviews contribute to this diversified spectrum of beliefs and how we approach, examine, and consequently conduct our lives.

So there is room for evolutionists to believe in God and simultaneously focus on scientific and methodological naturalism and some form of creationism (also known as the theistic evolutionist, evolutionary theist, and desist positions). Likewise, there is room for creationists to believe in scientific discoveries, theological supernaturalism, and some limited forms of evolution; this includes some strict/conservative and most liberal/progressive creationists. These philosophical and theological worldviews were discussed and shown to coexist or be somewhat compatible, as observed with the dialog model. This model demonstrated the possibility of detailed and validated scientific events "fitting" into Genesis' six "days of creation" scenarios while retaining their separate knowledge domains.

In addition, I believe it is essential to be flexible in one's beliefs on this subject. Otherwise, one can quickly go down a path that becomes problematic. (Cases of fideism or faith alone and scientism or science alone exemplify these extreme positions.) My research has shown that complete faith in an evolutionary way is weak. Lack of discoveries or evidence from fossils, artifacts, and genetic findings supports this conclusion. For example, evolutionary mechanisms have not been decisively shown, such as naturally selecting beneficial mutations to make positive changes to evolve one species into another over a gradual period.

Another example is the rapid (e.g., not gradual) "explosion" of completely formed species during the relatively short geological Cambrian era. This belief also applies to changing inorganic chemicals into organic biomolecules and eventually into the first primitive single cell. The "chicken-egg" dilemma highlights this situation. DNA (e.g., chicken) is used to produce proteins (e.g., egg), but proteins are involved in the production of DNA. Which comes first — DNA or proteins? Finally, the probability or odds of these events aligning to produce even the simplest organism that can survive and reproduce is nearly "zero."

Also, the evolutionary pathway of the early (ancient or archaic) hominids to modern humans or Homo sapiens *sapiens* and the migration of hominids around the globe is unclear. Molecular clock (genomic) analyses of DNA-to-DNA, gene-to-gene, and chromosome-to-chromosome comparisons between chimps, early hominids, neanderthals, and modern humans demonstrate significant anatomical, physiological, and behavioral differences. Modern humans have the most changes and are unique and special among all these and other organisms. Unlike other species, we can develop entire civilizations and significant technological innovations. In Genesis 1:27, "God created mankind in His own image, in the image of God He created them male and female he created them." Many philosophers say this ability to seek God is "wired into us" and resides in our consciousness or mind. Perhaps this ability answers the most critical question. That is, "Why are we here?" Only God can provide this answer. Science cannot. Based upon this belief, God divinely formed, shaped, and continually intervenes in our world. He did all of this for us so that, ultimately, we can have purpose and meaning in our lives and look forward to a life with Him in heaven. This concept is His ultimate plan for us if we believe in Him and give Him credit for our miraculous origins, regardless of knowing "how" He exactly did it. That requires faith or trust in Him.

We all have opinions regarding our origins, evolution, and creation, which supports my sincere belief that "it's all a matter of perspective!" In my opinion, the bottom line is that it is easier to believe in the biblical creation miracle by God than to believe in evolution strictly alone! My research on this controversial subject was not just an intellectual exercise but a real commitment to finding the truth. I am convinced that God is the Creator of everything in this world. I hope this book will help *you* on your journey through life. Socrates reminds us that "an unexamined life is not worth living." As revealed in Scripture, we all have the same choice to seek and know God and believe in His Word or not. Carefully studying God's perspective (e.g., Word) regarding His creation will strengthen your faith in Him. Additionally, of all God's creatures, only humans can anticipate future events. Hebrews 10:23 (NKJV) says, "Let us hold fast the confession of our hope without wavering, for He who promised is faithful." Even though the hope of heaven fills our thoughts, it is important for each of us to stay "grounded" in the presence with Him. Therefore, as Christians, we live in two worlds. As we walk with God, we should live with one foot on earth and one in heaven. God provides us the opportunity to understand His creation through our origins.

My wife, Laurel, often reminds me that "with time, all truth is revealed." God created time so that He could begin, form, develop, and sustain the universe and everything in it. Therefore, His timing is perfect in all events for life to exist for His purpose and ours. My journey to find the truth about our origins has given me the peace of "mind" to know that God really did it! Praise God!

"Our miraculous origins" are indeed a miracle from God! We are the ultimate recipients of His creation!

FIGURES

Introduction

Chapter 2: Survey of Five Origin Questions and Possible Answers

Chapter 4: Creation Accounts

Chapter 6: Consolidation of Religious/Theological, Philosophical, and Scientific Paths

Chapter 7: Evaluation of the Stellar and Chemical Theories of Evolution

Chapter 9: Discounting the Evolutionary Pathway to Humanity!

Chapter 10: Genesis and Science Compatibility Consideration?

Chapter 11: An Integrated Origins Perspective — a "Big" Picture Summary

TABLES

ABOUT THE AUTHOR

Michael brings over forty years of project management, science, and engineering education and experience together to address the complex and often controversial subject of our origins. Through his extensive research and study in several fields, he reaffirms God is the One true master Architect, Designer, Engineer, Creator, and Sustainer of the universe and everything in it. In that vein, Michael defends the idea that God created us — His greatest and most unique creation that was formed on the sixth day of creation, as declared in the book of Genesis chapters 1 and 2. Additionally, Michael believes God reveals His purpose in creating us, as observed in other books of the Bible.

In order to understand our origins, Michael carefully and comprehensively reviews and dissects leading evolution and creation models that interpret our origins. Based upon his study, he believes understanding how our origins happened is beyond our human comprehension or explanation. Specifically, Michael believes our origins cannot be understood without divine intervention of a supernatural God as the Creator and requires faith and evidence on our part to believe it is true.

Therefore, Michael delves into this subject and provides an overview of these miraculous events from a biblical perspective. He systematically integrates concepts from philosophy, religion, theology, and science into a "big" picture. Further, he develops five unique perspectives in the form of illustrations to help us "make sense of it all." He shows how these perspectives influence our worldview beliefs and daily lifestyles. Lastly, while he recognizes we all have a perspective on our origins, he hopes this basic review will help others to ultimately decide for themselves whether philosophically or theologically there is a God or no God. Finally, he believes spiritual discernment is needed to have faith in a Creator "God."

ENDNOTES

1   Dave Robinson and Judy Graves, *Introducing Philosophy* (Totem Books, 1999), 1

2   Wikipedia, "Separation of church and state," last modified February 12, 2024, https://en.wikipedia.org/wiki/Separation_of_church_and_state

3   Bruce Bickel and Stan Jantz, *Creation and Evolution 101* (Harvest House Publishers, 2001), 273

4   Tom Morris, *Philosophy for Dummies* (Wiley Publishing Inc, 1999), 26

5   Wikipedia, "Westminster Confession of Faith," last modified November 1, 2023, https://en.wikipedia.org/wiki/Westminster_Confession_of_Faith.

6   Ravi Zacharias, *Beyond Opinion: Living the Faith We Defend* (Thomas Nelson, 2007), 37

7   "What Is Secular Humanism," CFI, https://centerforinquiry.org/definitions/what-is-secular-humanism/

8   Wikipedia, "Secular humanism," last modified September 20, 2023, https://en.wikipedia.org/wiki/Secular_humanism

9   Zacharias, *Beyond Opinion*, 37–38

10   Ibid., 221

11   Max Funk, "Wokeism — the New Religion of the West," published October 20, 2020, https://www.convergemedia.org/wokeism-the-new-religion-of-the-west/

12   Ibid.

13   Ibid.

14   Ibid.

15   Ibid.

16   Ibid.

17   Betsy Cooper, Daniel Cox, Rachel Lienesch, Robert P. Jones, "Exodus: Why Americans Are Leaving Religion — and Why They're Unlikely to

Come Back," published September 22, 2016, https://www.prri.org/research/prri-rns-poll-nones-atheist-leaving-religion

18   "Evolution, Creationism, Intelligent Design," Gallup, https://news.gallup.com/poll/21814/evolution-creationism-intelligent-design.aspx

19   "Exploring Different Ways of Asking about Evolution," Pew Research Center, https://www.pewresearch.org/religion/2019/02/06/the-evolution-of-pew-research-centers-survey-questions-about-the-origins-and-development-of-life-on-earth/

20   Wikipedia, "Rejection of evolution by religious groups," last modified February 14, 2024, https://en.wikipedia.org/wiki/Rejection_of_evolution_by_religious_groups

21   Ibid.

22   Ibid.

23   Ibid.

24   Rick Warren, "What's Influencing Your Worldview?" published November 11, 2021, https://www.crosswalk.com/devotionals/daily-hope-with-rick-warren/daily-hope-with-rick-warren-november-11-2021.html

25   Bickel and Jantz, *Creation and Evolution 101*, 279

26   Lee Strobel, *The Case for a Creator* (Zondervan, 2004), 98

27   *Merriam-Webster*, "Occam's razor," https://www.merriam-webster.com/dictionary/Occam%27s%20razor

28   Strobel, *The Case for a Creator*, p. 102

29   Ibid., 113–114

30   Ibid., 113

31   Ibid., 113–114; Carl Sagan, *Cosmos: A Personal Voyage* (New York: Ballantine, 1993), 4

32   Deborah Zabarenko, Reuters News Agency, "Princeton Physicist Offers Theory of the Cyclic Universe," Orange County, CA, Register (April 26, 2002);

      etu, "New Theory Provides Alternative to Big Bang," published April 26, 2002, https://www.princeton.edu/news/2002/04/26/new-theory-provides-alternative-big-bang;

Wikipedia, "Cyclic model," last modified October 4, 2023, https://en.wikipedia.org/wiki/Cyclic_model

33   Strobel, *The Case for a Creator*, 116–117

34   Ibid., 117

35   Stephen Hawking, *A Brief History of Time: From the Big Bang to Black Holes* (New York: Bantam, 1988), 140–141

36   Strobel, *The Case for a Creator*, 113–117

37   Bickel and Jantz, *Creation and Evolution 101*, 27

38   Strobel, *The Case for a Creator*, 106

39   Ibid., 107

40   Ibid., 105–106

41   "The CMB: How an Accidental Discovery Became the Key to Understanding the Universe," The Conversation, published July 24, 2015, http://theconversation.com/the-cmb-how-an-accidental-discovery-became-the-key-to-understanding-the-universe-45126

42   9.newage.pdf (cornell.edu); "What Is the New Age Movement?" Got Questions, https://www.gotquestions.org/new-age-movement.html

43   Bickel and Jantz, *Creation and Evolution 101*, 29

44   Strobel, *The Case for a Creator*, 94–95

45   P. James E. Peebles, David N. Schramm, Edwin L. Turner, and Richard G. Kron, "The Evolution of the Universe," published October 1, 1994, https://www.scientificamerican.com/article/the-evolution-of-the-universe/;

Michael S. Turner, "Origin of the Universe," published May 21, 2013, https://www.scientificamerican.com/article/origin-of-the-universe-extreme-physics-special/

46   Bickel and Jantz, *Creation and Evolution 101*, 30

47   "How Does the Qur'an Compare to the Book of Genesis on the Great Events of History?" ChristianAnswers.Net, https://christiananswers.net/q-aig/quran-genesis.html

48   Monty White, "Hasn't Evolution Been Proven True?" https://answersingenesis.org/theory-of-evolution/evidence/hasnt-evolution-been-proven-true/

49   Bickel and Jantz, *Creation and Evolution 101*, 103

50   Ibid., 102

51   George W. Knight and James R. Edwards, *The Layman's Overview of the Bible* (Thomas Nelson Publishers, 1987), 13

52   Michael Morrison, "The Torah: Genesis 1: Are the Six Days of Creation Literal or Figurative?"

53   Hugh Ross, *A Matter of Days: Resolving a Creation Controversy* (NavPress, 2004), 66

54   Hugh Ross, *The Genesis Question: Scientific Advances and the Accuracy of Genesis* (NavPress, 2001), 195

55   Wikipedia, "Creation myth," last modified October 14, 2023, http://en.wikipedia.org/wiki/Creation_myth

56   Wikipedia, "Enūma Eliš," last modified January 20, 2024, https://es.wikipedia.org/wiki/En%C5%ABma_Eli%C5%A1

57   Ibid.

58   "Bodie Hodge," Answers in Genesis, http://answersingenesis.org/bios/bodie-hodge/;

        "Dr. Terry Mortenson," Answers in Genesis, http://answersingenesis.org/bios/terry-mortenson/

59   Knight and Edwards, *The Layman's Overview of the Bible*, 12

60   Ibid.

61   Bodie Hodge and Dr. Terry Mortenson, "Did Moses Write Genesis?" https://answersingenesis.org/bible-characters/moses/did-moses-write-genesis/

62   Ibid.

63   Ibid.

64   Ibid.

65   Eamonn O'Doherty, "The Conjectures of Jean Astruc, 1753" *Catholic Biblical Quarterly*, 15 (1953): 300–304;

        Wikipedia, "Creation myth"

66   Ross, *The Genesis Question*, 82

67   Ibid., 82-86

68   Ibid., 69–70

69   Michael Morrison, "The Torah: Genesis 1: Are the Six Days of Creation Literal or Figurative?"

70   Ibid.

71   Ibid.

72   Wikipedia, "Epic of Gilgamesh," last modified October 12, 2023, http://en.wikipedia.org/wiki/Epic_of_Gilgamesh

73   "Flood Mythology," https://www.bibliotecapleyades.net/mitos_creacion/mitos_diluvio01.htm

74   Wikipedia, "Creation myth"

75   Joshua J. Mark, "Eridu Genesis," https://www.worldhistory.org/Eridu_Genesis/;

    Wikipedia, "Eridu," last modified January 28, 2024, https://es.wikipedia.org/wiki/Eridu

76   "Flood Mythology"; Wikipedia, "Flood myth," last modified January 15, 2024, https://en.wikipedia.org/wiki/Flood_myth;

    The Editors of Encyclopaedia Britannica, "Flood Myth," last updated February 2, 2024, https://www.britannica.com/topic/flood-myth

77   Wikipedia, "Creation myth"

78   Morris, *Philosophy for Dummies*, 238

79   Ibid., 239–240

80   How Many Miracles Are Listed in The Bible — List of 150 Biblical Miracles; "What Are…miracles," ChristianAnswers.Net, last modified November 29, 2018, https://christiananswers.net/dictionary/miracle.html;

    How Many Miracles Of Jesus Are Recorded In The Bible? - Proven Way

81   Hugh Ross, "Fulfilled Prophecy: Evidence for the Reliability of the Bible," published August 22, 2003, https://reasons.org/explore/publications/articles/fulfilled-prophecy-evidence-for-the-reliability-of-the-bible;

    "Fulfilled Prophecy as Evidence for the Bible's Divine Origin: An Outline," Faith Facts, https://www.faithfacts.org/search-for-truth/maps/fulfilled-prophecy-as-evidence

82 "Death Penalty for Old Testament False Prophets," ad Dei Gloriam Ministries, https://www.addeigloriam.org/commentary/ot-law/death-penalty-false-prophets.htm

83 Ernst Mayr, *What Evolution Is* (Basic Books, 2001), 74

84 Edward J. Larson, *The Theory of Evolution: A History of Controversy* (The Teaching Company, 2002), 11

85 Ibid.

86 Ibid., 14–17

87 Nils Ch. Rauhut, *The Big Questions: Philosophy for Everyone* (Prisilla MeGeehon Publisher, 2006), 3–4

88 Ibid., 3

89 Ibid., 5

90 Mary Fairchild, "How Many Religions Are There in the World?" published March 22, 2021, https://www.learnreligions.com/how-many-religions-are-there-in-the-world-5114658;

Wikipedia, "List of religions and spiritual traditions," last modified February 15, 2024, https://en.wikipedia.org/wiki/List_of_religions_and_spiritual _traditions

91 Rauhut, *The Big Questions*, 248

92 Wikipedia, "Theism," last modified September 23, 2023, https://en.wikipedia.org/wiki/Theism;

Morris, *Philosophy for Dummies*, 237–238

93 New World Encyclopedia, "Henotheism," https://www.newworldencyclopedia.org/entry/Henotheism

94 Wikipedia, "Apatheism," last modified August 28, 2023, https://en.wikipedia.org/wiki/Apatheism

95 Wikipedia, "Philosophy of religion," last modified September 16, 2023, http://en.wikipedia.org/wiki/Philosophy_of_religion

96 Wikipedia, "Special revelation," last modified June 29, 2023, http://en.wikipedia.org/wiki/Special_revelation

97   Keith Mathison, "General and Special Revelation," published May 18, 2012, https://www.ligonier.org/learn/articles/general-and-special-revelation-reformed-approach-science-and-scripture

98   Dictionary.com, "theology," http://dictionary.reference.com/browse/theology

99   Theologians & Theology, https://www.theologian-theology.com;

Theology — Divine Nature, Bible Study, and Eastern Orthodoxy | Britannica

100   "What is general revelation and special revelation?" Got Questions, last updated January 4, 2022, https://www.gotquestions.org/general-special-revelation.html

101   Bickel and Jantz, *Creation and Evolution 101*, 23

102   Wikipedia, "Special revelation"

103   "The Belgic Confession," Reformed Church in America, https://www.rca.org/about/theology/creeds-and-confessions/the-belgic-confession/

104   "Arguments for the Existence of God," Existence of God, https://existenceofgod.org/arguments-for-the-existence-of-god/

105   Morris, *Philosophy for Dummies*, 269–278

106   "Faith: Historical Perspectives," Internet Encyclopedia of Philosophy, https://iep.utm.edu/faith-re/

107   Ibid.

108   Ibid.

109   Ibid.

110   Ibid.

111   "What Is Evidence?" Stack Exchange, last updated November 13, 2018, https://philosophy.stackexchange.com/questions/57038/what-is-evidence

112   "What Is the Difference between Philosophy, Religion, and Science?" Stack Exchange, last modified April 10, 2018, https://philosophy.stackexchange.com/questions/43233/what-is-the-difference-between-philosophy-religion-and-science

113   Bickel and Jantz, *Creation and Evolution 101*, 203

114   Morris, *Philosophy for Dummies*, 43–50

115   Ibid.

116   Ibid.

117   Norman Geisler, "The Current Debate on Creation and Evolution," published September 4, 2005, https://jashow.org/articles/the-current-debate-on-creation-and-evolution/

118   "What Is the Day-Age Theory?" Got Questions, https://www.gotquestions.org/Day-Age-Theory.html

119   Gerald L. Schroeder, "The Age of the Universe: One Reality Viewed from Two Different Perspectives," https://aish.com/the-age-of-the-universe-one-reality-viewed-from-two-different-perspectives/

120   Got Questions, "What Is the Day-Age Theory?"

121   Gerald L. Schroeder, *The Science of God: The Convergence of Scientific and Biblical Wisdom* (First Free Press, 2009), 163

122   Stephen C. Meyer, "Not by Chance," published December 1, 2005, https://www.discovery.org/a/3059/

123   Ibid.

124   Georgia Purdom, "Is the Intelligent Design Movement Christian?" https://answersingenesis.org/intelligent-design/is-the-intelligent-design-movement-christian/

125   William A. Dembski and Sean McDowell, *Understanding Intelligent Design* (Harvest House Publishers, 2008), 27

126   Ibid., 102–109

127   Ibid., 140–148

128   Ibid., 154–159, 162–166

129   Stephen C. Meyer, *Darwin's Doubt: The Explosive Origin of Animal Life and the Case for Intelligent Design* (HarperCollins Publishing, 2013), inside cover

130   Kitzmiller v. Dover Area School District, 04 cv 2688 (December 20, 2005), 69

131   Wikipedia, "Progressive creationism," last modified July 26, 2023, http://en.wikipedia.org/wiki/Progressive_Creationism

132   Ibid.

133   Ibid.

134   Ibid.

135   Clark S. Larsen, ed., *A Companion to Biological Anthropology* (2010), 555

136   Wikipedia, "Progressive creationism";

"What Is Progressive Creationism and Is It Biblical?" Got Questions, last updated January 4, 2022, https://www.gotquestions.org/progressive-creationism.html

137   Ronald Numbers, *The Creationists: From Scientific Creationism to Intelligent Design*, expanded ed. (Harvard University Press, 2006), 208

138   https://reasons.org/explore/publications/articles/creation-timeline

139   Bickel and Jantz, *Creation and Evolution 101*, 57

140   Fazale Rana and Hugh Ross, *Origins of Life* (NavPress, 2004), 42–45

141   "The Hope That We Have," Reasons to Believe, published April 2, 2015, https://reasons.org/explore/publications/articles/the-hope-that-we-have/

142   Stephen J. Gould, *The Panda's Thumb* (New York: W.W. Norton & Co., 1982), 82

143   Rana and Ross, *Origins of Life*, 42–45

144   Wikipedia, "Reasons to Believe," last modified August 27, 2023, http://en.wikipedia.org/wiki/Reasons_to_Believe

145   Wikipedia, "Progressive creationism";

Got Questions, "What Is Progressive Creationism and Is It Biblical?"

146   Ross, *A Matter of Days*, 81

147   "What Is the Gap Theory?" Got Questions, last updated October 5, 2022, https://www.gotquestions.org/gap-theory.html

148   Wikipedia, "Gap creationism," last modified June 22, 2023, https://en.wikipedia.org/wiki/Gap_creationism

149   "What Is the God of the Gaps Argument?" Got Questions, last updated January 4, 2022, https://www.gotquestions.org/God-of-the-gaps.html

150   Ibid.

151   Wikipedia, "Gap creationism"

152   Wikipedia, "Theistic evolution," last modified November 30, 2023, https://en.wikipedia.org/wiki/Theistic_evolution

153   Francis Collins, *The Language of God* (New York Free Press, 2007), 200

154   Wikipedia, "Theistic evolution"

155   Ibid.

156   Wikipedia, "Deistic evolution," last modified January 24, 2024, https://en.wikipedia.org/wiki/Deistic_evolution

157   Wikipedia, "Evolutionary creation," last modified January 27, 2024, https://en.wikipedia.org/wiki/Evolutionary_creation

158   Ibid.

159   Norman Geisler, "The Current Debate on Creation and Evolution"

160   Wikipedia, "Jewish views on evolution," last modified January 7, 2024, https://en.wikipedia.org/wiki/Jewish_views_on_evolution;

"Jewish Views on Evolution," The Spiritual Life, https://slife.org/jewish-views-on-evolution/

161   Wikipedia, "Islamic views on evolution," last modified September 30, 2023, http://en.wikipedia.org/wiki/Islamic_views_on_evolution

162   "The Creation/Evolution Continuum," National Center for Science Education, published January 22, 2016, https://ncse.ngo/creationevolution-continuum;

Pope John Paul II, "Cosmology and Fundamental Physics," https://www.ewtn.com/catholicism/library/cosmology-and-fundamental-physics-8135

163   Eugene C. Scott, *Evolution vs. Creationism: An Introduction* (University of California Press, 2009), 69

164   "Young Earth Creationism," National Center for Science Education, published January 22, 2016, https://ncse.ngo/young-earth-creationism

165   "What Is Young Earth Creationism?" Got Questions, last updated January 4, 2022, https://www.gotquestions.org/young-earth-creationism.html;

Edward J. Larson, *Trial and Error: The American Controversy over Creation and Evolution* (New York: Oxford University Press, 2003), 248–250

166   "Rejection of Evolution by Religious Groups," The Spiritual Life, https://slife.org/rejection-of-evolution-by-religious-groups/

167   Theodosius Dobzhansky, "Nothing in Biology Makes Sense Except in the Light of Evolution," *The American Teacher* (March 1973), 125–129

168   Edward J. Larson, *Evolution: The Remarkable History of a Scientific Theory* (New York: Modern Library, 2004), 251

169 Wikipedia, "Creation science," last modified October 16, 2023, http://en.wikipedia.org/wiki/Creation _Science

170 Wikipedia, "Rejection of evolution by religious groups," last modified 14, 2024, https://en.wikipedia.org/wiki/Rejection_of_evolution_by_ religious_groups

171 Eugenie C. Scott, *Evolution versus Creationism*, xii;

"Creationism vs. Evolution," Diffen, https://www.diffen.com/difference/ Creationism_vs_Evolution

172 Bickel and Jantz, *Creation and Evolution 101*, 101

173 Wikipedia, "Creationism," last modified February 12, 2024, https://en.wikipedia.org/wiki/Creationism

174 Ibid.

175 Ibid.

176 Ibid.

177 Ibid.

178 Ibid.

179 National Center for Science Education, "Young Earth Creationism"

180 "McLean v. Arkansas Board of Education," http://www.talkorigins.org/faqs/ mclean-v-arkansas

181 Wikipedia, "Creationism"

182 Ibid.

183 Ibid.

184 Norman L. Geisler, *Systematic Theology, Volume Two: God/Creation* (Minneapolis: Bethany House, 2003), 468–473.

185 RationalWiki, "Methodological naturalism," December 27, 2022, https://rationalwiki.org/wiki/Methodological_naturalism

186 Saul Mcleod, "Karl Popper: Falsification Theory," last updated July 31, 2023, https://www.simplypsychology.org/karl-popper.html; Wikipedia, "Falsifiability," last modified February 12, 2024, https://en.wikipedia.org/ wiki/Falsifiability

187 "Science, Religion, Evolution and Creationism: Primer," Smithsonian Museum of Natural History, last updated January 3, 2024,

https://humanorigins.si.edu/about/broader-social-impacts-committee/science-religion-evolution-and-creationism-primer

188   Anne Marie Helmenstine, "What Is the Difference Between Hard and Soft Science?" last updated November 29, 2019, https://www.thoughtco.com/hard-vs-soft-science-3975989

189   Wikipedia, "Consilience," last modified June 29, 2023, https://en.wikipedia.org/wiki/Consilience

190   "Lines of Evidence," Berkeley, https://undsci.berkeley.edu/glossary/lines-of-evidence/;

        "Science Relies on Evidence," Berkeley, https://undsci.berkeley.edu/understanding-science-101/what-is-science/science-relies-on-evidence/

191   Wikipedia, "Consilience"

192   Ibid.

193   Richard Osborne, *Philosophy for Beginners* (Writers and Readers Publishing Inc, 1992), 6

194   Robinson and Groves, *Introducing Philosophy*, 15

195   Larson, *The Theory of Evolution*, 11

196   Mayr, *What Evolution Is*, 74

197   Larson, *The Theory of Evolution*, 11

198   Wikipedia, "Natural selection," last modified February 16, 2024, https://en.wikipedia.org/wiki/Natural_selection;

        "Darwin's Theory of Natural Selection," Biology Wise, https://biologywise.com/darwins-theory-of-natural-selection

199   Wikipedia, "Natural selection"

200   Larson, *The Theory of Evolution*, 11

201   Ibid., 12.

202   Heather Scoville, "8 People Who Inspired Charles Darwin," last updated July 10, 2019, https://www.thoughtco.com/people-who-influenced-charles-darwin-1224651;

        "3.1: Darwin History and Influences," LibreTexts, https://bio.libretexts.org/Workbench/

Bio_1130%3A_Remixed/03%3A_Natural_Selection-_History_and_
Evidence/3.01%3A_Darwin_history_and_influences

203   Mayr, *What Evolution Is*, 23–30

204   "Auguste Comte — The Work," https://web.pdx.edu/~tothm/theory/
DeadSoc/Comte/Auguste%20Comte%20-%20The%20Work.htm;

Wikipedia, "Auguste Comte," last modified February 14, 2024,
https://en.wikipedia.org/wiki/Auguste_Comte

205   White, "Hasn't Evolution Been Proven True?"

206   "How Could the Big Bang Arise from Nothing?"
published January 3, 2022, https://theconversation.com/
how-could-the-big-bang-arise-from-nothing-171986

207   Wikipedia, "Evolution as fact and theory," last updated January 13, 2024,
https://en.wikipedia.org/wiki/Evolution_as_fact_and_theory

208   Ibid., 1–2

209   White, "Hasn't Evolution Been Proven True?"

210   Wikipedia, "Evolution as fact and theory"

211   Ibid., 2–3

212   Ibid., 5

213   Wikipedia, "Progressive creationism"

214   Bickel and Jantz, *Creation and Evolution 101*, 66

215   Ibid.

216   Phillip E. Johnson, "Excerpts from Defeating Darwinism by Opening
Minds," http://www.sedin.org/propeng/defeat1.htm;

R. Michael Duffy, "An Easy-to-Understand Guide for Defeating Darwinism
by Opening Minds," https://faithalone.org/journal-articles/book-reviews/
an-easy-to-understand-guide-for-defeating-darwinism-by-opening-minds/

217   Cynthia L. Mills, *The Theory of Evolution: What It Is, Where It Came From,
and Why It Works* (Wiley and Sons Inc, 2004), 20

218   "Darwin's delay the stuff of myth," University of Cambridge,
https://www.cam.ac.uk/research/news/darwins-delay-the-stuff-of-myth;

"'Darwin's delay' the stuff of myth," phys.org, https://phys.org/news/2007-03-darwin-myth.html

219   The Human Origin Project, "Darwin's Theory of Evolution in 5 Easy Points," published February 20, 2019, https://medium.com/@humanoriginproject/darwins-theory-of-evolution-in-5-easy-points-7682f47986ad;

"Darwin, Evolution, & Natural Selection," Khan Academy, https://www.khanacademy.org/science/ap-biology/natural-selection/natural-selection-ap/a/darwin-evolution-natural-selection

220   Dan Falk, "The Complicated Legacy of Herbert Spencer, the Man Who Coined 'Survival of the Fittest,'" published April 29, 2020, https://www.smithsonianmag.com/science-nature/herbert-spencer-survival-of-the-fittest-180974756/;

Who proposed the survival of the fittest? – TeachersCollegesj

221   "Social Darwinism," HISTORY, https://www.history.com/topics/early-20th-century-us/social-darwinism;

Wikipedia, "Social Darwinism," last modified January 27, 2024, https://en.wikipedia.org/wiki/Social_Darwinism

222   Bickel and Jantz, *Creation and Evolution 101*, 269

223   "Mendel's Laws of Inheritance," Byju's, https://byjus.com/biology/mendel-laws-of-inheritance/;

"Laws of Inheritance," toppr, https://www.toppr.com/guides/biology/principles-of-inheritance-and-variations/laws-of-inheritance/

224   Mahak Jalan, "Gregor Mendel's Laws of Inheritance: Law of Segregation, Dominance, Independent Assortment," last updated October 19, 2023, https://www.scienceabc.com/humans/gregor-mendels-laws-of-inheritance-law-of-segregation-dominance-independent-assortment.html

225   Richard Peachey, "Major Twentieth Century Theories of Evolution: The Neo-Darwinian Synthesis and Punctuated Equilibrium," published January 20, 2010, https://creationbc.org/index.php/major-twentieth-century-theories-of-evolution-the-neo-darwinian-synthesis-and-punctuated-equilibrium/

226 David Sloan Wilson and Kevin Laland, "Empowering the Extended Evolutionary Synthesis," published April 7, 2016, https://www.prosocial. world/posts/empowering-the-extended-evolutionary-synthesis

227 Wikipedia, "Modern synthesis (20th century)," last modified October 14, 2023, https://en.wikipedia.org/wiki/Modern_synthesis_(20th_century);

Vassiliki Betty Smocovitis, "The Modern Synthesis," last modified October 25, 2018, https://www.oxfordbibliographies.com/display/document/obo-9780199941728/obo-9780199941728-0115.xml

228 Philippe Huneman and Denis M. Walsh, eds., *Challenging the Modern Synthesis: Adaptation, Development, and Inheritance* (Oxford University Press, 2017), 76;

Barth F. Smets and Tamar Barkay, "Horizontal Gene Transfer: Perspectives at a Crossroads of Scientific Disciplines," *Nature Reviews Microbiology 3* (September 1, 2005): 675–678, https://doi.org./10.1038/nrmicro1253

229 Wikipedia, "Rejection of evolution by religious groups," last modified September 22, 2023, https://en.wikipedia.org/wiki/Rejection_of_evolution_by_religious_groups

230 "Quote by Carl Sagan," goodreads, https://www.goodreads.com/quotes/178439-the-cosmos-is-all-that-is-or-was-or-ever

231 "Secular Philosophy," All about Worldview, https://www.allaboutworldview.org/secular-philosophy.htm;

"Julian Huxley Quotations," quotetab, https://www.quotetab.com/quotes/by-julian-huxley;

Wikipedia, "Secular humanism"

232 Wikipedia, "Existence of God," October 17, 2023, https://en.wikipedia.org/wiki/Existence_of_God

233 "What Is Theistic Evolution?" Got Questions, last updated January 4, 2022, https://www.gotquestions.org/theistic-evolution.html

234 "Timeline of the Universe Image," NASA, last updated December 21, 2012, https://map.gsfc.nasa.gov/media/060915/index.html

235 Paul Sutter, "What Triggered the Big Bang? It's Complicated (Op-Ed)," published November 23, 2015, https://www.space.com/31192-what-

triggered-the-big-bang.html;

"What Is the Big Bang?" NASA Science Space Place, last updated March 17, 2021, https://spaceplace.nasa.gov/big-bang/en/

236   Ross, *The Creator and the Cosmos: How the Latest Scientific Discoveries Reveal God* (RTB Press, 2018), 101–106

237   Patrick Koppenburg and Hilary Cliff, "Scientists Discover 4 New Particles," published March 14, 2021, https://earthsky.org/human-world/cern-lhc-4-new-particles/;

Mark Bustos, "CERN Scientists Discover Four New Elementary Particles," *The Science Times*, March 15, 2021, https://www.sciencetimes.com/articles/30130/20210315/cern-scientists-discover-four-new-elementary-particles.htm

238   Ross, *The Creator and the Cosmos*, 69;

A. T. Crities, J. W. Henning, P. A. R. Ade, K. A. Aird, J. E. Austermann, J. A. Beall, A. N. Bender, B. A. Benson, L. E. Bleem, J. E. Carlstrom "Measurements of E-Mode Polarization and Temperature-E-Mode Correlation in the CMB from 100 Suare Degrees of SPTPOLData," *The Astrophysical Journal* 801, no. 1 (May 18, 2015): id. 36, https://doi.org/10.1088/0004-637X/805/1/36

239   Ross, *The Creator and the Cosmos*, 42

240   "What Is the Anthropic Principle?" Got Questions, last updated January 4, 2022, https://www.gotquestions.org/anthropic-principle.html

241   Ross, *The Creator and the Cosmos*, 195–198

242   Ibid., 176–194

243   Rana and Ross, *Origins of Life*, 48–49

244   Stephen C. Meyer, *Signature in the Cell: DNA and the Evidence for Intelligent Design* (HarperOne, 2009), 46

245   Ibid., 46–47

246   Rana and Ross, *Origins of Life*, 22

247   Meyer, *Signature in the Cell*, 131

248   Ibid., 238

249   Ibid., 54

250 Jerry Bergman, "Why the Miller-Urey Research Argues Against Abiogenesis," https://answersingenesis.org/origin-of-life/why-the-miller-urey-research-argues-against-abiogenesis/

251 Rana and Ross, *Origins of Life*, 26–27

252 Meyer, *Signature of the Cell*, 239–240

253 Ibid., 241

254 Ibid., 134

255 Ibid., 170-175

256 Rana and Ross, *Origins of Life*, 137–138

257 Meyer, *Signature in the Cell*, 201–205

258 Rana and Ross, *Origins of Life*, 124

259 Ibid., 123–124

260 Wikipedia, "Homochirality," last modified December 8, 2023, https://en.wikipedia.org/wiki/Homochirality;

Hugh Ross, "Homochirality and the Origin of Life," published November 7, 2011, https://reasons.org/explore/publications/articles/homochirality-and-the-origin-of-life

261 Rana and Ross, *Origins of Life*, 124

262 Ibid., 125–128

263 Ibid., 129–130

264 Ibid., 131–132

265 Robert Shapiro, "Prebiotic Cytosine Synthesis: A Critical Analysis and Implications for the Origin of Life," *Proceeding of the National Academy of Sciences* 96, no. 8 (1999): 4396–4901

266 Robert Shapiro, "The Prebiotic Role of Adenine: A Critical Analysis," *Origins Life Evol Biosphere* 25(1995), 83–98

267 Rana and Ross, *Origin of Life*, 115

268 Ibid., 151–158

269 Ibid., 94

270 Ibid., 95

271 Ibid., 100

272 Ibid., 101

273 Ibid., 101

274 Ibid., 104

275 Meyer, *Signature of the Cell*, 201–210

276 Ibid., 210–211

277 Ibid., 138

278 Ibid., 138

279 Ibid., 138

280 Ibid., 208

281 Rana and Ross, *Origins of Life*, 37;

Hubert P. Yockley, *Information Theory, Evolution, and the Origin of Life*, 151–152

282 Meyer, *Signature of the Cell*, 212

283 Ibid., 213

284 Ibid., 213

285 Ibid., 222

286 Ibid., 235–237

287 Michael Anisimov, "How Many Proteins Exist?" last modified October 2, 2023, https://www.allthescience.org/how-many-proteins-exist.htm;

Wikipedia, "Protein," last modified January 26, 2024, https://en.wikipedia.org/wiki/Protein

288 Fazale Rana with Hugh Ross, *Who Was Adam?* 2nd ed. (Covina: rtbPress, 2015), 35

289 J. William Schopf and Bonnie M. Packer, "Early Archean (3.3-Billion to 3.5-Billion-Year-Old) Microfossils from Warrawoona Group, Australia," *Science* 237, no. 4810 (July 1987): 70

290 Meyer, *Darwin's Doubt*, 58–61

291 Kevin J. Peterson, James A. Cotton, James G. Gehling, and Davide Pisani, "The Ediacaran Emergence of Bilaterians: Congruence between the Genetic and the Geological Fossil Records," *The Royal Society* 363, no. 1496 (April 27, 2008)

292   Simon Conway Morris, "Evolution: Bringing Molecules into the Fold," *Cell* 100, no. 1 (January 7, 2000): 5

293   Meyer, *Darwin's Doubt*, 62

294   Ibid., 79–85

295   Ibid., 55

296   Mills, *The Theory of Evolution*, 10–11

297   "A Geologic Time Scale Shows Major Evolutionary Events from 650 Million Years Ago to the Present," gettyimages, https://www.gettyimages.com.mx/detail/fotograf%C3%ADa-de-noticias/geologic-time-scale-shows-major-evolutionary-fotograf%C3%ADa-de-noticias/143064422;

      "Geologic Time Scale," Britannica Kids, https://kids.britannica.com/students/assembly/view/183845

298   Bob Strauss, "10 Steps of Animal Evolution: From Fish to Primates," last updated January 30, 2020, http://www.thoughtco.com/evolution-of-vertebrate-animals-4040937

299   Meyer, *Darwin's Doubt*, 79–85

300   Douglas Erwin and James Valentine, *The Cambrian Explosion: The Construction of Animal Biodiversity*, 66–70

301   Meyer, *Darwin's Doubt*, 56–58

302   Richard Monastersky, "Ancient Animal Sheds False Identity," *Science News* (August 1997)

303   Meyer, *Darwin's Doubt*, 101

304   Gregory A. Wray, Jeffrey S. Levinton, and Leo H. Shapiro, "Molecular Evidence for Deep Cambrian Diverges among Metazoan Phyla," *Science* 274, no. 5287 (October 25, 1996): 568–573

305   Monastersky, "Ancient Animal Sheds False Identity"

306   Meyer, *Darwin's Doubt*, 163

307   NIH, "An Illustration of How Epigenetic Mechanisms Can Affect Health", https://www.nature.com/scitable/content/an-illustration-of-how-epigenetic-mechanisms-can-33372/

308   Ibid., 272–282

309 James W. Valentine, "Late Precambrian Bilaterians: Grades and Clades," *Proceedings of the National Academy of Sciences* 91, no. 15 (July 19, 1994): 6751–6757

310 Meyer, *Darwin's Doubt*, 162

311 Ibid., 163

312 Ibid., 163

313 Ibid., 163

314 Stephen J. Gould, *Wonderful Life: The Burguess Shale and the Nature of History*, 125–136;

Graham E. Budd, "The Morphology of Opabinia Regalis and the Reconstruction of the Arthropod Stem-Group," *Lethaia* 29, no. 1 (March 1, 1996): 1–14

315 Jochen J. Brocks, Graham A. Logan, Roger Buick, and Roger E. Summons, "Archean Molecular Fossils and the Early Rise of Eukaryotes," *Science* 285, no. 5430 (August 13, 1999): 1033–1036

316 Douglas H. Erwin, James W. Valentine, and J. John Sepkoski, "A Comparative Study of Diversification Events: The Early Paleozoic versus the Mesozoic," *Evolution* 41, no. 6 (November 1, 1987): 1183

317 Ibid.

318 "New Genome Comparison Finds Chimps, Humans Very Similar at the DNA Level," National Human Genome Research Institute, https://www.genome.gov/15515096/2005-release-new-genome-comparison-finds-chimps-humans-very-similar-at-dna-level

319 "Frequently Asked Questions," Smithsonian National Museum of Natural History, last updated July 11, 2022, https://humanorigins.si.edu/education/frequently-asked-questions

320 Wikipedia, "Evolution of primates," last modified February 8, 2024, https://en.wikipedia.org/wiki/Evolution_of_primates

321 Ardipithecus - Early Hominin, Fossil Evidence, Primate | Britannica

322 Michel Brunet, Franck Guy, David Pilbeam, Hassana Taisso Mackaye, Andossa Likius, Djimdoumalbaye Ahounta, Alain Beauvilain, Cécile Blondel, Hervé Bocherens, Jean-Renaud Boisserie, Louis De Bonis, Yves Coppens, Jean Dejax, Christiane Denys, Philippe Duringer, Véra Eisenmann, Gongdibé Fanone, Pierre Fronty, Denis Geraads, Thomas

Lehmann, Fabrice Lihoreau, Antoine Louchart, Adoum Mahamat, Gildas Merceron, Guy Mouchelin, Olga Otero, Pablo Pelaez Campomanes, Marcia Ponce De Leon, Jean-Claudee Rage, Michael Sapanet, Mathieu Schuster, Jean Sudre, Pascal Tassy, Xavier Valentin, Patrick Vignaud, Laurent Viriot, Antonine Zazzo, and Christoph Zollikofer, "A New Hominid from the Upper Miocene of Chad, Central Africa," *Nature* 418 (2002), 145–151

323 "Human Family Tree," Smithsonian National Museum of Natural History, last updated January 3, 2024, https://humanorigins.si.edu/evidence/human-family-tree

324 Taxonomy | Basic Biology; "Levels of Taxonomy Used in Biology," ThoughtCo., thoughtco.com/levels-of-taxonomy-1224606

325 Fazale Rana with Hugh Ross, *Who Was Adam?* (NavPress, 2005), 140;

Wikipedia, "Evolution as fact and theory"

326 Rana with Ross, *Who Was Adam?* 141–142

327 Ibid., 84

328 How did bipedalism affect brain size? – Sage-Answer

329 Rana with Ross, *Who Was Adam?* 157–159;

Meave G. Leakey, Fred Spoor, Frank H. Brown, Patrick N. Gathogo, Christopher Kiarie, Louise N. Leakey, and Ian McDougall, "New Hominid Genus from Eastern Africa Shows Diverse Middle Pliocene Linages," Nature 410 (2001): 433–440;

Daniel E. Liberman, "Another Face in Our Family Tree," Nature 410 (2001): 419–420

330 Rana with Ross, *Who Was Adam?* 162–163

331 Ibid., 157

332 Ibid., 164

333 Ibid., 63-64;

Ann Gibbons, "Calibration of the Mitochondria Clock," *Science* 279 (1998): 28–29;

Lois A. Tulley, Thomas J. Parsons, Robert J. Steighner, Mitchell M. Holland, Michael A. Marino, and Valerie L. Prenger, "A Sensitive

Denaturing Gradient Gel Electrophoresis Assay Reveals High Frequency of Heteroplasmy in Hypervariable Region of the Human mtDNA Central Region," *American Journal of Human Genetics* 67, no. 2 (2000): 432–443

334   Rana with Ross, *Who Was Adam?* 2nd ed., 263

335   Ibid., 265;

Phillip Endicott, Simon Y. W. Ho, Mait Metspalu, and Chris Stringer, "Evaluating the Mitochondrial Timescale of Human Evolution," *Trends in Ecology and Evolution* 24 (2007), 515–521

336   Rana with Ross, *Who Was Adam?* 2nd ed., 266;

Adrian Rieux, Anders Eriksson, Mingkun Li, Benjamin Sobkowiak, Lucy A. Winert, Vera Warmuth, Andres Ruiz-Linares, Andrea Manica, and François Balloux, "Improved Calibration of the Human Mitochondrial Clock Using Ancient Genomes," *Molecular Biology and Evolution* 31 (2014): 2780–2792

337   Rana with Ross, *Who Was Adam?* 2nd ed., 266;

Qiaomei Fu, Alissa Mittnik, Philip L. F. Johnson, Kirsten Bos, Martina Lari, Ruth Bollongino, Chengkai Sun, liane Giemsch, Ralf Schmitz, Joachim Burger, Anna Maria Ronchitelli, Fabio Martini, Renata G. Cremonesi, Jiří Svoboda, Peter Bauer, David Caramelli, sergi Castellano, David Reich, Svante Pääbo, and Johannes Krause, "A Revised Timescale for Human Evolution Based on Ancient Mitochondrial Genomes," *Current Biology* 23 (2013), 553–559

338   Rana with Ross, *Who Was Adam?* 2nd ed., 267

339   Ibid., 266;

Fulvio Cruciani, Beniamino Trombetta, Andrea Massaia, Giovanni Destro-Bisol, Daniele Sellitto, and Rosaria Scozzari, "Revised Root for the Human Y Chromosomal Phylogenetic Tree: The Origin of Patrilineal Diversity in Africa," *American Journal of Human Genetics* 88 (2011), 814–818

340   Rana with Ross, *Who Was Adam?* 2nd ed., 264–265, 347–352;

Dennis Venema and Darrel Falk, "Does Genetics Point to a Single Primal Couple?" Biologos Forum (blog), posted April 5, 2010;

"Adam, Eve, and Human Population Genetics: Responses to Popular Arguments," BioLogos, published November 12, 2014, http://biologos.org/blog/does-genetics-point-to-a-single-primal-couple;

Nuha Elhassan, Eyoab Iyasu Gebremeskel, Mohamed Ali Elnour, Dan Isabirye, John Okello, Ayman Hussein, Dominic Kwiatksowski, Jibril Hirbo, Sara Tishkoff, Muntaser E. Ibrahim, "The Episode of Genetic Drift Defining the Migration of Humans Out of Africa Is Derived from a Large East African Population Size," *PloS One 9* (May 2014), https://doi.org/10.1371/journal.pone.0097674;

Lev A. Zhivotovsky, Noah A. Rosenberg, and Marcus W. Feldman, "Features of Evolution and Expansion of Modern Humans, Inferred from Genomewide Microsatellite Markers," *American Journal of Human Genetics* 72 (2003): 1171–1186

341   Rana with Ross, *Who Was Adam?* 2nd ed., 267;

G. David Poznik, Brenna M. Henn, Muh-Ching Yee, Elzbieta Sliwerska, Ghia M. Euskirchen, Alice A. Lin, Michael Snyder, Lluis Quintana-Murci, Jeffrey M. Kidd, Peter A. Underhill, and Carlos D. Bustamante, "Sequencing Y Chromosomes Resolves Discrepancies in Time to Common Ancestor of Males versus Females," *Science* 341, no. 6145 (August 2013): 560–562

342   Rana with Ross, *Who Was Adam?* 2nd ed., 350

343   Ibid., 351;

Renaud Kaeuffer, David W. Coltman, Jean-Louis Chapuis, Dominique Pontier, and Denis Réale, "Unexpected Heterozygosity in an Island Mouflon Population Founded by a Single Pair of Individuals," *Proceedings of the Royal Society B: Biological Sciences* 274, no. 1609 (February 2007): 527–533

344   Rana with Ross, *Who Was Adam?* 2nd ed., 351

345   Ibid., 215;

Roderick D. M. Page and Edward C. Holms, *Molecular Evolution: A Phylogenic Approach*, 251–261

346   Rana with Ross, *Who Was Adam?* 2nd ed., 215;

Charles G. Sibley and Jon E. Ahlquist, "The Phylogeny of the Hominoid

Primates, as Indicated by DNA-DNA Hybridization," *Journal of Molecular Evolution* 20 (February 1984): 2–15;

Sibley and Ahlquist, "DNA Hybridization Evidence," 99–121;

Adalgisa Caccone and Jeffrey R. Powell, "DNA Divergence among Hominoids," *Evolution* 43, no. 5 (August 1989): 925–942

347   Rana with Ross, *Who Was Adam?* 2nd ed., 215;

Pascal Gagneux, Christopher Wills, Ulrike Gerloff, Diethard Tautz, Phillip A. Morin, Christophe Boesch, Barbara Fruth, Gottfried Hohmann, Oliver A. Ryder, and David S. Woodruff, "Mitochondrial Sequences Show Diverse Evolutionary Histories of African Hominoids," *Proceedings of the National Academy of Sciences* 96, no. 9 (April 1999): 5077–5082;

Satoshi Horai, Kenji Hayasaka, Rumi Kondo, Kazuo Tsugane, and Naoyuki Takahata, "Recent African Origin of Modern Humans Revealed by Complete Sequences of Hominoid Mitochondrial DNAs," *Proceedings of the National Academy of Sciences of the United States of America* 92, no. 2 (January 1995): 532–536

348   Rana with Ross, *Who Was Adam?* 2nd ed., 63

349   Ibid.;

Robert Boyd and Joan B. Silk, *How Humans Evolved*, 3rd ed. (New York: Norton, 2003), 390–391

350   Rana with Ross, *Who Was Adam?* 36

351   Ibid., 38

352   https://rationalwiki.org/wiki/assimulation-model/

353   Rana with Ross, *Who Was Adam?* 2nd ed., 353–354;

Chiara Batini and Mark A. Jobling, "The Jigsaw Puzzle of Our African Ancestry: Unsolved, or Unsolvable?" *Genome Biology* 12 (June 2011), https://doi.org/10.1186/gb-2011-12-6-118

354   Rana with Ross, *Who Was Adam?* 2nd ed., 354

355   Ibid., 78, 354

356 Wikipedia, "Population bottleneck," last modified January 3, 2024, https://en.wikipedia.org/wiki/Population_bottleneck

357 https://www.languagesoftheworld.info/historical-linguistics/atkinsons-theory-of-language-origins.html

358 Wikipedia, "History of human migration," last modified January 17, 2024, https://en.wikipedia.org/wiki/History_of_human_migration

359 Rana with Ross, *Who Was Adam?* 84

360 Rana with Ross, *Who Was Adam?* 2nd ed., 272–273;

Elizabeth Pennisi, "Tracking the Sexes by their Genes," *Science* 291, no. 5509 (March 2001): 1733–1734;

Carl Zimmer, "After You Eve," *Natural History*, March 2001, 32–35

361 Rana with Ross, *Who Was Adam?* 2nd ed., 274;

Shannon A. Mahan, Tammy M. Rittenour, Michelle S. Nelson, Nina Ataee, Nathan Brown, Regina DeWitt, Julie Durcan, Mary Evans, James Feathers, Marine Frouin, Guillaume Guérin, Maryam Heydari, Sebastien Huot, Maryank Jain, Amanda Keen-Zebert, Bo Li, Gloria I. López, Christina Neudorf, Naomi Porat, Kathleen Rodrigues, Andre Oliveira Sawakuchi, Joel Q. G. Spencer, and Kristina Thomsen, "Guide for Interpreting and Reporting Luminescence Dating Results," *GSA Bulletin* (September 2022): 1480–1502.

362 Rana with Ross, *Who Was Adam?* 2nd ed., 274;

Pallab Ghosh "Cave Paintings Change Ideas about the Origin of Art," *BBC News*, October 8, 2014

363 Rana with Ross, *Who Was Adam?* 2nd ed., 274;

Adrian Rieux et al., "Improved Calibration of Human Mitochondrial Clock Using Ancient Genomes," *Molecular Biology and Evolution* 31 (2014): 2780–2792

364 Rana with Ross, *Who Was Adam?* 2nd ed., 322–323;

Jianzhi Zhang, David M. Webb, and Ondrej Podlaha, "Accelerated Protein Evolution and Origins of Human-Specific Features: FOXP2 as an example," *Genetics* 162 (2002), 1825–1835;

Jianzhi Zhang, David M. Webb, and Ondrej Podlaha, "Accelerated Protein Evolution and Origins of Human-Specific Features: FOXP2 as an Example," *Genetics* 162, no. 4 (December 2002): 1825–1835

365 Rana with Ross, *Who Was Adam?* 84;

Richard G. Klein, *The Human Career: Human Biological and Cultural Origins*, 2nd ed. (Chicago: University of Chicago Press, 1999), 520–529;

Olga Soffer, "Late Paleolithic," in *Encyclopedia of Human Evolution and Prehistory*.

366 Rana with Ross, *Who Was Adam?* 89;

Achim Schneider, "Ice-Age Musicians Fashioned Ivory Flute," http://www.nature.com/news/2004/041213/pf/041213-14_pf.html/

367 Rana with Ross, *Who Was Adam?* 89;

Tim Appenzeller, "Evolution or Revolution?" *Science* 282 (1998): 1451–1454

368 Rana with Ross, *Who Was Adam?* 92;

Richard G. Klein with Blake Edgar, *The Dawn of Human Culture: A Bold New Theory on What Sparked the "Big Bang" of Human Consciousness* (New York: Wiley, 2002), 261

369 Rana with Ross, *Who Was Adam?* 92, 264–270

370 Rana with Ross, *Who Was Adam?* 2nd ed., 95–96

371 Ibid., 76–77;

Ralf Kittler, Manfred Kayser, and Mark Stoneking, "Molecular Evolution of Pediculus Humanus and the Origin of Clothing," *Current Biology* 113 (2003): 1414–1417;

J. Travis, "The Naked Truth? Lie Hint at a Recent Origin of Clothing," *Science News* 164 (2003);

David L. Reed, Vincent S. Smith, Shaless L. Hammond, Alan R. Rogers, and Dale H. Clayton, "Genetic Analysis of Lice Supports Direct Contact between Modern and Archaic Humans," *PloS Biology* 2 (October 2004): e340, https://doi.org/10.1371/journal.pbio.0020340

372 Rana with Ross, *Who Was Adam?* 90;

Klein, *The Human Career*, 550–553

373 Rana with Ross, *Who Was Adam?* 90–91;

Klein, *The Human Career*, 550-553

374 Ibid.

375 Rana with Ross, *Who Was Adam?* 71

376 Rana with Ross, *Who Was Adam?* 213;

Asao Fujiyama, Hidemi Watanabe, Atsushi Toyoda, Todd D. Taylor, Takehiko Itoh, Shih-Feng Tsai, Hong-Seog Park, Marie-Laure Yaspo, Hans Lehrach, Zhu Chen, Gang Fu, Naruya Saitou, Kazutoyo Osoegawa, Pieter J. de Jong, Yumiko Suto, Masahira Hattori, and Yoshiyuki Sakaki, "Construction and Analysis of a Human-Chimpanzee Comparative Clone Map," *Science* 295 (January 2002): 131–134

377 Rana with Ross, *Who Was Adam?* 213;

Ingo Ebersberger et al., "Genomewide Comparison of DNA Sequences Between Humans and Chimpanzees," *American Journal of Human Genetics* 70 (2002): 1490–1497

378 https://genesisapologentics.com/faqs/human-and-chimp-dna-is-it -really-98-similar/

379 Broad Institute Communications, "Comparison of Human and Chimpanzee Genomes Reveals Striking Similarities and Differences," published August 31, 2005, https://www.broadinstitute.org/news/comparison-human-and-chimpanzee-genomes-reveals-striking-similarities-and-differences

380 Jeffrey Tomkins, "Separate Studies Converge on Human-Chimp DNA Dissimilarity," Act & Facts 47 (2018): 9;

David A. DeWitt, "What about the Similarity between Human and Chimp DNA?" www.answersingenesis.org/articles/nab3/human-and-chimp-dna/

381 Broad Institute Communications, "Comparison of Human and Chimpanzee Genomes";

Maria V. Suntsova and Anton A. Buzdin, "Differences between Human and Chimpanzee Genomes and Their Implications in Gene Expression, Protein Functions and Biochemical Properties of the Two Species," *BMC Genomics* 21 (2020)

382   E. Wijaya, M.C. Frith, P. Horton and K. Asai, "Finding Protein-coding Genes through Human Polymorphisms," *PloS One* 8 (2013)

383   Yoav Gilad, Alicia Oshlack, Gordon K. Smyth, Terence P. Speed, and Kevin P. White, "Expression Profiling in Primates Reveals a Rapid Evolution of Human Transcription Factors," *Nature* 440, no. 7081 (March 2006): 242–245

384   Philipp Khaitovich et al., "Regional patterns of Gene Expression Profiles," *Proceedings of the National Academy of Sciences*, USA 101 (2004): 1462–1473

385   Wolfgang Enard et al., "Molecular Evolution of FOXP2, a Gene Involved in Severe Speech and Language Disorder," *Nature* 418 (2002): 869–872

386   Jacquelyn Bond, Sheila Scott, Daniel J. Hampshire, Kelly Springell, Peter Corry, Marc J. Abramowicz, Ganesh H. Mochida, Raoul C. M. Hennekam, Eamonn R. Maher, Jean-Pierre Fryns, Abdulrahman Alswaid, Hussain Jafri, Yasmin Rashid, Ammar Mubaidin, Christopher A. Walsh, Emma Roberts, and C. Geoffrey Woods, "Protein-Truncating Mutations in ASPM Cause Variable Reduction in Brain Size," *American Journal of Human Genetics* 73 (2003): 1170–1177

387   Maria C. N. Marchetto et al., "Differential L1 Regulation in induced Pluripotent Sem Cells of Humans and Apes," *Nature* 503 (2013): 525–529

388   Jeffery P. Demuth, Tijl De Bie, Jason E. Staijich, Nello Cristianini, and Matthew W. Hahn, "The Evolution of Mammalian Gene Families," *PLOS ONE* 1, no.1 (2006): e85

389   S. Kakuo, K. Asaoka, and T. Ide, "Human Is a Unique Species among Primates in Terms of Telomere Length," *Biochem. Biophy. Res. Commun.* 263 (September 1999): 308–314

390   Jeffrey P. Tomkins, "Documented Anomaly in Recent Versions of the BLASTN Algorithm and a Complete Reanalysis of Chimpanzee and Human Genome-Wide DNA Similarity Using Nucmer and LASTZ," *Answers Research Journal* 8 (October 2015): 379–390.

391   Ann Gibbons, "Which of Our Genes Make Us Human?" *Science* 281 (1998): 1432–1434

392   Nathaniel T. Jeanson, "Purpose, Progress, and Promise, Part 4," published December 30, 2014, http://www.icr.org/article/purpose-progress-promise -part-4

393   Harrison Wein, "Neanderthal Genome Sequence," published May 24, 2010, https://www.nih.gov/news-events/nih-research-matters/ neanderthal-genome-sequenced#

394   William L. Straus Jr. and A. J. E. Cave, "Pathology and the Posture of Neanderthal Man," *The Quarterly Review of Biology* 32 (1957): 348–363;

      William L. Straus Jr. and A. J. E. Cave, "Pathology and the Posture of Neanderthal Man," *The Quarterly Review of Biology* 32, no. 4 (December 1957): 348–363;

      Rana with Ross, *Who Was Adam?* 2nd ed., 184

395   Christopher Stringer and Robin MeKie, *African Exodus: The Origins of Modern Humanity*, (New York: Henry Holt, 1996), 85–114;

      Klein with Edgar, *The Dawn of Human Culture*, 172–180;

      Rana with Ross, *Who Was Adam?* 2nd ed., 185

396   Sedeer el-Showk, "Neanderthal Clues to Brain Development in Humans," *Nature*, July 24, 2019, https://www.nature.com/articles/ d41586-019-02210-6

397   Rana with Ross, *Who Was Adam?* 2nd ed., 311

398   "Ancient DNA and Neanderthals," Smithsonian National Museum of Natural History, last updated January 3, 2024, https://humanorigins.si.edu/ evidence/genetics/ancient-dna-and-neanderthals

399   David Gokhmam et al., "Reconstructing the DNA Methylation Maps of the Neanderthal and the Denisovans," *Science* 344 (2014): 523–527

400   Rana with Ross, *Who Was Adam?* 2nd ed., 311;

      Ian Tattersall, *Masters of the Planet: The Search for Our Origins* (New York: Palgrave Macmillan, 2012), 168

401   Rana with Ross, *Who Was Adam?* 246

402   Ibid, 246

403 News, "Has a Superintellect Monkeyed with Our Universe's Physics?" published August 14, 2022, https://mindmatters.ai/2022/08/has-a-superintellect-monkeyed-with-our-universes-physics/

404 Jerry Bergman, "The Ape-to-Human Progression: the Most Common Evolution Icon Is a Fraud," *Journal of Creation* 23, no. 3 (2009), https://creation.com/images/pdfs/tj/j23_3/j23_3_16-20.pdf

405 Göran Burenhult, *People of the Past* (San Francisco: Fog City Press, 2003), 50–51

406 Russell Miller and The Reader's Digest Association, *The Truth About History: How New Evidence Is Transforming the Story of the Past* (New York: Barnes & Noble, 2007), 11

407 Jerry Bergman, "The Ape-to-Human Progression"

408 Editorial, "Racism still runs deep: even the most well-meaning liberal harbor hidden prejudice," *New Scientist* 197(2643):5, 16 February 2008

409 Wikipedia, "Relationship between religion and science," last modified February 13, 2024, https://en.wikipedia.org/wiki/Relationship_between_religion_and_science

410 Keith Ward, *The Big Questions in Science and Religion* (Templeton Press, 2008)

411 Casey Luskin, "Intelligent Design Theory, and the Relationship between Science and Religion"

412 William Lane Craig, "What Is the Relation between Science and Religion," https://www.reasonablefaith.org/writings/popular-writings/science-theology/what-is-the-relation-between-science-and-religion

413 Ibid.

414 Bickel and Jantz, *Creation and Evolution 101*, 56–57

415 Hugh Ross, *Improbable Planet: How Earth Became Humanity's Home* (Baker Books, 2016), 182–215

416 Wikipedia, "Chronology of the universe," last modified February 15, 2024, https://en.wikipedia.org/wiki/Chronology_of_the_universe

417 Wikipedia, "History of the Earth," last modified June 20, 2023, https://simple.wikipedia.org/wiki/History_of_the_Earth

418   Sutter, "What Triggered the Big Bang?"; David J. Eicher, "How Did the Big Bang Happen?" published July 1, 2019, https://www.astronomy.com/science/how-did-the-big-bang-happen/

419   Wikipedia, "History of the Big Bang theory," last modified October 24, 2023, https://en.wikipedia.org/wiki/History_of_the_Big_Bang_theory

420   Wikipedia, "Lambda-CDM model," last modified February 12, 2024, https://en.wikipedia.org/wiki/Lambda-CDM_model

421   "Kevin Peterson: The Evolution of a Paleontologist," Dartmouth, published October 20, 2011, https://home.dartmouth.edu/news/2011/10/kevin-peterson-evolution-paleontologist

422   Meyer, *Darwin's Doubt*, 86–87

423   Michel Brunet et al., "A New Hominid from the Upper Miocene of Chad";

       Bernard Wood, "Hominid Revelations from Chad," *Nature* 418 (2002): 133–135;

       Ann Gibbons, "Paleoanthropology. First Member of Human Family Uncovered," *Science* 297, no. 5579 (2002): 171–172

424   Rana with Ross, *Who Was Adam?* 2nd ed., 286

425   Wikipedia, "Homo sapiens idaltu," last modified April 11, 2023, https://simple.wikipedia.org/wiki/Homo_sapiens_idaltu;

       Wikipedia, "Herto Man," last modified January 22, 2024, https://en.wikipedia.org/wiki/Herto_Man

426   Charles Q. Choi, "Who Were the Denisovans?" last updated August 29, 2022, https://www.livescience.com/denisovans-extinct-human-relative

427   "Americans' Perception of Conflict between Science and Religion," Pew Research Center, published October 22, 2015, https://www.pewresearch.org/science/2015/10/22/perception-of-conflict-between-science-and-religion/

428   Smithsonian National Museum of Natural History, "Science, Religion, Evolution and Creationism: Primer"

429   Ibid.

430   Bickel and Jantz, *Creation and Evolution 101*, 274

431   Reasons to Believe, "The Hope That We Have"

432   Glenn T. Seaborg, *The Nature of Science* (American Association for the Advancement of Science, 1990);

"Chapter 1: The Nature of Science," Science for All Americans, http://www.project2061.org/publications/sfaa/online/chap1.htm;

Wikipedia, "Scientific theory," last modified February 14, 2024, https://en.wikipedia.org/wiki/Scientific_theory

433   Wikipedia, "Scientific theory"

434   Jon Bloom, "The Insanity of Leaning on Our Own Understanding," published March 7, 2014, https://www.desiringgod.org/articles/the-insanity-of-leaning-on-our-own-understanding

435   Bickel and Jantz, *Creation and Evolution 101*, 272

436   "What Does God Mean When He Says, 'My Ways Are Higher than Your Ways' in Isaiah 55:9?" Got Questions, last updated April 28, 2022, https://www.gotquestions.org/my-ways-are-higher-than-your-ways.html

437   "What Is Divine Providence?" Got Questions, last updated January 4, 2022, https://www.gotquestions.org/divine-providence.html

Printed in the USA
CPSIA information can be obtained
at www.ICGtesting.com
CBHW071953090724
11357CB00006B/104